Hope and Healing in a Troubled World

Hope and Healing in a Troubled World

Stories of Women Faith Leaders

Roberta Swan

iUniverse, Inc.
New York Lincoln Shanghai

Hope and Healing in a Troubled World
Stories of Women Faith Leaders

iUniverse, Inc.

For information address:
iUniverse, Inc.
2021 Pine Lake Road, Suite 100
Lincoln, NE 68512
www.iuniverse.com

Quotations of prayers and poems in this book are either from traditional sources, or specific permission and origin are listed at the entry.

ISBN: 0-595-31109-1

Printed in the United States of America

To all the women who still struggle to find their way in a world that seems to offer more promise of success but is full of hidden barriers to its achievement, but especially to those women who forge new pathways through those barriers for the rest of us to follow.

Contents

Preface xiii

Prayers and Poems:

Introduction to Prayers and Poems 1

Karyl Huntley: by Karyl Huntley 2

Jan Heglund: Jeremiah 29:11 3

Denise Wylie: by Denise Wylie. 4

Lama Palden: Buddhist Prayer 6

Carolyn Kellogg: by Monica Kaufer 7

Susannah Malarkey, O.P.: by Susannah Malarkey. 8

Louise Franklin: Principles of Attitudinal Healing. 9

Aline O'Brien: Traditional by Doreen Valiente. 10

Linda Cutts: Buddhist, Hymn to Perfection 11

Sue Severin: by Sue Severin. 12

Mary Neill, O.P.: St. Augustine 13

Nahid Angha: Fatiha, the Opening, Holy Qur'an. 14

Meredith Cahn: by Dolores Wilkenfeld 15

Margaret Hough: a Baha'i Prayer 17

Fu Schroeder: Contrary Ways from the Dhammapada 18

Betsy Rosen: by Dag Hammarskjold. 20

Allen Yan-Chamberlin: by Jan L. Richardson 21

Sara Vurek: by Mattie J.T. Stepanek 23

Linda Compton: by Rabbi Abraham Joshua Heschel 25

Ann Eichhorn: by Ann Eichhorn 26

Jan West: St. Theresa of Avila 27

Joanne Abrams: by Doris Panoff 28

Veronica Goines: Matthew 11 :28-30 and Veronica Goines 30

Janie Spahr: by Miriam Therese Winter 32

Carolyn Logan and Kelly Thomas: Psalm 34:1-3 33

Carol Hovis and Gervaise Valpey, O.P.: Micah: 6:8 34

Betty Pagett: adapted by Betty Pagett 35

Renee Geiger: by Joyce Rupp 37

Sylvia Boorstein: the Buddha's Words on Loving Kindness 38

Carol Saysette: Wisdom of Solomon 7 21:28 40

Stories:

Introduction to the Stories 41

Joanne Abrams, Jewish Convert 42

Nahid Angha, Sufi Leader 49

Sylvia Boorstein, Buddhist Teacher 55

Linda Compton, Agency Director 60

Linda Cutts, Buddhist Abbess 67

Ann Eichhorn, UCC Minister and Activist 73

Deanna Euritt, Hospice Chaplain 78

Louise Franklin, Agency Leader 84

Stacy Friedman, Rabbi 91

Renee Geiger, Lutheran Minister 97

Veronica Goines, Presbyterian Minister 104

Jan Heglund, Police Chaplain 110

Margaret Hough, Bahai 117

Carol Hovis, Non Profit Chaplain 122

Karyl Huntley, Religious Science Minister 128

Carolyn Kellogg, Catholic Change Agent 133

Theresa Kime, Unitarian Universalist Minister 138

Carolyn Logan, Licensed Missionary 144

Susannah Malarkey, O.P., Retreat Center Leader 150

Mary Neill, O.P., Spiritual Director 151

Aline O'Brien, Pagan Ambassador 156

Betty Pagett, Housing Advocate 163

Lama Palden, Sukhasiddhi Foundation 170

Carol Saysette, Pastoral Counseling 176

Fu Schroeder, Buddhist Teacher 182

Sue Severin, Quaker Activist 189

Janie Spahr, Lesbian Activist 196

Kelly Thomas, Choir Director 202

Gervaise Valpey, O.P., Catholic Educator 207

Sara Vurek, Merging Traditions 213

Jan West, Episcopal Priest 218

Denise Wylie, American Baptist 225

Allen Yan-Chamberlin, Methodist Minister 231

Acknowledgements

The original interviews were made possible with grants from the Marin Community Foundation, the E. Rhodes and Leona B. Carpenter Foundation and the Sufi Women Organization. The conference which allowed the interviews to be shared with the public was co-sponsored by the Dominican University of California Institute of Leadership Studies and the Dominican University of California Department of Humanities. The original idea to survey and interview women of faith was conceived in a conversation with Susan Kirsch who with Dana Curtin held my hand and gave valuable feedback. And the idea would not have gotten any farther without the support and help of Dr. Nahid Angha who helped me find women to interview, shared her funding contacts and acted as great moral support throughout the process. The women in the study not only gave me time out of busy schedules for the interview, but either allowed me to take their photograph or found one for me to use in the exhibit, then they found wonderful inspirational quotes as my ideas expanded, and finally almost all took a day on February 15, 2003 to share their story with a very interested public. Deborah Lattimore provided excellent transcription service to get the interviews from voice to word. My friend, Lynn Peterson, lent me her large color xerox machine when sufficient funding for the display did not materialize as well as the use of a commercial display system. My husband, James Swan, and son, Andrew Swan, spent innumerable hours cutting, pasting, carrying and setting up. And, although advise and help was given by many, my final decision on all copy renders me responsible for any mistakes or errors in this manuscript.

Preface

My journey to find a spiritual core for my life led me to talk to a large number of women religious leaders. Their stories and favorite prayers are collected in this book.

In the fall of 2001, just after 9/11, like so many others in America I began to re-examine my life and priorities. I had a job that I was not happy with and was searching for new directions both professionally and spiritually. I began to want to know more about spiritual traditions. I had been searching for a spiritual home for a few years and although I had met some wonderful people and felt more spiritually grounded than when I began my search I still felt something was missing.

I had always been interested in how women moved into places in society where they had previously been banned and what effects that move had both on the women and their work. I began to wonder about women in ministry. How far had they come, what changes had they made, and how did they feel about being leaders? I wrote a proposal, secured some grant money and set out to interview women leaders in faith.

My stated goal with the project was to find the best cross section of beliefs, age, and ethnicity available in the local area, to conduct interviews with the women and then to create a public event to share what I had found with the wider community. The goal in my heart was to continue to explore my own spiritual path and to see if I could find what was missing for me.

The material in this book is the result of that study. I was able to interview 34 women with representatives from Bahai, Buddhist (Zen, Vipassana, and Tibetan), Christian (American Baptist, Catholic, Church of Religious Science, Episcopal, Lutheran, Methodist, Pentecostal, Presbyterian, Quaker, Unitarian Universalist, and United Church of Christ), Jewish, Muslim, Pagan and alternative healing. The individual stories in this book are edited from recorded interviews with each woman who was than asked to submit a prayer, poem or inspirational message to accompany her story.

As I conducted the interviews I felt great joy and connection with the women I was meeting. I wanted to join every church and movement because I was so impressed by the depth of love, wisdom and hope that I found in each person. To be immersed in the lives of these women was balm for my spirit; I had found the human spirit at its best. My own quest still goes on. I joined an interfaith group at the invitation of one of the women I interviewed and am looking at a meditation group led by another. I searched for ideology and found 10,000 mothers and now find myself nourished daily because of the work I have done.

Introduction to Prayers and Poems

When I put together a display with quotes and pictures from the Women in Leadership in Faith study I wanted to show a more direct connection to the spiritual life of the women in the study. Because I wanted the display to reflect something about their spiritual practice I asked each woman to give me a prayer, a poem or an inspirational saying that was not more than one page in length. Five of the women wrote an original prayer or poem, most of the others gave me quotes from the Bible, Buddhist texts, or the Koran and traditional sources. A few gave me prayers and poems from contemporary sources.

In our world where conflict and chaos are so frequently encountered we all need time to center and reflect, to pray for ourselves and the world around us. This collection is meant to be read slowly and savored. The words are chosen to be balm for the spirit as we allow ourselves to participate in an interfaith sharing of tradition and evolving wisdom.

I have read this collection over many times and have arranged the material in a cycle that continues to remind me that we are women searching for answers. I have tried to weave themes together with prayers and poems interspersed with traditional texts to remind us as we read the traditional works that these works have inspired at least one woman of faith.

I asked women who were not included in the original survey to submit prayers or poems and there are two in this book (Cahn and Rosen). And although every woman I interviewed submitted a prayer or poem there are three that are not included (Euritt, Friedman and Kime), primarily due to copyright complications.

Karyl Huntley Prayer

May the Infinite Divine Presence, from which we all came and to which we all return, who birthed the universe out of Itself, whose power is creative, unifying and sustaining—may this loving Presence be with the women of the world now, empowering them to do the work which is being called forth to be accomplished.

May all mothers and grandmothers of every earthly culture, all wise women in every walk of life, and all holy women from every spiritual path now be the hands and heart and voice of God.

May the wisdom and love of the Infinite One move through all women on earth at this time, healing separation, uniting that which has been torn apart, and celebrating all that is life-giving.

May all that is nurturing be lifted up, given away, multiplied, and well used so that this precious system of earthly life be re-established in harmony, balance, and peace.

May all this divine work that can be done through women be done by women now and all work that can be done through me be done in perfect ways for the good of all.

Let these words become manifest in our world now. Amen

A Prayer for the Women
by Karyl Huntley
(Rev. Huntley is a minister in the Church of Religious Science)

Jan Heglund Prayer

For I know the plans I have for you
declares the Lord,
plans to prosper
and you are not to harm you,
plans to give you hope
and a future.

Jeremiah 29:11
(Rev. Heglund is an Episcopal Deacon and a Police Chaplain)

Denise Bowman Wylie Prayer

Compassionate God,

At Starbucks and Nordstrom they know us by name. Their computers reveal our choices, our vices seemingly benign.

Time management defeats us! Completely filled with doing important tasks for our family, our friends, and our community, our days provide no respite, no margin, and no peace. Amid the stressors of our routine, please meet us with Your peace. Satisfy our longing to live significant lives.

We fear missing an opportunity to develop our children's potential. We imagine that mastering carpool conundrums may ensure their enrichment and our Palm Pilots will keep us in order. Please, guide our scheduling with Your values. Help us to securely ground their experiences with Your wisdom and let our own lives reflect our respect for You.

And what about our potential? In the struggle for competing priorities we often lose ourselves. There is so much to do. We cut ourselves so little slack. It's just not in our wiring! Or, is it? You created us. You know us inside and out, wiring included. Help us to know You. May we perceive Your presence amid the chaos, love ourselves as You designed us and delight in our relationship with You.

Our gracious homes are not consistently grace-filled. The mortgage alone ups the ante. We have indentured ourselves to our shelter. Remind us of our greater liability to You. May our grateful hearts be reflected in true hospitality toward all You send our way. May our words be kind and our welcome be sincere.

Yoga, Pilates or Spinning Class may stretch our frames. We ask You to stretch our vision. May we see those in pain, distress and grief with caring eyes then respond with healing actions. Help us reach out with Your grace.

You have blessed us with so much. We are among the richest in the world. As we live in the tension between realizing our own abundance and recognizing other's scarcity, help us to join You in righting the balance. Give us the daily courage to act selflessly.

We need Your Spirit's constant encouragement and Jesus' bold example. Thank you for providing both the blessing and the challenge. Help us to reflect Your love in the choices we make.

Amen

by Denise Bowman Wylie
(Rev. Wylie is a minister in the American Baptist Church)

Lama Palden Prayer

May all beings have happiness and the causes of happiness!
May all beings have no suffering or the causes of suffering!
May all beings have the supreme bliss which is free from all suffering!
May all beings live in the great equanimity which is free from all attachment and aversion!

Buddhist Prayer
(Lama Palden teaches Tibetan Buddhism through the Sukhasiddhi Foundation)

Carolyn Kellogg Prayer

Holy One,
your many names are holy.
May your presence prevail everywhere
and in our hearts.
Give us daily bread
for body, mind, and spirit.
Cover us with your compassion
and open our hearts
to all our sisters and brothers.
Guide our steps on the journey
and surround us with your love.
Holy One,
abide with us now and forever.
Amen.

by Monica Kaufer for A Critical Mass
(Ms. Kellogg is a counselor in private practice. She works with the women's
Catholic group, A Critical Mass, and for women's ordination.)

Susannah Malarkey, O.P.,
Prayer

One Earth
One People
One Love

by Susannah Malarkey, O.P.
(Sister Malarkey is a Dominican nun. She runs a retreat center.)

Louise Franklin Prayer

1. The essence of our being is love.

2. Health is inner peace. Healing is letting go of fear.

3. Giving and receiving are the same.

4. We can let go of the past and of the future.

5. Now is the only time there is and each instant is for giving.

6. We can learn to love ourselves and others by forgiving rather than judging.

7. We can become love finders rather than fault finders.

8. We can choose and direct ourselves to be peaceful inside regardless of what is happening outside.

9. We are students and teachers to each other.

10. We can focus on the whole of life rather than the fragments.

11. Since love is eternal, death need not be viewed as fearful.

12. We can always perceive ourselves and others as either extending love or giving a call for help.

The Principles of Attitudinal Healing, written by Jerry Jampolsky, M.D., and distributed by the Center for Attitudinal Healing
(Ms. Franklin is the Chief Operating Officer for the Center for Attitudinal Healing)

Aline O'Brien Prayer

Sing, feast, dance, make music and love,
all in My presence,
for Mine is the ecstasy of the spirit
and Mine also is joy on earth.
My love is law unto all beings...
Nor do I demand aught of sacrifice,
for behold, I am the Mother of all things,
and My love is poured out upon the earth."

by Doreen Valiente, Traditional throughout Craft
(Ms. O'Brien, a.k.a. M. Macha NightMare, is a priestess and a witch. She has co-written *The Pagan Book of Living and Dying* and gives workshops around the country.)

Linda Ruth Cutts Prayer

Homage to the Perfection of Wisdom, the lovely, the holy.

The Perfection of Wisdom gives light.

Unstained, the entire world cannot stain her.

She is a source of light, and from everyone in the triple
world she removes darkness.

Most excellent are her works.

She brings light so that all fear and distress may be forsaken,
and disperses the gloom and darkness of delusion.

She herself is an organ of vision.

She has a clear knowledge of the own being of all dharmas,
for she does not stray away from it.

The Perfection of Wisdom of the Buddhas sets in motion the
Wheel of Dharma.

Hymn to the Perfection of Wisdom
"We chant these words in our daily service. It is an excerpted version from an
ancient hymn to transcendental wisdom. The Perfection of Wisdom is icono-
graphically a woman figure."
(Rev. Cutts is a Buddhist priest and is abbess at a Buddhist Zen Center.)

Sue Severin Prayer

"I have a mantra I use whenever I'm feeling frustrated, annoyed, or something's not going my way, which helps me to regain and maintain my balance."

If this is my biggest problem...
then I have nothing to worry about.

"It's amazing how much this concept helps to put things into an appropriate context, and frees me up to move forward in appropriate ways."

by Sue Severin
(Ms. Severin is a Quaker, a peace advocate, and a volunteer who travels frequently to Central America as teacher, witness, and observer.)

Mary Neill, O.P., Prayer

O Christ, for thy sacred name's sake,
for thy bitter passion's sake,
for thine infinite mercy's sake,
forgive and forget what I have been;
pity, oh pity what I am;
satisfy for what I deserve and
grant what I desire;
oh, My Savior thou sought me
when I fled from thee;
do not reject me now that I seek thee.

St. Augustine

As soon as you trust yourself,
you will know how to live.

Goethe
(Mary Neill, O.P. is a Dominican nun. She is retired from teaching theology and works as a spiritual counselor.)

Nahid Angha Prayer

In the name of Allah, Most Gracious, Most Merciful
Praise be to Allah, the Cherisher and the Sustainer of the worlds
Most Gracious, Most Merciful
Master of the day of Religion.
It is You that I worship, and it is from You that I seek help
Show me the straight path, the way of those on whom You have bestowed your
Grace,
Those whose portion is not wrath, and who go not astray.

Fatiha, the Opening, Holy Qur'an
(Dr. Angha is a teacher in the Muslim Sufi tradition. She is the author of numerous books and the founder of the Sufi Women Organization.)

Meredith Cahn Prayer

This is my journey to become a blessing
It is a journey I make alone-but not alone
For with me is a well-packed bag
Of belongings I cherish
Even when they seem a burden.

At the heart, placed for greatest protection,
My family,
Surrounded by the people I embrace as friends
Supported by the women I know as sisters
Lined with the fabric of congregation and community
Covered by the canvas of the world in which I live.

Sometimes, it seems too much for me to carry
And I am tempted to remove something from the load.
But, would I want the bag to be any less full?
Would I want my life to be any less meaningful?

Perhaps, a little lighter
Perhaps, a little easier
So that the quality of its contents could be more deeply appreciated,
The beauty of its contents more thoroughly enjoyed,
So that the love and care with which it is fastened
Could be more visible and enduring.

But, whatever the weight or route to be taken,
It is my precious cargo which I carry with hope and promise
And the prayer that You will be with me
As I continue my journey
To become a blessing.

This, then, is our prayer
To become a blessing
To our faith and our God
To our people and our universe
To our congregations and our families
To ourselves and to each other.

by Dolores Wilkenfeld, From SACRED CIRCLE, an installation for the WRJ 43rd Assembly, (c)2001 by Women of Reform Judaism, The Federation of Temple Sisterhoods
(Ms. Cahn is a feminist activist in the Reform Jewish movement.)

Margaret Hough Prayer

Create in me a pure heart, 0 my God, and renew a tranquil
conscience within me, 0 my Hope!

Through the spirit of power confirm Thou me in Thy Cause, 0 my Best-Beloved,
and by the light of Thy glory reveal unto me Thy path, 0 Thou the Goal of my
desire!

Through the power of Thy transcendent might lift me
up unto the heaven of Thy holiness, 0 Source of my being, and by
the breezes of Thine eternity gladden me, 0 Thou Who art my
God!

Let Thine everlasting melodies breathe tranquility on me, 0
my Companion, and let the riches of Thine ancient countenance
deliver me from all except Thee, 0 my Master, and let the tidings
of the revelation of Thine incorruptible Essence bring me joy, 0
Thou Who art the most manifest of the manifest and the most
hidden of the hidden.–

Baha'u'llah, A Baha'i Prayer
(Ms. Hough is a member of the Baha'i faith. She has been an active leader but is
now retired.)

Fu Schroeder Prayer

What we are today comes from our thoughts of yesterday, and our present thoughts build our life of tomorrow; our life is the creation of our mind.

If a man or a woman speaks or acts with an impure mind, suffering follows them as the wheel of the cart follows the beast that draws the cart.

What we are today comes from our thoughts of yesterday, and our present thoughts build our life of tomorrow; our life is the creation of our mind.

If a man or a woman speaks or acts with a pure mind, joy follows them as their own shadow.

"He insulted me, they hurt me, she defeated me, he robbed me." Those who think such thoughts will not be free from hate.

"She insulted me, he hurt me, they defeated me, he robbed me." Those who think not such thoughts will be free from hate.

For hate is not conquered by hate; hate is conquered by love. This is the law eternal.

Many do not know that we are here in this world to live in harmony. Those who know this do not fight against each other.

Contrary Ways

"This poem is a portion of the first verse of the Dhammapada (The Path of Truth), the Buddha's simple teachings of compassion and wisdom compiled in the 3rd century BCE."

(Rev. Schroeder is a Buddhist priest. She serves as the head of practice at a Zen Buddhist center.)

Betsy Rosen Prayer

For all that has been-Thanks!
To all that shall be—Yes!

Markings, 1964, the diary of Dag Hammarskjold,
"He was a person who, while fully engaged with the world,
maintained a deeply spiritual private life."
(Rev. Rosen is an Episcopal Deacon who serves as a hospital chaplain.)

Allen Yan-Chamberlin Prayer

We remember unnamed women,
  who wove the threads of history;
  who gave to the world
      their music, their labor,
      their children, their struggle,
      their art. their visions,
      their laughter, their wisdom,
      their words, their lives;
  who survived in wars;
  who died in death camps;
  who told the stories;
  who made a way out of no way;
  who gave life to women
      who do so still:
  who minister as priests in the underground church in the former Soviet Union
whose ordination is not recognized by the Catholic Church;
  who fight for freedom in South Africa;
who pray for their missing children in El Salvador. Argentina,
      Chile, Guatemala;

  who live with AIDS and other illnesses;
  who work as healers, teachers, mothers,
      laborers, community organizers;
  who bear the cup of life;
  who poured it out to heal the ground on which you stand;
  who bid you taste and see
      how good it is.

Come, Spirit of Memory,
    and stir up in us
remembrance of all
    who passed us this cup.

Thirsting for memory,
    we cry out their names;
fill us, 0 Wind,
    transform us, 0 Flame!

(Rev. Yan-Chamberlin is a Methodist minister.)

Sara Vurek Prayer

For Our World
We need to stop.
Just stop.
Stop for a moment
Before anybody
Says or does anything
That may hurt anyone else.
We need to be silent.
Just silent.
Silent for a moment
Before we forever lose
The blessing of songs
That grow in our hearts.
We need to notice.
Just notice.
Notice for a moment
Before the future slips away
Into ashes and dust of humility.
Stop, be silent, and notice
In so many ways, we are the same.
Our differences are unique treasures.
We have, we are, a mosaic of gifts
To nurture, to offer, to accept.
We need to be.
Just be.
Be for a moment
Kind and gentle, innocent and trusting,
Like children and lambs,
Never judging or vengeful
Like the judging and vengeful.
And now, let us pray,

Differently, yet together,
Before there is no earth, no life,
No chance for peace.

September 12, 2001
by Mattie Stepanek, From *Hope Through Heartsongs*, Copyright © 2002 Mattie
Stepanek. Reprinted by permission of Hyperion.
(Rev. Vurek is pastor of a United Church of Christ church.)

Linda Compton Prayer

Living is not a private affair of the individual.
Living is what we do with God's time
What we do with God's world.

Rabbi Abraham Joshua Heschel
(Rev. Compton is an ordained Presbyterian minister who is Executive Director of a non-profit agency for disabled and seniors.)

Ann Eichhorn Prayer

Gracious and Holy One, We pray for guidance and wisdom as we wake each day.

Enable us to discern the myths that seek to control our actions, and separate us from the rest of your human family.

Empower us with courage to speak out against injustice; strength for the long struggle in the sharing of life giving resources in equitable ways.

Guide us towards peaceful solutions, sparing human life and dignity by intentionally putting aside violent behavior and responses.

Grant us insight and humility when faced with adversity, that we might listen also to what is not being said, and act first out of the principles of love for the other.

Bless us in your work to be done on earth. Amen

by Ann Eichhorn
(Rev. Eichhorn serves as co-pastor of a United Church of Christ Congregation.)

Jan West Prayer

Christ has no other arms but ours
to do his work in the world.

St. Theresa of Avila

They do not need to know
how wonderful you are,
they need you to love them
so they will know
how wonderful they are.

Traditional
(Rev. West is an Episcopal priest. After a number of years as the spiritual advisor at a non-profit, she is now serving as an assistant pastor in an Episcopal congregation.)

Joanne Abrams Prayer

There was a woman
whose hands
were empty of purpose
and Sisterhood made them full.

There was a woman
whose burdens were great
and Sisterhood helped to lighten them.

There was a woman who yearned
to express her joy in Judaism...
her love for her family...
as well as her concern
for the human family
and Sisterhood gave her the tools.

For Sisterhood can be
the instrument in our hands...
the sensitive pen with which
we write our message.

Let us dedicate ourselves
to that purpose
to do good, to do more, to do it now
as Jewish women in a changing world
...while unchanged...

deep within us...
is our faith...
the faith of our fathers and mothers...
our beloved Judaism

(Ms. Abrams is a wife and mother who is active in Women of Reform Judaism and other Jewish organizations.)

Veronica Goines Prayer

For over seven years I have extended an invitation to the congregation following the proclamation of the Word of God. Visitors, members and friends, touched by the love of God expressed through song, prayer, the passing of the peace, and the preaching of the Good News, come forward indicating a desire for new or renewed commitment to Jesus Christ. The piano sounds, the church stands, a verse of spirit-filled song is sung. And above the music these words ring out:

"Come to Me, all you who labor and carry heavy burdens, and I will give you rest. Take my yoke upon you and learn from Me, for I am gentle and humble in heart, and you will find rest for your souls. For My yoke is easy, and my burden is light."
Matthew 11 :28-30

These words of Jesus were spoken to a group of weary people, struggling under a system of political and religious oppression over two thousand years ago. Yet, the words for many are compelling still.

Just recently, feeling totally overwhelmed by the enormity of ministry, I wondered, "Am I supposed to feel like this, or is something wrong?" I began to make it a matter of intentional prayer. Trying my best to turn it over to Jesus, I prayed, "Lord, I'm struggling so right now. I am not experiencing the abundant life that Jesus talked about. I feel overwhelmed and under-supported. I know that you've called me to the ministry, but I hope this is not what you had in mind. Lord, help me."

My feelings of frustration and exhaustion began to dissipate as light and clarity broke through the haze. The very Words that I extend on Sunday morning, the Words Jesus spoke to the weary masses, were the Words He so sweetly whispered in my heart:

"Come to Me, all you who labor and carry heavy burdens, and I will give you rest. Take my yoke upon you and learn from Me, for I am gentle and humble in heart, and you will find rest for your souls. For My yoke is easy, and my burden is light."
Matthew 11 :28-30

This message crystallized for me as I read a copy of Pulpit Helps, in which appeared an article by the title: Are you Wearing the Wrong Yoke, or Wearing the right yoke wrongly?" The title itself was confirmation that Jesus was calling me back, and to learn from him how to wear this yoke rightly.

I know no greater challenge in this life than that of spiritual leadership. Yet, as great as it is and can be, there is a greater source than we. I hope that others will find in these words liberation. I am experiencing, again, a greater sense of abundant life, as I learn to listen more carefully to the voice of Jesus, to discern clearly the yoke he has for me, and how not to carry yoke intended for others. I can affirm that his yoke is easy, and his burden is light.

by Veronica Goines
(Rev. Goines is pastor of a Presbyterian church.)

Janie Spahr Prayer

O for a world where everyone respects each other's ways,
where love is lived and all is done with justice and with praise.

O for a world where goods are shared and misery relieved,
Where truth is spoken, children spared, equality achieved.

We welcome one world family and struggle with each choice
that opens us to unity and gives our vision voice.

The poor are rich, the weak are strong, the foolish ones are wise.

Tell all who mourn; outcasts belong, who perishes will rise.

O for a world preparing for God's glorious reign of peace,
where time and tears will be no more, and all but love will cease.

"O for a World"
Text by Miriam Therese Winter
© Medical Mission Sisters 1990.
(Rev. Spahr is a lesbian activist and an ordained Presbyterian minister who heads
the organization, "That All May Freely Serve.")

Carolyn Logan Prayer

"To God be the glory for the things that He has done!"
I will bless the Lord at all times:
his praise shall continually be in my mouth.
My soul shall make her boast in the Lord:
the humble shall hear thereof, and be glad.
O magnify the Lord with me and let us exalt his name together.

Psalm 34:1-3
(Ms. Logan is a Pentecostal "Licensed Missionary" and the Women's Ministry Director of a Pentecostal congregation.) *This passage was also submitted by Kelly Thomas.*

Gervaise Valpey, O.P., Prayer

This is what Yahweh asks of you,
only this:
to act justly,
to love tenderly and
to walk humbly with your God.

Micah: 6:8
(Sister Valpey is a Dominican nun. She recently retired as the principal of a K-12 school and now serves as their Director of Development.)

Carol Hovis Prayer

God has told you,
O mortal,
what is good;
and what does the Lord require of you
but to do justice,
and to love kindness
and to walk humbly with your God?

Micah 6:8
New Revised Standard Version, Old Testament
(Rev. Hovis is an ordained Presbyterian minister who serves as the spiritual director for a non-profit agency.)

Betty Pagett Prayer

"Choose life, that you and your descendents may live!"
Deuteronomy 30:19

As we reflect on our Biblical story and on our faith, we find ourselves looking at our own moments of exodus and exile. We find in our own stories a connection to those who are 'exiles' in our midst. What self-interest do those of us who are not poor have in investing in the poor? The future of children who grow up with our children? Our own elderly and disabled parents, uncles, cousins? The bottom line is that it is in our mutual interest to respect the full humanity of all our neighbors, even those de-humanized and robbed of their dignity by unemployment, low wages, homelessness, illness and age.

We examine our own lifestyles. Where do we shop? How do our lifestyles relate to our economic systems, what resources are used? Where do our sales taxes go? Is our consumption out of proportion to the needs of others? Working together, we can make choices that build just and caring communities.

Our children need to see us meet human need and solve community problems more than they need to see us isolate them from those who are different or who have urgent and troubling needs. It is from *us* that our children learn what it means to be human!

In these most challenging times, we will be asked as individuals and as families, as congregations and as communities, to choose between differing policies and programs that will have considerable impact on millions of lives. 'Choose life, that you and your descendents may live!'

We are the ones to remember the faces.

We are the ones to keep in our hearts the stories of the real people on waiting lists and in shelters and on the streets.

We are the ones to keep focused on the big picture–the children of the future.

The communities we shape will continue long after us.

We are called to take practical steps, for the Love we are called to embody is practical love.

We *can* create and sustain caring communities.

Working together, we celebrate our common humanity, we tell and re-tell the stories and make our choices.

Together, we seek a way home for all.

The Reverend Betty Strathman Pagett, adapted from "The Way Home," <u>Christian Social Action,</u> January, 1998.

(Rev. Pagett is an ordained Methodist minister. She serves as Director of Education and Advocacy For Affordable Housing for a non-profit agency.)

Renee Geiger Prayer

Holiness is knowing we have tasted God and knowing that we can never be satisfied with just that taste.

It is choosing, in spite of our fear, to go more deeply.

Holiness is facing the pain of the world and crying out with its suffering.

Holiness is stopping to gasp in amazement at how love stirs in the joy and beauty of ordinary events.

Holiness is feeling an awesome restlessness that pursues us even though we try to run away from it.

Holiness is choosing to keep on struggling and believing that there is such a thing as eternal life, that there is such a one as eternal love.

Excerpted from *Fresh Bread and Other Gifts of Spiritual Nourishment* by Joyce Rupp. Copyright © 1985 Ave Maria Press, P.O. Box 428, Notre Dame, IN 46556, www.avemariapress.com. Used with permission of the publisher. (Rev. Geiger serves as pastor of a Lutheran church.)

Sylvia Boorstein Prayer

This is what should be done
By those who are skilled in goodness,
And who know the path of peace:
Let them be able and upright,
Straightforward and gentle in speech.
Humble and not conceited,
Contented and easily satisfied.
Unburdened with duties and frugal in their ways.
Peaceful and calm, and wise and skillful,
Not proud and demanding in nature.
Let them not do the slightest thing
That the wise would later reprove.
Wishing; in gladness and in safety,
May all beings be at ease.
Whatever living being there may be;
Whether they are weak or strong, omitting none,
The great or the mighty, medium, short or small,
The seen and the unseen,
Those living near and far away,
Those born and to-be-born—
May all beings be at ease!
Let none deceive another,
Or despise any being in any state.
Let none through anger or ill-will
Wish harm upon another.
Even as a mother protects with her life
Her child, her only child,
So with a boundless heart
Should one cherish all living beings;
Radiating kindness over the entire world:
Spreading upward to the skies,

And downward to the depths;
Outward and unbounded,

Freed from hatred and ill-will.
Whether standing or walking, seated or lying down,
Free from drowsiness,
One should sustain this recollection.
This is said to be the sublime abiding.
By not holding to fixed views,
The pure-hearted one, having clarity of vision,
Being freed from all Sense desires,
Is not born again into this world.

The Buddha's Words on Loving Kindness
(Ms. Boorstein teaches and writes about Buddhism. She is the author of numerous books including *Don't Just Do Something Sit There*.)

Carol Saysette Prayer

For in wisdom there is a spirit intelligent and holy
unique in its kind yet made up of many parts
subtle, free-moving, lucid, spotless, clear, invulnerable,
loving what is good, eager, unhindered, beneficent,
kindly towards men, steadfast, unerring, untouched by care,
all-powerful, all surveying, and permeating all intelligent,
pure, and delicate spirits.

For wisdom moves more easily than motion itself,
she pervades and permeates all things
because she is so pure.

Like a fine mist she rises from the power of God,
a pure effluence from the glory of the Almighty;
so nothing defiled can enter into her by stealth.

She is the brightness that streams from everlasting light,
the flawless mirror of the active power of God
and the image of his goodness.

She is but one, yet can do everything;
herself unchanging, she makes all things new;
age after age she enters into holy souls and makes them
God's friends and prophets.

Wisdom of Solomon 7 21:28
(Rev. Saysette is an ordained Presbyterian minister and a spiritual counselor.)

Introduction to the Stories

There are many ways you can read the stories of these women leaders in faith. The stories contain information on the great variety of belief systems and the many paths that lead to the divine. The women in the stories tell of how they came to follow their particular path, usually they have to complete a search of their own hopes, dreams and motives that is instructive. In all cases the need to serve is strong, in most the need to change outmoded thoughts and patterns is stronger.

My goal in doing the study was not to be scientific but to give clear images of real women who have had many of the struggles that all women face. I wanted to share the stories of how the discovery of a path actually happened for each individual.

The following transcripts are edited from one-hour interviews. This is the way these women speak, not the way they write. In many cases I changed the order of thoughts and words in the actual interview to make it more readable but I always tried to leave the sense of an individual voice. I eliminated all the pauses and repetitive words that most of us are unaware of in our spoken conversations, and I edited out tangents and dead ends. I hope my editing has brought clarity of thought and not muddled anyone's story. I had a wonderful transcription company who got the words from tape to paper (or computer) but the editing work is entirely mine as are any and all errors in the text.

Joanne Abrams Story

JEWISH CONVERT

Claiming Judaism

I was raised Catholic and had a very strong Catholic upbringing. I went to parochial school through grammar school and high school at Mercy Burlingame. When I was in high school I was very active in an organization called Sodality. We would visit people in retirement homes and convalescent hospitals. As a senior in high school, I was president of Sodality, and I was the first person to bring a weekend retreat to our high school.

Recently I was looking at an old high school yearbook, and it described Sodality as a way for the girls to find spirituality in their lives. And I thought, boy, I really haven't fallen very far from the tree, when I think about that. I'm still a very spiritual person, but it's taken a different path.

I was always interested in Judaism, even as a child. There was something about the mystique of it. I don't know what it was, but I just felt the connection. And always dated Jewish boys, never dated Catholic boys. Of course, the nuns were appalled by that. And I ended up marrying a Jewish man, Fred.

His family celebrated Christmas and Easter, and they were Jewish in their heritage and nationality. His dad had been a Hebrew scholar, but for some reason he never would talk about it. I wanted to get married by a rabbi, and, of course, they didn't know any rabbis. Thinking about it now, that was twenty-five years ago, we probably wouldn't have been able to find a rabbi to marry us, because at the time I was still Catholic. So we were married by a Congregationalist.

When our son, Nathan, was two, we decided to send him to the Jewish day school in Oakland. That started this whole thing with me of being Jewish, because he would come home and he would have his little prayers. Fred and I would sit there and say "What?" We were totally clueless.

I started becoming involved in the day school and ended up being on the committee for the nursery school. It was part of the Oakland Jewish Community

Center. As a result of that, I was on the board of the Jewish Community Center. Still had not converted to Judaism. A few years later Nate went to kindergarten and we felt that we were losing our connection to Jewish life because he was going to a public school. So we decided to visit Temple Sinai in Oakland, which is a Reform temple.

I'll never forget it. The first time I walked into that synagogue for shabbat service, I felt like I had come home. This warmth came over me, and I felt a connection, that this was where I belonged. I started taking classes on Judaism. And, Fred and I and the two boys took a family education course. We were learning the prayers and starting to do high holyday services at our home and attending services, and would meet with the rabbi, Rabbi Steven Chester, who's a real *mench*, just a wonderful person, and talk to him about what I needed to do to convert. He said, "You don't have to do very much, because you're already a Jew in your heart." He was just this incredibly sweet person.

Sisterhood

I have since been very active in the Women of Reform Judaism which we usually refer to as the Sisterhood. It's an international organization which our synagogue belongs to. We have a gift shop which is our fundraising arm. Our gift shop is successful and we put the money that we receive back into the synagogue.

We support the religious school. We give them money every year for the holiday so that we provide *gelt* at Chanukah and *hamentaschen* cookies at Purim. We provide money for scholarships for children to go to Jewish camps and to Israel, money to the rabbis so that they can visit college students. We provide money toward the senior lunch program.

We want to provide a way for Jewish women to come together as a community to help meet their spiritual needs. This is our fifth year to sponsor a retreat. Meredith Cahn and myself, we're the ones that originated this five years ago with Rabbi Stacy's help. The first two years it was a one-day retreat. Now we do a two-day retreat off-site.

Also we have what we call shabbatons, which is on Saturday, or shabbat. We have a woman's service that is written by women for women. About thirty women attend and we pray together, study together, laugh, and talk about women's issues. We put on programs regarding women's health issues. We do fun things like go to Jewish museums, maybe to a Jewish film festival, and have dinners. And we do a woman's seder.

I have been programming chair, president, and I'm currently treasurer of our Sisterhood, as well as serving on our district board. I am serving my second term as a director at the district level. As a director, I am responsible for five other Sisterhoods within the Bay Area, and I contact them to see how they're doing, if they're having problems with membership or volunteers, or if they need programming ideas. I've been nominated to become the treasurer at the district level.

Every other year we have a national convention which brings about 2,000 women together from all over the country for three days. The United American Hebrew Congregations come together at the same time as the Sisterhood convention is happening. So on Friday night for shabbat service and on Saturday morning for shabbat, there's usually about 5,000 of us altogether for services.

Sisterhood has a seat on the UN, and we contribute money toward the Religion Action Coalition, which is a lobby for the Congress so that we make sure that women and children's rights are looked at. We were in the forefront recommending the acceptance of gay marriages to the Reform movement. The Medical Marijuana Initiative was initiated here within our district and then taken to the national convention and was passed at the national convention. We look at rights not only within the United States, but international human rights as well.

It's a very powerful organization. The president and the executive director of the international organization meet with dignitaries from all over the world. We have a very strong presence nationally and internationally and it's something we're all very proud of.

Torah

We're still trying to break through the glass ceiling as far as how the Torah is approached, because the Torah that we read is really a patriarch document. Women either have no names or they're these women that are in cahoots with trying to get their sons into power. There's not much commentary that is written from a women's approach. It has really only been in the last twenty years, but more so in the last ten years, that we're seeing new commentary and women taking time to look at what is their role in Judaism today.

One of the things that we have done with WRJ is to commission a complete Torah commentary done by women for women. We started about five years ago. The first booklet that came out took three different chapters from the Torah and did women's commentary on that. We hired a woman rabbi who will be the editor of this commentary on the complete Torah. So we hope with in the next four years, we'll have a complete document. I definitely think that there are still places for women to push. There are no women scribes to write a Torah. That's not accepted. It has to be a male scribe.

The Torah scroll itself is all handwritten on parchment skins. And, for it to be considered kosher, it must be written by an Orthodox scribe. We thought "wouldn't it be nice if we could have women write a Torah?" But all Orthodox scribes are male. So we got around this in a very funny way. Eight years ago we commissioned a Torah that would travel with dignitaries from the international organization, or our own Sisterhood chapters could request to have the Torah brought to us.

First we had to hire a scribe. The first scribe appalled all the women at the convention as he belittled women. And there was this huge outcry, "No way we're going to pay for this guy to do it." So we hired a second scribe, a wonderful man named Neil Yerman. He comes to conventions and local retreats, bringing the scroll. We made an arrangement that for a fee women could go and put their hand on his hand as he would write a letter in the Torah. It is the most incredible experience. And he teaches us about the Torah and the thought and the process that goes into writing a Torah scroll.

The Torah was completed at our convention in December 2001. It was the most incredible experience that we ever had. Most of us have written at one point over the four years once or twice in the Torah scroll. We had this incredible ceremony where the Torah was presented. Everybody was dressed in white, and the Torah was opened up. They unfurled the whole Torah, and they wrote the first word at the beginning of the Torah and the last word at the end of the Torah. Then it was blessed and rolled.

We have a video of it; it was so powerful. Women were getting up and dancing and crying. Neil Yerman got up that day, he said, "Well, my sisters," and everybody just got emotional and started crying. He's a *mench*. He's an incredible person and we learned so much from him. So the Torah scroll has been completed, and though it's not written by a woman, women have touched that Torah.

Women's Seder

One of our big highlights of the year, is the women's seder. We have it catered, so none of the women have to be in the kitchen preparing the meal, which is a big role for women at home at Passover. We use a service that has been written by women of the congregation. So it's more of a matriarch's approach to the story of the fleeing of Egypt to Israel. We sing and we dance.

Traditionally when I think of seder, I think of the women in the kitchen, because there's all this food that has to be cooked. The patriarchs of the family are leading the service, and, of course, the whole story is told from a male point of view. It's about Moses and from Egypt. You always think of the women with the piles and piles of dishes, because you'd have so many ceremonial foods that you traditionally eat.

When we decided to do a women's seder we decided that we didn't want to cook. We want to be out there having fun. So we hired a caterer. We've had a caterer now for the last five years.

The first year, everyone that came had to bring a symbol of personal oppression, because Passover is about an oppressed people. Some people brought serious things, about quality of pay or health issues that affect women. Or they brought funny things. I brought a paper bag, because I feel all I ever do is make lunches every single day for kids. Somebody else brought pantyhose. It was a mix of serious and funny things. Then the following year the theme was freedom. So everybody had to bring a symbol of personal freedom. Now we've moved away from those themes, and it's more to get women connected. We have about 100 to 110 women that come to this event every year.

Spirituality

I find spiritual renewal in solitude at retreats, in nature, with other women and with my family. The retreat's really a time for me to step back within myself and look at who I am and my connection with God. I really like that period of silence, of meditation. I feel closest to spirituality and God when I'm in nature. If I can be out in nature and take time to breathe and to reflect and to feel around me what's happening, I feel a connection to a god.

I also feel spiritually renewed by services. But we don't go to services often because it's really hard when you have children, on a Friday night to get everybody through dinner and to get to the temple. We began to ask, "what was the point of rushing dinner? Shouldn't we be taking time to have dinner as a family?" Shabbat really should be a celebration in the home.

When we do come together as a family and light our shabbat candles it feels like a time out which I like. It's a time out of time. There's a ritual of when you light the candles, that you bring your hands from the flame to your face three times, and then you put your hands over your eyes and close your eyes as you're saying this blessing over the candles. Then when you take your hands away and you open your eyes, it's the beginning of shabbat. There is an actual moment where everything is changed.

Shabbat starts Friday night and goes to sundown on Saturday night. On Saturday I don't get on the computer. It's a simple thing, but I will not get on the computer at all. I won't make phone calls if I can help it. If someone calls me, I will take the phone call, but I try not to use the phone.

More recently I have been trying to just not feel guilty about not doing the laundry or running errands on Saturday. I'll work in the garden or I'll read or do needlepoint. I'll do something that's for me. Fred and I try to relax and find more spiritual activities. That's what it's supposed to be. It's a time out of time.

Women's Day Off

I'm involved with a group of eight women who meet once a month. It is a time for women pray and study together, it's called Rosh Chodesh. The story behind the Rosh Chodesh is that when Moses was up on the mountain getting the Ten Commandments, they built the golden calf. They were collecting jewelry and gold from the people.

There's a *midrash*, which is a story, about women at this time. It's not in the Torah but it's an interpretation, that the women refused to give their gold. And as a result of that, God granted them, on the new moon, a day of rest, when they do not cook, they do not do housekeeping. It's their day of study and prayer.

That holiday wasn't celebrated for many, many, hundreds of years. About thirty years ago it was reintroduced through Sisterhood. Many women have established these Rosh Chodesh groups, where they get together at the time of the new moon. My group is from our congregation. And once a month we meet at somebody's house in the morning.

First, we do a check-in. Everybody goes around and says how they've been for the last month. Then we read from the Torah portion and we discuss it. Sometimes personal issues come up. It's always very confidential. Whatever happens with this group of women stays with the group. We have developed this incredible community. We take time for silent meditation and socializing also as well. But we've become a tight community. It's really wonderful.

Role Models

The more that I'm involved with women's groups, the stronger I feel about women and how powerful we really are. When I was growing up, I could relate better to men than I could to women. But as I've gotten older, I find myself relating more to women and the sisterhood of women.

Therefore, I think it's important, that we have role models that are women, and spiritual leaders that are women, because they bring to the table their own personal experiences as a woman. Not that men aren't great spiritual leaders, because there are some rabbis in my life who are men, who I think the world of and who I draw energy from, and who have made me feel better spiritually. But women also can do the same and yet they bring it from a different aspect. They can relate to the roles women perform (professional, mother, daughter, wife, sister, daughter, friend, etc.) And to have women in a spiritual role, is really important for young girls so that they can see that they can be whatever they want to be.

Joanne Abrams is a wife and mother who has served as a board member and officer of Women of Reform Judaism and other Jewish organizations.

Nahid Angha Story

SUFI LEADER

Iran Was A Different Country

Iran before the revolution was a different country. Women were in leadership positions, making their own decisions, etc. They were entitled to do what anyone else was entitled to do. I don't know what is going on in Iran right now, and, after the revolution. But one thing I know, and that is, Iranian women are strong. If politics push them away, they will come back to claim their seats, as Iranian women do not take the second seats.

My Father Was My First Teacher

I was born into an atmosphere of spirituality. I was also interested in what my father was teaching. I loved my father so much, and I wanted to know what he knew. When I was a child, I always wanted to be just like him. I was interested in what he was doing, which was not only teaching Sufism and spirituality, but he was also an acclaimed philosopher, scientist, and poet. That's how I was introduced to this path, through its wholesomeness and beauty. It remained my path until now, and to future.

My father was a very open minded teacher, he assigned women to teach and lead, including myself. He did not make the path of Sufism a male dominated path of spirituality and leadership. He made it open to whoever was knowledgeable, whoever was qualified, and whoever was ready to take the responsibility.

The history of Sufism has been abundant with many outstanding teachers; some of these teachers were women. Yet not much about them is known, perhaps they have been mentioned as footnotes under the biography of their male students. But ignoring their teachers is the shortcoming of cultures. And I am sure this is a case for many cultures regardless of their religious practice. I am hoping that many of these women were recognized during their own time.

Sufi's Are Muslims

The Sufis are those Muslims who practice more than just the rituals of the religion. They have made the pursuit of knowledge, a teaching of the Prophet, their duty and responsibility. They become more open-minded toward understanding, it is not your color, gender, nor your culture that prevents you from pursuing the knowledge of God. Nothing should prevent you. However, sometimes, you, or your ego, become the obstacle preventing you from pursuing such knowledge.

Islam is not only a spiritual religion toward understanding God; it is also a social justice religion, meaning that when you become a knowledgeable person, it is your duty to serve your community. Your duty does not end with you serving yourself. That is actually in conflict with the teaching of the Prophet. One does not serve one's ego thinking one is serving God, one does not mistake one's ego as God. When you learn, you learn to serve humanity as humanity is the sacred creation of God. Your serve God, and through that you serve humanity.

So when you become spiritual, you also choose to serve your family, your society, and your greater human family. At the same time, you have to be knowledgeable, because the more you know the more valuable servant you will become. The less you know, the lesser value you will provide to your community.

As long as we are alive, the door of knowledge is not closed. As long as we change, we are open to learning.

I practice as other Muslims. During the month of fasting, Ramadan, I am aware that I am not only teaching my body to learn to take less food, but I also give the money I save as a result to the poor or to education. I am thankful for such teaching. And most importantly, through such practice, I learn humility and compassion.

True Spirituality Can Only Come From Deep Conviction

My personal opinion is that: in order to have a religion, you need to have a longing first. Religion is not something that you can dictate to yourself, nor can someone else. That is why I do not believe in converting or being converted. That is not how "having a religion" or "believe" works. This is a wrong approach. Everybody is free to come to a religion; such is a longing in the depth of someone's heart. So you find it, you come to terms with it, you are at peace with it, and it becomes you.

In order to become a spiritual person I have to learn to remain present in my heart, so to understand what it means that God is present wherever I am. That is the only way you see the presence of God in all His creation. You become more observant, more alert.

Moving To The United States

When I came to the United States, I wanted to teach and share my knowledge with a different culture and nation. I have found the people of this nation open, interesting and interested. So my husband and I established the International Association of Sufism. There were many people who, internationally, nationwide and also locally, helped to create this organization. It began with a few of us and developed into an international, well-respected association. It has supporters from around the world, teachers from around the world, and we have accomplished many goals.

The Creation Of The Sufi Women Organization

One of the greatest accomplishments of the International Association of Sufism is the creation of Sufi Women Organization that now has chapters and representatives around the world. And we are taking a great many steps for human rights, with focus on women's rights, in Muslim and non-Muslim countries.

One of the local projects is a prison project. We have volunteers who go to women prisons here in Marin County. They teach stress reduction, anger management, health education like breast cancer early detection. There are so many positive things that we can do for female prisoners in the Marin County jails. Nationwide, we write letters and send books for prisoners. And this is not only women; it is men and women. It is open to all prisons.

With Sufi Women Organization, I have created an online dialogue that has members from around the world, where we address issues that are important to women. We have people from Australia, Indonesia, Europe, Africa, United States, Canada, and Middle East. Sometimes we share information and address issues that are not so much known either in one's county or even other countries, because the media does not always address facts. The women tell you what is happening, so you are informed, you are connected with the women and their issues in their own countries.

One of the greatest accomplishments that we had was after the rioting in Indonesia when some of the buildings and orphanages were destroyed. Our chapter in Indonesia sent a note that maybe one of the things we need to do is to rebuild some of the orphanages. So we began to collect money, and we called it Chocolate Box Collection. And the story goes that you buy a chocolate box, and you empty the chocolate and keep the box in your house or your office, and every Saturday put some money in that chocolate box. As soon as it goes in that box, it is not yours any longer. It belongs to Sufi Women Organization and is saved for those humanitarian efforts that we all agreed upon.

We were able to collect chocolate box money from around the world to send to Indonesia, and they were able to rebuild an orphanage. The importance of this accomplishment is not that they were able to build an orphanage; it was the trust that all of us created amongst ourselves.

I also encouraged and am encouraging many women, many Sufi women of the present time, to write their biography so their biographies are not lost in history and in culture. As the result of the first attempt, I was able to collect, compile and publish the *Journey Towards the Beloved*, the biographies of the Sufi women of the present time written by themselves. This is the first book in a series, and I am hoping to continue this project.

The Importance Of Women's Role As Mother

Women have such a greater natural opportunity than their brothers do, sometimes we underestimate that. The opportunity is the trust of nature in entrusting you with the creation of life. It doesn't mean if you have a child or if you do not have a child, it has nothing to do with bearing children. It has everything to do with that natural trust of capability to bear and care for life. That is the trust bestowed upon you by the intelligent nature. As a woman, you have that trust. As a man, you do not have that trust.

The teacher of any human being is a mother. Thus it is necessary for us to recognize the contributions of these teachers of humanity to human civilizations. Sometimes we may ignore to acknowledge that. Sometimes we do not think of ourselves as the educators. We are not just mothers feeding a child; we hold the pulse of the civilization. We cannot forget our responsibilities.

This is such an important issue. I think many human societies have forgotten this simple, yet important fact, including us. There is no leader in the society, anywhere in the world, whose teacher was not a mother. Either it was a mother, a nurse, or a grandmother. Most children are not trusted to their fathers or to their grandfathers or to a male nurse. They are trusted to a female, and that is an important observation.

If the world is wrong, then we have to ask ourselves: "Where did we go wrong, as mothers?" Did I not teach my son to respect all lives, did I not teach my daughter to stand for her own rights? It is not enough to blame the world for its wrong direction; I am the mother of all humanity, so I have to learn my art, so I have to stand for the wellbeing of my human family.

Women Need To Educate Themselves For Leadership

Women, who are in leadership position, need to take the responsibility, educate and open doors for other women, and other women should take the opportunity. However, we need to stand up first, and we have to qualify ourselves for leadership. Leadership comes with hard work. Leadership is a part of healthy, positive competition. Thus we need to set goals, and, means to accomplish those goals. Achievement accompanies qualification, and qualification comes with clear understanding of one's goals and one's capability. We need to educate ourselves, not only on social level but also on academic level. Education is a great tool. It teaches us patience, it sets goal for us, and it helps us endure hardship, creates friendship, and satisfies our thirst for positive contribution.

Sometimes we may choose not to work outside the home, that is our choice. But we have to be independent in our thoughts, in our action. When one stays home to take care of her family, she really has to stand up and make sure she is helping and providing for her family the means to make all the right decisions. So she is not only providing them with food but also providing them ground for a sound future, with morality, with best kind of opportunity that they can have.

Sometimes when we are not acting to our potential it is because others tell us that we do not have potential, and we believe them. It is a pity, they limit our opportunity, so it becomes a struggle for us to expand and open a door for ourselves. And sometimes it becomes frustrating and we give up. That is why women need to come together, to network, to exchange ideas. We must learn not to fail at the feet of frustration. Don't give up because others tell you that you do not have what it takes.

Women Lead By Example

In 1994, we had our first Sufism symposium. It was in that conference that I sat in the circle praying with all my Muslim brothers. And, probably that was the first time, to my knowledge, that a woman sat in the center circle with men. That act opened a great many doors for other women, I made sure of that. And my spiritual brothers were very supportive. Perhaps they did not know how to take the first step, so I had to make it easy. I made it easy for them through communication, through mutual respect. I believe in doing in what I teach. If I am teaching respect, I have to have respect for myself and for others. If I'm teaching honor, I should be an honorable person myself. I also have to qualify myself for whatever I am trying to achieve.

Women are great peacemakers; they can offer ground for peaceful resolutions. We have done it through our parenting and teaching, so we are experienced. At the same time, our children have learned to listen to our mediation. So as grown-ups why shouldn't we expect them to continue listening to our peacemaking solutions?

Offering peaceful ground for resolution is an art that women are qualified for. We have been successful in creating peaceful ground for resolution in our home; I do not see why we may not offer the same ground to our greater human family?

Dr.Nahid Angha is a member of the board of the International Sufi Association, sits on several interfaith boards, teaches, writes, translates Sufi writers and is the founder of the Sufi Women Organization.

Sylvia Boorstein

BUDDHIST TEACHER

Personal

My own work in consciousness began in 1968. I had graduated from social work school, and I was working in San Rafael. A friend of mine called and said, "There's a yoga class at the Jewish Community Center. Do you want to go?" I went, and it seemed to me, in terms of ambiance, very ordinary. It was held on the basketball court of the old Jewish Community Center. The teacher, Magana Baptiste, played quiet music–probably Stephen Halpern—on a record player.

I loved the class. It was wonderful. Nothing amazing happened in terms of "psychic" experiences. But I knew after just one class, that there was something Magana knew, something that gave her a quality of calm confidence that I needed to know.

After that series of yoga classes ended, I became a student of Magana and traveled often to San Francisco and her yoga studio. The ambiance at the studio was much more unusual, more contemplative, more "new age," than the Jewish Community Center. There were bells and gongs and incense. Although a part of me wondered, "What am I doing here? This is not like me at all," I became a regular.

Magana would say what seemed to me some very odd things like, "Now, let your consciousness rest in your lower abdomen." I would think, "What an unusual thing to say." Or, she might say, "Feel your abdomen surrounded by the color orange."

I probably thought, "That's so peculiar!"

But, what was more strange was my discovery that if I followed her instructions they worked. I began to understand that consciousness is not equivalent to thought, wasn't located in my head; I began to feel my body as more alive, and that the suggestion, "Wake up your awareness, here or there," woke it up. That discovery played a key part in my growing interest in consciousness and meditation.

Contemplative Practice

I think that the growing interest in this country in Eastern religion practice is the awareness that contemplative experience, meditation, is an important aspect of a complete spiritual life and has largely been absent in modern Western religious practice. I first learned of Buddhist practice, specifically Zen practice, by reading the books of Thomas Merton, a Roman Catholic monk. I was influenced by Merton's books, very moved by his spiritual dedication. His discovery that his life as a religious practitioner was deepened by Zen practice, that it illuminated his liturgical and prayer life, was inspiring.

It is also true that the Buddha's teachings on the difference between pain and suffering–that pain is inevitable in life and that suffering, the extra tension in the mind suffering with pain, can be lessened through meditation–is compelling to people whether they think of themselves as religious or not. The teaching of Buddha is known as the Dharma. It's very accessible. It's straightforward; it's not mystical. People find it easy to understand. The Buddha is said to have said, "I've come to teach one thing and one thing only. Suffering and the end of suffering." People resonate to that.

Basic Dharma

One of the first things I heard at the first meditation retreat I attended was a teaching of the Buddha to the people of Kalama. He said, "Don't believe anything I say. Don't believe anything that anybody says. Not if it's a friend, not if it's a respected personage, not if it's a noted teacher, not even if it's a Buddha. Don't believe it. You try out what I'm saying to you, and if it makes a difference in your life, then you'll know that it's true. You don't have to believe it's true."

That was tremendously interesting to me because it made it immediately clear that there isn't anything about practice that needs to be accepted *a priori* as an act of faith. Mindfulness was presented as a personal practice, not as a set of beliefs to be taken on. So it can be a useful practice for people with connections to other religious traditions, as well as to people who are not religious.

The Buddha was acknowledged as being Enlightened, entirely free of suffering caused by confusion. My sense is that beginning meditators these days are not thinking about becoming enlightened; I think they are meditating in order to feel less trapped by their mind, less stressed, more peaceful. I also think that, as Westerners raised in a culture whose religious ethos is social responsibility, people are practicing meditation because they want to make a positive difference in the world.

The Dalai Lama can describe Buddhism in four words. Someone said, "Is Buddhism a religion?" And he said, "Yes." "What kind of religion?" And he said, "My religion is kindness."

It's not kindness that we take on as a, "Okay, ready, set, go, I'll be kind." It's the kindness that naturally arises from really seeing how very difficult life is. It is the spontaneous response to suffering. However lovely or pleasant or exciting our lives are, or the lives around us are, we are all also continually being presented by situations that upset us. The challenge, I think, is to be able to keep our hearts responsive, relaxed and alert, able to respond wisely.

Buddhism and Psychology

I became a psychotherapist in 1967, and I went on my first Buddhist retreat in 1977. People often asked me where do they overlap, and when are you doing therapy and when are you doing spiritual direction, or how does your insight meditation color how you are with people. I think my therapy training was very useful in helping me to recognize patterns of psychological response that were unique to me, or to the person I was working with, based on our former experiences. To whatever degree habit patterns are illuminated, they cause less pain. The patterns, though, don't entirely go away.

I think I became a better therapist because I began to see how my patterns cause suffering. I catch myself in a pattern sooner and undo it sooner. I am less frightened of my own suffering, and I've become less frightened other people's suffering because I am, generally, more at ease.

The Buddha's insight about the inevitable suffering inherent in life, in the challenge that changing physical health, changing circumstances, presents for us all is an insight we all share. In psychology we might call it existential angst. I think it's a good thing to realize that life is difficult. Perhaps it is this very realization—Life is difficult that's just the truth of it—that leads people to spiritual practice, to a search for a way of cultivation a mind (and heart) that can respond to difficulty with compassion rather than with despair.

Women Teachers

I've been noticing that these days there seem to be more women students in retreats at Spirit Rock than there are men. This face, I think, makes it more important than ever for us to have women teachers. Historically, women have not had prominent roles as Buddhist teachers, but the emerging Western Buddhist community is, in keeping with the recently changed Western consciousness, more egalitarian.

I recently led a retreat at Spirit Rock, a gathering of nearly a hundred men and women, at which both of my associate teachers were women. Our teaching teams, for the most part, are both men and women, so the fact that we were all women was somewhat unusual. I'm guessing that it might have been meaningful to the people on the retreat, but no one mentioned it at all. So perhaps it felt as normal to them as it did to us.

On Behalf of All Beings

It is said that after the Buddha's Enlightenment, his deep understanding of suffering in the world was what motivated him to teach "on behalf of all beings." Sometimes I think of the world as a graveyard, the summary of everyone who has come before us, who, like us, tried to remedy suffering. That makes me think of the world as holy ground.

The Buddha taught that the roots of evil are greed, hatred and delusion, and when I think about this world, this holy ground, and all the troubles that are happening to it now: the wars between nations, the civil wars within nations, the unequal distribution of the riches of the planet among its inhabitants, I sometimes feel overwhelmed. I recently said to a friend, "You know, maybe the pain and the turmoil in the world is too far gone. Maybe we should just give up." He looked a me and said, "Sylvia, you know that's not an option." He was right, of course. He needed to remind me because in my distressed confusion, my faith had wavered. I am grateful for my opportunity to teach because I see that as my chance to remind myself and everyone who hears me that transforming my own heart towards peace on behalf of the world is the only option.

I think the troubles of the world continue because we haven't yet seen clearly that pursing our own selfish ends as people and as nations perpetuates the pain of the world. Just as the Buddha became Enlightened, understood clearly the cause and the end of suffering, I am hoping that the whole world will suddenly wake up and say, "Wait, we are doing this wrong. We can stop. We can befriend each other. We can convert our hearts to kindness and the planet to peace.

Sylvia Boorstein has written several books on Buddhism, including *Don't Just Do Something, Sit There*. She is one of the founders of Spirit Rock Meditation Center and teaches there and around the country.

Linda Compton Story

AGENCY DIRECTOR

The Call

I was not raised in the church, and actually, being a child of the sixties, had a bit of an adversarial relationship with organized religion and, I think, some smugness around that, too. I had seen neighbors or friends who attended church on Sundays and then did things the other days of the week that I as a "heathen" or an "infidel" wouldn't be caught dead doing, mainly because I feel I'm a person of conscience and integrity. So I had a real bias against organized religion.

Then in 1979, when I was working for a multinational corporation in healthcare management, I had a very dramatic "Saul, Paul, Damascus road" conversion experience, which literally and indelibly changed my life. As I like to say, it was not on my things-to-do list, to become a Christian, it was certainly not in my five-year goals and objectives. It was a very life-changing and transforming experience, which has informed and guided my career path from there.

I was reading an article on the shroud of Turin, the reputed burial cloth of Jesus, and there was a rather lengthy article in the December '79 issue of the *Santa Barbara News & Review*, which is like our *Pacific Sun*. There was this scientific research team that had been invited to Turin, Italy, to try and document the authenticity of the shroud in 1978. Brooks Institute, which is a photography school in Santa Barbara, was named to have the photographers on the trip. So there were astrophysicists and other scientists, but all the photographers that were invited on this team were from Brooks Institute in Santa Barbara.

I was sitting in my living room, alone on my couch, and reading about this trip and the local photographers who had gone over there and been part of the research. I was reading it with sort of a smug, touch-in-cheek, intellectual curiosity, thinking, "Oh, well, this is interesting. I have a bachelor's degree in philosophy with an emphasis in Eastern thought. I've traveled and studied in India. So I can read about this."

I got to a certain point in the article where it was explaining that there was this phenomenon that to this day is still inexplicable, and that is that every time this linen, this sixteen-foot piece of cloth, is photographed, the image is actually inverted. So when you take a picture, you have a negative in your camera. You take that and you develop it and then you have a positive print. The shroud is actually a negative, so the light and dark images are inverted or reversed. This happens every time this reputed burial cloth is photographed. Doesn't matter what the camera is, the speed of film, the process, it's always the same.

So I thought to myself, "Well, this just can't be." I've done work in the dark-room, and so I couldn't wrap my mind around this. There was no category where it would fit. So there was just this moment where I think I set aside my smugness and my skepticism and said, "Huh. How can this be? I wonder. I wonder if this could be true, if this might be real," and at that moment I opened up to the possibility.

My entire living room just flooded, filled, and flooded with this blinding light that didn't hurt my eyes, but my fanny was riveted to the couch, and I couldn't move or speak, and it was almost like smoke clearing. I found myself in the presence of this most incredibly loving, perfectly loving, lighted being, and we had a conversation, not audibly, but I heard it from the inside.

I remember thinking about this song or hymn, "Amazing Grace," and somewhere along the line as a young girl I had heard that. I remember thinking how offended I was by it. My sensibilities were offended, and I used to think, "Gosh, how absurd. I may not be perfect, but I'm certainly not a wretch." You know, just my ego, my humanness was offended by that lyric, and that was the only part of the song I remember.

It was from somewhere in my past, but I remember thinking at that point that I was absolutely aware for the first time, of my wretchedness, my creatureliness, not because there was any sense of judgment coming from this loving, luminous being, but because over against that, my self-understanding was that I was so small, that I was so petty, that my worldly ambitions were so insignificant, and I felt this creatureliness and felt absolutely loved and accepted at the same time.

At one point in this inner dialogue I was invited to read John. After some period of time, that I don't know chronologically, but maybe an hour later, after this experience subsided, I remembered that I had an old Gideon Bible that I had stolen while in high school from the Disneyland Hotel as a joke, and it was upstairs in a box in the back of my closet.

I thought, "Read the gospel of John," or, "Read John." I didn't know what that was, but I had a sense it was probably in that book. So when I was able, I went upstairs and I dug through this old box of stuff, and I found this Gideon Bible. I finally get to the gospel according to St. John in the table of contents, and I know that's it. So I start reading this chapter, and it's talking about Jesus being the light of the world, and I realized that that was what I'd just been blinded by.

Several things happened after that, but one was that I went to work the following Monday. I had a staff of about a hundred nurses who worked for me and several physical therapists, and one of my physical therapists, who never came to the office or made appointments with me, called that morning and said, "I have to see you today."

My day was booked, but my assistant said, "You know, she's really insistent that she wants to see you sometime today." So I rearranged some appointments and saw her after lunch. It was amazing, because she said, "God told me to come see you today." I said, "What do you mean?" We'd never had a conversation like that. "What do you mean?" She had been given a dream to come talk to me. So I told her what happened. Then she recommended a church which I visited the following Sunday. I ended up joining that church and being baptized the following Easter.

The subsequent pastor of that same church visited with me. I went to talk to him and told him some of the things I was struggling with, and it was harder and harder to hear those sermons on Sunday morning and not do something about it, you know. He said, "You know, I think you have all the signs and symptoms." I said, "For what? I feel fine." He said, "I think you're being called to the ministry."

The Work

I think of Marin County as my congregation. The values and the theology that I hold dear call me to look at everyone who is entrusted to my care, which is anyone and everyone that I interact with, as a congregant. After I finished seminary I worked as the Executive Director of the Marin Interfaith Council and then as the Religion Program Officer at the Marin Community Foundation. I enjoyed the work at the Marin Community Foundation and had no plans to leave.

But the headhunter for Whistlestop called me three times over a five-week period and encouraged me to apply, and I said, "I'm honored and humbled and that's great, but it's a mess. It's too big. I don't want it. I'm just learning to be effective at the foundation and love my colleagues here and what I'm learning. I feel I'm doing some effective work." But the third time she called me to consider applying here, she said, "Look. Let's just go to lunch. There's one thing I want to say to you, and then we can talk about other issues." And I was familiar with the agency and some of its challenges and also the good work that it does.

So, again, kind of like reading that article about the shroud of Turin, I had this smugness, and I thought, "Well, it doesn't matter. Whatever she tells me, I'm not interested," and it was still in that "Thanks, but no thanks" mode that I accepted her gracious invitation to come to lunch.

We were sitting at lunch and she handed me the qualifications for the ideal candidate and she said, "Now, we're not going to talk about this now. You just take this home and read it at your leisure. But this is what I want to tell you." She leaned forward, and she looked me right in the eye, and she said, "Linda, what these people and this agency, what they need more than anything else, is a healer." And I looked at her, and I smiled and said, "You dirty dog." She really got me with that.

And I went home and I read the brochure and literally got down on my knees to pray about this. Within ten or fifteen seconds, I was sobbing, just sobbing. What I feel is that I'm told where I'm supposed to be. I do feel called, and I've never doubted for a moment that I'm supposed to be here at this time. And it was for healing. It was for a kind of spiritual infusion of values and vision that would heal the agency and take it to that next level. The staff is different today because of that conviction. They didn't want a minister for their executive director, but they called *me* to be here, and I am a clergyperson, and I bring that. That is who I am. So I've been referred to—and I like this, actually—as a monk in the marketplace, and the marketplace needs monks badly.

The agency and the community are my congregation. I try not to impose my theology on anyone, but I do have a responsibility to share my sense of mission, values, and accountability.

We work with people who are vulnerable. So our population, by virtue of our mission and our services, means that we are serving the least of those among us. We serve elderly and persons with disabilities, which means that by some definition, they're vulnerable and they need care and they need assistance. We're not just delivering over 100,000 meals a year to seniors; we're providing service, a real human connection, and we're showing that care and compassion to someone who has a need, a very specific need. So it's not just a service delivery system, but it's a system of compassion and service as well.

The Need For Faith

It weighs heavily on my heart that we've had such a—I don't like to use the word *crisis*. I think it's overused. But I do think there has been some kind of spiritual crisis in this country because of maybe the sixties and then the greed of the eighties and nineties. Just the lack of trust in organized religion in general is very painful. Because I wasn't raised in the church, I wasn't wounded or betrayed by the institution, but I've seen that and the repercussions of that. I think part of the fabric of our created being is that we are spiritual and that there's a hunger and there is a restlessness until we find our rest in God, however we conceive of that.

There's a wonderful quote, and I don't know whose it is or even when I heard it, it wasn't attributed to anyone. But it was not that we're human beings on a spiritual journey, but we're spiritual beings on a human journey, and I love that. I believe that, especially with my clinical death experiences. I believe that with all of my heart, that we are spiritual beings on this human journey.

So to the extent that organized religions, that institutionalized religions, have abused their powers and hurt and done harm where they were supposed to do healing and good, I do think there's a crisis. I think there has been kind of a phoenix experience where new expressions are coming out of those ashes of betrayal and disappointment. But it's hard.

I have so many people who come and want to talk to me, and they say, "You know, there's something about you that's just different. I'm not a religious person. I don't want to talk about religion, but I'm wondering if there's something that is missing, and do I have to be like you to have that?"

That's hard to hear, because what people are saying underneath is, "I don't trust the church. I don't trust these faith traditions. I don't trust these spiritual leaders who have abused their power. But I'm still hungry. I'm still searching."

Near Death Experience

My own faith has been strengthened by the near death experiences I have had. I've had two clinical death experiences, or what are called NDEs, near-death experiences. There's a universal theme that runs through all of those stories of people who've experienced NDEs, and that certainly reinforced and heightened my conviction that we are connected one to another and that we are in relationship one with another and we are accountable. Ultimately we are responsible. I take that very seriously.

The first one was after an emergency surgery. It's almost comical, the first part, because I was in the recovery room after the surgery, and I had some awareness that there was some poor woman who was just having a hell of time breathing, and I could hear her, and then I heard the physician, the recovery room personnel, or nurses saying, "Oh, oh, she's in trouble. Oh, we're losing her. We're losing her."

Then I'm hovering above my body, and I look down, and I'm looking at this poor pathetic little shell, and it's me. You know, we're not quite so glorious when you're outside looking. I thought, "Oh, that poor thing down there." The nurses and the folks there are doing their CPR stuff.

I'm looking down and I'm trying to reach down to just touch them on their shoulder and tell them, "I'm fine. Relax. Don't worry. It's okay." I can't quite reach them, but I just wanted to tell them that, "Don't worry." Then there was this radiant, glorious tunnel of light, and I was being drawn up into that and saw these figures similar to my conversion experience, that just lighted, luminous from the inside out, just magnificent radiance, and, oh, I wanted to go and be with them.

Then someone came in and filled the tunnel, and said, "Your work's not finished. You need to go back." I said, "Oh, no, no, I don't want to go back. I don't want to go back. Work? I have more work to do? No, no, no." Then I'm just looking up, and they're saying, "You're okay. You're going to make it. You're fine." And I went, "Oh, oh, no."

That experience was an incredible gift of grace, because my mother was dying. She'd been an alcoholic and had severe cirrhosis of the liver. We'd been quite estranged, and she was critically ill, and I took her to the doctor's. She looked nine months pregnant with death. She had severe ascites and was bloated.

He said, "Take here home. Do the best you can do. She may die tonight." There was a waiting list for beds at the acute hospital. Now, I was in healthcare management. I had a hundred nurses who worked on my staff. I ran a home health agency. But this was my mother, and I was paralyzed.

I said, "What do you mean take her home, do the best we can do, she may die tonight?" Well, they couldn't give her anything because it breaks down. It's toxic. So she was in tremendous pain. She didn't die that night. She lived for seven months, and she didn't drink. She was lucid. They wrote her up in the medical journals because she didn't have DTs or anything.

It was about midway through this period I had emergency surgery, and I think I had the clinical death so I could tell her with real authority and conviction there was absolutely nothing to fear, because she was terrified of dying. So I prayed with her, and I told her about this experience, and it completely changed her.

Then she had a dream one night shortly before she died. I was sitting up with her all night. You know, when you're up all night and you're exhausted and you're sad and it's about four in the morning and you're just kind of rummy? Well, I was in that place, and she woke up with a start and she said, "I just had the most remarkable dream. It was so perfect."

Then she started crying because *perfect* was such a pitifully inadequate word for the grandeur of what she had witnessed. She was by a beach, and they had given her these shells to listen to that reoriented her inner harmonics.

I said, "Mom I think God just gave you a vision of the other side so that you wouldn't be afraid to go." Everything shifted after that, and she had no fear. It was an incredible gift of grace, but I think that first experience was given to me so I could comfort her in her passing.

Linda Compton is currently Executive Director of Whistlestop, a non-profit agency serving seniors and disabled in Marin County.

Linda Cutts Story

BUDDHIST ABBESS

Personal History

Where did my journey start? I guess I would say that my serious turning toward a spiritual life happened when I was eighteen. During the first quarter of my freshman year at the University of Minnesota, the Fall of '66, I became pregnant. As often happened during those years pre-Roe. V. Wade, I was sent away to a foster home and my family and I lied about my situation. This was a very difficult time in my life. After I had the baby, and gave him up for adoption, I just went into a deep, deep depression. It was a major trauma, I guess you could say. I returned to school the following year and the world was very different. I was in a very different place than the rest of my classmates, and nothing made much sense anymore. I was really in despair. And then, with that mind, I was introduced to meditation.

A friend had come out to San Francisco to practice with the Japanese Zen Master Suzuki-roshi. He showed me how to sit in meditation and I was very interested in the practice. When he dropped out of his Ph.D. program to come to Zen Center, I thought, "Well, I'm going to check out Zen Center, too." There was a group of western students at that time, who had gathered around Suzuki-roshi to practice meditation and I just joined in with this group for a week in 1968. There was something different about the people and how they were. Just seeing people prepare food, chopping vegetables, sitting zazen (meditation), relating to their teacher was very important to me. I could barely say what it was that I saw that was so different, but there was something about the way they handled the kitchen utensils, and the attention they paid to the activities of everyday life that spoke to me, that met me. I left there thinking, "This is what I want to do with my life." I was twenty at the time. After going to Italy for a Junior year abroad program, and staying another year on my own, I transferred to UC Berkeley and moved into San Francisco Zen Center in 1971. I went right from Zen Center to Green Gulch Farm and then to the monastery, Tassajara Zen Mountain Center, and lived there for about five years, was ordained as a priest at that time, and have just been continuing to practice at Zen Center for all these years.

Zen Practice

I was raised in the Reform Jewish tradition-and my religion of origin did not meet my need for practice. In Zen the word practice is used a lot. In retrospect I realize that although there were many meaningful cultural and family practices, I did not feel drawn to the spiritual side of the practice. Even though there are Jewish meditation practices, I was never exposed to them, there was nothing that was offered where I grew up in that way, in part because Reform Judaism was moving away from many of the traditional practices. I think this is not so uncommon in other religious backgrounds. How the practice informs everyday life may not be so clear for us in our religion of origin. In Zen there is an emphasis on informal everyday life practice and the formal practice of zazen and other ceremonies. Zazen means "seated Zen" but zazen refers to both seated meditation and also a wider zazen mind. And it is that practice that allows you to bring understanding into your everyday life. There are many practices offered: mindfulness, doing each thing completely, awareness while walking, sitting, standing, and lying down, bringing your attention and clarity and awareness to each activity. This all seemed so fresh to me. No one had ever talked about "when you cut the carrots, just cut the carrots," just be there with the cutting board and the knife. That felt like the key to life. It felt so important. Rather than a once a week thing, it was each moment of each day.

I could feel it, feel the aesthetic that comes out of being awake and being present with each day, each activity. That is the informal practice. In the zendo or meditation hall, there is the formal practice. There are certain forms, certain postures of the hands (mudras) and ways to stand and move, ways to enter the zendo, take your place, bow, sit down and fold your robe. And sometimes practicing with these kinds of forms, people might feel, "Oh, it's so rigid, there's no freedom." I find however, that I am encouraged to wake up through this formal practice. I am helped by actually working with this body and mind in a very particular container, the forms. In this way the everyday-ordinary and the spiritual-extraordinary, are not so different. I feel that being exposed to this practice is a relief. Instead of some lofty practice there is the groundedness of the everyday practice as an expression of our understanding.

Becoming A Priest

I became a priest in 1975 when I was 27. At Zen Center just what is a priest, is one of those age-old questions that we have been looking at. Suzuki-roshi acknowledged that our practice was not exactly a lay practice and not exactly a classic priest practice. He had a group of committed people who were practicing zazen daily and thoroughly, going to Tassajara monastery, and they were lay. In Japan, the laity are more like a Sunday congregation who support the local priest, relate to the Temple for ceremonial occasions, but they're not necessarily Zazen students.

Perhaps he thought, "I don't know what you are." And we are still working on this, clarifying the paths of a committed lay and priest practitioner. Basically, if someone wants to become a priest, there are certain prerequisites. A person has to be in the community for at least five years, has to have sat a certain number of long retreat weeks (called sesshin), has to have participated in a certain number of Tassajara practice periods, and one needs to have a teacher, someone who is working closely with you. The main intention is to devote yourself to conveying the wisdom and compassion of the Buddha in order to help all beings. In Suzuki-roshi's lineage, this intention is conveyed through zazen and the forms as well as everyday activities, and that's your basic life's work. Some people, after training, go on and do other things. As a priest, they may be teaching in an academic situation, doing hospice work, be a doctor or do chaplaincy work or psychotherapy...many possibilities. But for one's initial training, it's very clear. We also ask people, after they've been ordained, to be closely working with their teacher for a minimum of four years, and for most people it is longer.

I think that the emphasis on everyday mind and conveying the teaching through everyday life lends itself very well to being a teacher and working with children. There is a woman who was ordained and did her initial training, and after four or five years was the head monk, lived here in the community, and now is a very gifted teacher in the Mill Valley school system. So it may be traceless. You may not know that a person was ordained. The traditional way of living the life of a priest, doing pastoral work, leading ceremonies, grief counseling, other kinds of work with traditional Buddhist teaching and classes, may not be what one ends up doing one's whole life.

At least within the context of the San Francisco Zen Center there are many different ways to live as a priest. You can be a priest and be working down in the fields. In fact, we have people who are asked to work on the farm in order to help bring the sense of practice, Zen mind, to working in the fields. They become teachers in the fields, working with apprentices. Or one's work could be cooking. The job of the head cook in the monastery is traditionally given to a person who has matured in Zen practice. There's not a big dichotomy between your work and spiritual practice. It's one seamless expression of your understanding of life.

Women In Buddhism

Women have a complex history in Buddhism. From the beginning women have been drawn to the teaching and practice of the Buddha Way. The Buddha lived over 2500 years ago. The legend is that his mother died soon after childbirth and her sister, Mahapajapati, became his foster mother-aunt who raised him. After the Buddha's enlightenment he began teaching and she and a number of other women of his clan and the neighboring area wanted to become part of the Buddha's order which had been established for men. They asked for permission to ordain and there is a story that at first he refused to allow this. After repeated requests and the intercession of his closest disciple, he allowed the "going forth" of women, and a nun's order was established, very soon after the monk's order. So right from the beginning, the Buddha allowed the women's order because he said there's no difference between men and women in terms of spiritual understanding or ability to realize Buddha nature, their true self.

Buddha was not a revolutionary in trying to change the way the society related culturally to issues of men and women, although he was very egalitarian. Anybody could become a monk or nun if they had the proper prerequisites. He didn't uphold the Indian caste system within the order. Women had a separate order and they had various rules that were unique to them including being hierarchically beholden to monks. For example, in their ordination and in some other rituals, a monk had to be present. The nuns couldn't teach monks, but monks could teach nuns, so the education of women lagged behind, and the donations to women from the laity, which often go along with teaching, also lagged, and eventually the nun's order in India died out.

But the nuns' order got passed to Thailand and Sri Lanka and also into Tibet and Mongolia and into East Asia and Korea, Vietnam and China and Japan. So there always were monks and nuns. The spiritual teachings given were equal, but institutionally they were unequal. Because of cultural norms in all of those countries, the women's teachings and lineage were not valued and are therefore lost. Here at Zen Center we offer a dedication during the morning chanting service saying, "To all the women teachers known and unknown, remembered through these names," and then we name some of the women's names that we do have, but through the millennia most were lost.

When Buddhism came to the West it coincided with feminism, psychology, democracy, and all these other western things, and right from the beginning there have been an equal number of women and men involved with Zen Center, fifty-fifty. And Suzuki-roshi accepted that everybody was going to practice together and sit together in the same zendo, even though in Japan and other countries they are separate. It's a double standard in Japan, male priests can marry and women priests don't marry. When Zen came to the States it wasn't going to happen that way, and Suzuki-roshi just accepted that there were men and women practicing equally. He only ordained one woman, who ended up not continuing with her formal training, but he had a lot of lay women students. And Tassajara, the first monastery, was established as coed, rather than separate monasteries. And also administrative responsibilities and monastic responsibilities were pretty much shared.

So right from the start Zen Center had that as a value. But, just the way the culture is androcentric [male centered], I think Zen Center also was at first. I remember when the first woman was asked to be the head monk, head student of a practice period at Tassajara. It was a big deal. And now nobody even brings it up. It's just who ever is ready is asked. "Well let's have Kathy do it," "Well, how about John?" It doesn't get a blip in terms of the gender issue.

I believe I was the first woman to be head of practice (Tanto), in the city center in San Francisco. I remember what the abbot at the time said to me. I had just given birth to my daughter who was 6 months old, and he asked, "Are you still nursing?" I was indeed nursing and he thought that it was wonderful for the head of practice to be a nursing mother.

I feel Zen Center now has just about total equality for women. Even though Suzuki-roshi did not ordain many women, his successors did. Many women at that time and through the years were strongly encouraged to practice and took major responsibilities within all areas of Zen Center life.

Spiritual Journey And The Feminine

Wisdom and compassion are Buddha's mind, and compassion is very important. This loving kindness and nurturing and care and compassion traditionally are likened to that of a mother and this imagery is used in our liturgy. Some people had trouble with that imagery because of their own background and asked, "Well, why don't we use "parent" instead of mother?" But my feeling is that society is so out of balance in terms of valuing the feminine, we need these images. Even though we may have complicated relationships with our mothers, still it is an old and traditional image that people understand, that kind of love, I think it's a very positive image. And I feel it's the image that can be used for men and women, and maybe you could say, for men it is about developing their own feminine and enacting that wholeness.

Part of one's spiritual journey is realizing our true self. Who are we, really? There is the false self, made up of what's been internalized through the society and our families, in which we live for the approval of others etc. It is interesting how difficult this is to talk about, because the true self is neither male nor female and is beyond our conceptualization, but also we each take form. We manifest a form in this life. We are men or women. That's how it is. I don't find these two things at odds with one another. It's like finding one's true self is not separate from finding one's true form in our female or male body.

There is a Buddha or Awakened one, called Tara Buddha who is female. She made a vow to always return life after life in the body of a woman. That's Tara's vow. But at the same time, one can find in Buddhist writings that you have to be reborn in a male body in order to realize Buddhahood. So it is possible to find androcentric and misogynous teachings as well.

Now, this may come out of the fact that women in India had a hard time and a difficult life. They had very little freedom and were under the protection of their father, then their husband, then their son. Without that kind of protection, they were nobody. So maybe out of that kind of social vision, you might say, "Well, yes, in order to fully express yourself, you need to come back in a male body."

But Tara vowed to always return in a female body. That's how she wanted to manifest and teach. And she's the Tara Buddha. She is the fully awakened one in female form. It was very healing for me to encounter her. She is not necessarily a Zen figure, Tara comes out of an Indian and Tibetan tradition, but coming upon that teaching was very important to me, very empowering. It helped me to understand and celebrate the particularity of how my true nature is expressed in this lifetime.

Linda Cutts is currently the abbess at Green Gulch Zen Center in Marin County.

Ann Eichhorn Story

UCC MINISTER AND ACTIVIST

A Long Slow Call

I've always been a part of the church. My grandmother began to take me to church when I was three years old, every Sunday. I'm one of those people who had a whole shoulderful of good attendance bars till I was a senior in high school. It has always been a part of my life and a very important part of my life, but there was a period in which I had a lot of unanswered questions and confusion about the role religion played in my life.

Before I became a minister I worked for nineteen years as a delivery room nurse and an emergency room nurse. If you weren't busy in delivery room, you got pulled either to surgery or emergency room, so I went to emergency room. Because I was primarily working with women and girls who were pregnant I was exposed to what was happening in the early sixties and early seventies to women who did not have access to abortion rights or safe abortions. They did not have a real choice in whether or not they got pregnant.

I also worked in a Catholic hospital as a Protestant minister's wife. So I had a lot of questions about what religion is doing to our practices and our policies surrounding health care and people's choices and their own value systems. I was confused.

I entered seminary in 1975 to figure out for myself the answer, if there was an answer to some of these religious questions. Also, as a feminist, I was trying to figure out if there was anything in the Bible I believed anymore, and if it was all dominated by a patriarchal society I was asking if there was a place for me and my faith and my religion at that time.

I felt as though I was a part of a pioneering front. I couldn't see clearly what was behind me. I knew there were other women in seminary. I didn't have very many role models. In fact, relatively few at that point. I sensed it could be a lonely direction and it was, for me, for a number of years, but I felt okay about it.

I felt like I was called to it, that I was answering a call that had been there a long time before I recognized it, and that I was doing what I was meant to be doing.

When I was in my last year at seminary I knew that there were not very many positions available in the church for women. And, in particular, and for women my age. So I worked with a model, with permission from the seminary's senior program, to put together what I called Pieces Ministry, to see whether or not women could create or develop ministries of their own that would produce an income.

I did three pieces. I did family life consulting for our denomination's conference office here in San Francisco. And I was the California organizing coordinator for the Religious Coalition for Abortion Rights. Finally, the third piece was a program that we developed in a local church where my husband was serving, where I did outreach to the community, working with refugees from South Asia. We ended up co-sponsoring a twelve-person Vietnamese family. Those were the three projects. So where most of my colleagues had one or two supervisors who met with the department at the end of the year for evaluation and discussion about the future of ministry for the student, I had twelve people who were my committee.

When I was close to graduation I put together a proposal to be what we called an educational outreach minister and I became a missionary to the community. Mill Valley Community Church liked that idea and they said, "Let's go for it." So I decided, "Okay, I will go into ministry in this direction," and I was ordained in October of 1979.

A History Of Service

In 1984 my husband and I took a sabbatical to Germany and we worked with a church in Essen, Germany. The church had five pastors, one of whom was a woman, and we experimented and explored with what it would mean to be a co-ministry team.

We decided that we liked this model and that we thought we could do it. So we came back again to the States feeling as though we would most likely be leaving the area to float a proposal about co-ministry. Again we were advised, "Why don't you ask the church you're serving before you assume that they wouldn't be interested." We asked them and, lo and behold, they were interested.

So in '84 we were made co-ministers, which primarily meant that I was able to preach a couple times a month and also do weddings and memorials and baptisms and counseling, and Bill was also able to do outreach. So it helped us blend our ministries in that way.

We served that church from '84 to '89, and then we left there and went on our denomination's national staff. We moved to New York City, where we were elected to run the mission division for the denomination. We had a staff of fourteen program staff, and a number of clerical staff and consultants. We managed about fifty folks who provided mission support and project support to 6,300 churches and thirty-nine conferences from Puerto Rico to Hawaii.

We moved to New York knowing that the headquarters would be moved to Cleveland, and that part of our task was to be involved in that transition with staff and program. At the end of '93, a decision from Cleveland was before us. Did we do some lateral moves in other parts of the country, or what were we going to do. I had had cancer in '91, and we decided we wanted to come back to California where our home was, our adult children were, and our friends were. We left that ministry not thinking we would be back into ministry in the local church, but figuring that both of us would be working in nonprofits that were, from our perspective, mission oriented.

I worked as a development director for a couple years. After that I was an executive director of a nonprofit in the city. Then I took a job back in the county where I began a federal program for low-income people matching seniors with either children with special needs—that's a foster grandparent program—or with homebound elders—that's senior companion. I still do that program twenty hours a week.

Bill and I were members here at this church since 1993. It's had a very troubled history for the last about fifteen years. It lost its minister again in December of '99 in a rather quick resignation, and the board approached us and asked if we would be acting ministers. We thought about it and prayed about it and said, "Yes, we think we will." A part of our task on the national staff was to do some troubleshooting in other churches, and we thought it was time we helped this troubled church. And in April they decided that we seemed to be the team they needed and asked if we would consider it for a full-time position. So we share a full-time position here since April of 2000. That's how we got here.

As co-ministers there is an underlying question always in boards and sessions about where does the—quote— "buck stop," and the reality in a co-ministry is, with both of us. For folks that are still kind of hooked onto a patriarchal or a hierarchical structure, they want to see somebody over and in charge and with authority. So to have a shared or blended or a more egalitarian model is still somewhat experimental.

Working For Justice

I was probably radicalized with my faith through several issues. The first issue was the journey of women around the freedom of choice issue. The second issue was the journey with immigrants around their incredible torture and the things that were happening to them in the name of our government. And the third issue revolved around the gay and lesbian members of our congregation who we joined in the struggle for recognition. We helped get the first homosexual—out homosexual—ordained in any denomination. I don't think I would have chosen any of those issues, but, you know, God put them on our doorstep and you did what you had to do.

But the seeds for my radicalization came from when I was a nurse in the sixties in the Midwest which I'll leave unnamed at this point. I was a night charge nurse in a delivery room, after I helped women deliver their babies, I had to move them to their next place for recovery. In the hospital in which I worked in there were procedures where I was to put all the black patients on the non-air-conditioned floors and all the white patients on the air-conditioned floors and in the single rooms, and blacks in the wards. I got into a bit of difficulty a number of times because I bent the rules at night. So people who were supposed to go to the wards could have a sense of the coolness of air conditioning in a very hot place and a few more hours to recover before they had to go into less advantageous places.

This situation made me very conscious of racism and the implied privileges and assumptions that were behind racism that people weren't treated equally. I'm incensed by that wherever it happens, so I think all these places where I've been led and I've had to take an advocacy role have just been further examples of working with discrimination and inequity and injustice.

Ministry In Marin

I'm always interested in inviting others to journey with us in their faith, and to join with others in that journey, but I'm not interested in proselytizing a particular brand of religion. I think the most important thing we can be doing here at CCC is to be a community. And, at the same time we can open that community continually to others who might want to join it or be with us to practice our faith to the best of our abilities.

I experienced larger numbers of people in churches in some of the other settings like in a small Midwestern town. There the church may play a much more prominent role in people's life because it's about the only social event happening in the community. In this community we're in competition all the time with out-side activities. I think the opportunity that this gives us is that the people who come here to explore or to deepen their own faith are serious explorers. They are already grounded in their faith in some way that brings them together in a com-munity to celebrate God and find ways to serve in the wider community.

My real concern is about how we reach young people today to counterbalance the cultural values and the difficult and sometimes immensely negative messages that they get from the culture with something of joy and of positive self-esteem. I think there's a larger discussion that needs to happen, not only out of religious communities, but out of homes and parental responsibilities.

Finding Inner Peace

For personal spiritual renewal I like to walk the labyrinth. I got interested in the labyrinth about a decade ago. I didn't have very many opportunities to walk a labyrinth until the last few years. One of the things that thrilled me about this congregation, which is one of the reasons we joined here when we came back to California, was it was in the process of beginning to think about putting an out-door labyrinth in. We currently have an inside canvas labyrinth.

I'm the president of the board of directors of Veriditas, of Grace Cathedral in San Francisco, which is connected to the worldwide labyrinth movement. My work with Veriditas has me engaged in the labyrinth and people who understand it as a meditation tool and a grounding vessel.

I have a lot of interest in the right and left brain and how that works with us in terms of who we are and who we become. I'm absolutely convinced that the laby-rinth, with the way it leads and its pattern, is somehow linked to our brain func-tion; that we get both a right and a left brain fix, if you will, out of the labyrinth.

The labyrinth is not a maze. It has one way in and one way out, so you can't get lost on it. Even if you got turned around you'll still end up either in the center or back out. It's a place where you can go in mindless or you can go in troubled or you can go in agitated. By the time you come out, you're different. You've either calmed down, or you've got an answer to the question you took in, or you've moved from a mindless place to something that's become clearer or more focused. It's a very important place for me. It's sacred.

Ann Eichhorn currently serves as co-minister at the Community Congregational Church in Marin County.

Deanna Euritt Story

HOSPICE CHAPLAIN

History

When I was in my twenties, I wanted to be a social worker, but was not exactly the right profession for me to be in, so I decided to become an accountant instead. I wanted to balance being both a practical-minded person to make sure that I had a good career, with my desire to help other people. I struggled with that for many years, the social worker-accountant piece of me.

I used to live in Arizona where I contracted Valley Fever, which affected my lungs, my breathing, and my energy level. I had extreme fatigue, and it lasted for about five years, and I was able to work, but it was difficult. During that time, as everything in my life seemed to be unraveling, I was drawn more and more toward the church. I went to a community church, which had more of a Baptist perspective, but it was an evangelical, community-based church. The spirit of that church touched my heart, and I enjoyed being there. It was something that helped me get through my period of illness as well as gave me hope and inspiration. But I didn't like the theology.

I was beginning to have an interest in ministry. I was beginning to feel called by God to do something to help other people. I talked to the male minister of my church. He patted me on the head and basically said, "Go away, little girl, and do your accounting. That's much more practical." I walked out of there feeling very heartbroken.

So, I decided to visit this Presbyterian church that was in my neighborhood, it had co-pastors, a husband and wife team, and they were wonderful pastors. That was when I first realized, yes, women can in fact be in ministry. That would have been about twenty years ago about 1982.

Around that period of time, when I first began thinking about ministry, I had some dreams and visions. I felt God was extending a helping hand to me, to actually give me energy and strength, because I was so weak from the illness. I felt a very strong presence of God in my life that I had never felt before, and that really changed my life from that point on. Rather than viewing God as some hovering parent figure up there in the sky, God became very much a part of my life and not something or someone I thought about once a week on Sundays.

I decided to go off to seminary. I packed up my house and put it on the market. I farmed out my two little beagles to friends of mine. I got a U-Haul trailer, hooked it to my old Oldsmobile, and took off for California. I headed toward San Anselmo, which is where the San Francisco Theological Seminary is. I graduated in 1990 and was ordained in the United Church of Christ. My direction was to be a pastor in a church, to preach, to teach, to do pastoral care. But that's not what God had in mind for me.

First Church

I did end up going to a parish in Duluth, Minnesota, for a little less than two years. I had been raised in Iowa, and it was quite an adjustment to be back in the Midwest again after being gone for over twenty years. But it was a wonderful church, a wonderful experience, really, really good folks. I was an associate pastor at a church of about five, six hundred people.

I had been married for about fifteen years but was divorced before I went to the seminary. When I was in seminary, I realized that I had a lesbian orientation. That was a big surprise to me, as it was to many of my friends. So when I went to Duluth, my reputation preceded me. By the time I got into town, there was a front page newspaper article about this lesbian minister coming to town. They didn't name the person, but I was the only woman minister coming to town that month, so most people figured it out.

A lot of ministry that I did when I was in Duluth included the gay/lesbian community. It was a very mixed community of some very conservative and some very liberal people. I could not believe the number of people knocking on my doors wanting spiritual direction during that period of time. They didn't want to reconnect with the church, because they had been hurt by the church. They didn't feel welcome. But they would come to see me, because they wanted something in their lives. They wanted some kind of spiritual religious framework. I attended a lot of events, and it was a huge support for the people at that time to have somebody who represented the church tradition.

Coming to Hospice

I knew all the time I was in Duluth that I would not stay, it was an intuitive sense. Eventually I came back to California, and I was hired part-time by Hospice of Marin. I am now here full time as the Spiritual Services Manager. The work has been very diverse. I do patient care, counseling, community services and outreach.

Patient care consists of being with people who are admitted to hospice, being with patients, to help them deal with the end-of-their-life issues, which may be existential questions. Their faith may be enhanced or diminished by their experience, by their illness, by their grief. The same thing for family members, they may have a crisis of faith because of what they're dealing with.

It becomes heavy sometimes, and I think almost all of the staff members at Hospice have some sense of spirituality. We represent different traditions and beliefs, but we have a sense of spirituality. We all believe in something much, much more than just what's on this earth and our own mortal lives, and that gives us the ability to do this work. I think if we didn't have that kind of belief, we couldn't do this work. It would then be depressing because that would be the end, and that would be all there is.

We've seen a lot of love and beauty and just wonderful times for families in the face of death, that's been heart-warming. Families come together, and they're supportive and they're caring in ways that probably they hadn't been before. We find that a lot of families are really moved by this whole event called death, and they actually find it to be for them a sacred moment in their life. There are many spiritual, wonderfully spiritual experiences that we're witness to, and it feels like a privilege for us to be invited into a sacred space like that. That's what allows us to keep going.

We have a wonderful staff here, and we have good support. We have support groups. We always take a few moments to talk about the ones who have died and to hold them in our hearts. We have a staff memorial service every month in which we light a candle for each person who's died, and we read their names. We do those kinds of things so that we have a way to grieve. It's a loss to us too, especially if we've been very involved with patients and their families over a period of time.

But then we also are always reminding each other to take care of ourselves and to set boundaries. Very few people work more than forty hours a week, and that's true for me, too. There are times when I do, but it's usually because I'm doing something that is non-patient care.

Hospice Model

The concept of hospice in the United States began 30 years ago with the realization that people who were dying, and they were mostly dying in hospitals, were often put in the rooms that were farthest away from the nurses' station. Dying people had very little interaction with staff. They were basically alone, isolated, and had no one to talk to about their experience. It wasn't because people didn't care; it was that they didn't know what to do.

The Hospice model in the United States staffed mostly by volunteer female nurses, clergy and community members was started to help deal with quality of life compassionate care, symptom control, pain management, when cure was not an option. And that was totally radical. That was totally radical for the medical community, because the medical community had been geared toward curing, fixing, helping a person to get back on their feet again.

People simply were not trained to deal with pain control, symptom management, and death and dying. It was almost as if it didn't exist in our culture, this huge denial, and we still see a lot of that. Physicians are very supportive of hospice services but 30 years ago not as much was known about the dying process.

Death and Dying Experiences

We have heard may stories that people tell us of their own experiences just prior to death. I have been present on several occasions when people start having visions of loved ones who have died before them. Most understand that they're being helped along the way and as part of their journey, and that they're not going to be alone at the time of death. Oftentimes they'll see an aunt, uncle, mother, father, brother, or sister at the end of their bed or in the corner of the room.

Several years ago I was seriously ill and the disease was life-threatening. A couple of times I felt I was going to die, and that's when I felt God's presence and God's hand extending to me. So that was my first brush with death, and it helped me to work through some of my fears. But I think that this work has really done that, because it's helped me to reprioritize my life, to sometimes evaluate what's most important.

What seems to be most important over and over again is the love and care that we have for one another. Without that, life doesn't seem really important. When facing the end of life most people find hope in their faith and in the love of family and friends.

The Need for Volunteers/Interns

Our program has grown so much. I used to be the only chaplain, but now I function as a manager supervising other chaplains. We currently have three chaplains and two interns on staff. I'm trying to develop more of a volunteer corps to help fill in the peaks and valleys in our case load. If they'll commit to a period of a year and so many hours a week, then I will train them to be chaplains.

Women Are Still the Caregivers

One of things that I've noticed in this work is that women still are the caregivers. In families, it's almost always the women who are doing the caregiving, although I've seen some wonderful men who are actually doing the hands-on physical care. Our staff is 80% women, but we also have several wonderful male staff members.

There were many people who came together to make Hospice happen, including psychologists, physicians and priests. But I think it's primarily the nurses, the women nurses, who are nurturing, caring people by nature who realized that the dying process could be different. This could be more than just medication, procedures or placement. This could be about caring for a person, nurturing a person in a way that we've never thought of in medicine before.

And it's the often women who are saying, "Let's look at compassionate quality of life. Let's look at the more holistic ways that we can treat people. I think women have a greater sensitivity and are more intuitive about people's needs. I would attribute that to women nurses. Hospice was a movement led by women as well as a radical movement within the health care field.

Mary Taverna, our Foundation President, who helped to launch Hospice of Marin was a nurse and truly a wonderful pioneer. She was inducted into the Marin Women's Hall of Fame last year as a leader in the health care industry, and she really did forge the way. She started out as a volunteer herself when hospice was only staffed by volunteers. It was ten or fifteen years later before Medicare began to reimburse. Women nurses led the way and believed that this should happen, that people deserve to have dignity, comfort and care at the end of their lives.

Women As Spiritual Leaders

I think it's very important to have women spiritual leaders who are willing to lead not only in traditional institutions, but in nontraditional institutions. I think it often takes a woman with a strong sense of spirituality to be able to really make a difference in the world.

The first time I preached, before I went to seminary, I was terrified. I had all these physical symptoms of stress that you have when you do something like that, and I barely was conscious of what I said, because I probably had memorized the whole thing, and it just came out. Yet, because I was passionate about what I had to say, I was able to deliver the message.

So each time I do something new, I remember that, and I think, "You know, I stood up, and I was able to say what was truly in my heart."

The work that I do here can be important not only just in terms of the lives that I touch on a one-to-one basis, but also the outreach work I do in the community. I do some writing, some speaking, and I've done some workshops. I think that it's important to move from my heart into the public arena, to be able to put forward the kind of compassion that we need to have for people with end-of-life issues. Because of my spirituality, I lead with my heart. I lead with what I believe to be true, and that gives me the courage to go forth and have a voice.

Deanna Euritt is currently the Spiritual Services Manager for Hospice of Marin.

Louise Franklin Story

CENTER FOR ATTITUDINAL HEALING

History

I discovered the Center through one of Dr. Jampolsky's books, *Teach Only Love.* (Jampolsky is the founder of the Center.) At that time, I was going through a period that I would now describe as intense personal discovery and healing. It was as if I was coming out from under a heavy blanket–after years of suffering and struggle due to a series of events in my teens and twenties that had left me in a state of frozen grief and low-grade depression. I was experimenting with many kinds of alternative healing methods including meditation, intuitive and psychic states of consciousness, body work, twelve-step programs and counseling. In a way, I was beginning to feel as if I was in a kind of blessed state, or state of grace, because it seemed I was being led to particular experiences, people and organizations. At the same time, I was deeply concerned about my brother, who seemed to be developing a serious problem with drugs and alcohol. We had lost our father to suicide and I could not bear what seemed to be the likely outcome for my brother–an untimely death.

During this period, I worked in graphic and package design and had a successful business. Although I was a successful businesswoman, I felt increasingly split and unfulfilled. There was a growing yearning inside me-to integrate my spiritual life with my every day life. I think that when the heart is really asking for something, even if you are not consciously aware of it, it has a way of showing up. That's certainly what happened for me.

I never envisioned or planned to work for The Center for Attitudinal Healing. However, running an organization like this certainly provides me with an ongoing opportunity to integrate my spiritual path and practice with my professional life. My role as a member of the staff at the Center is multi-faceted. It not only involves managing the business side of the organization, it also includes working directly with clients.

I began my involvement with the Center in the 80's by volunteering in the teen program. I've always had an interest in teens, probably because it was such a hard time in my life and the lives of my siblings. After five years as a volunteer, I joined the staff in a part-time position as the Director of the Teen and Young Adult Program. At that time, we only served teens coping with illness. I had a particular interest in providing support for teens coping with bereavement and I was getting a lot of calls from parents with children who were not ill but troubled. These parents asked "Don't you have anything for my kid? They're having trouble with depression, grades, drugs, relationships, etc." At the same time, I noticed that the young people in our program who had survived their illness had emerged from the process with great life skills. I realized that the experiences these young people were having in the Center's programs could be helpful to any young person and I created the Power to Choose School Project.

The Power to Choose School Project has grown by leaps and bounds, thanks to a dedicated team. We conduct ongoing programs in schools that work with anger management and emphasize responsibility and making choices. We also act as a crisis response team to schools when there has been a death, illness, or other traumatic event. For instance, we visited schools after the September 11 attack and we supported students and teachers at a local high school after a fatal acci-dent-that-many of the students had witnessed. We also provided support at another high school that had a series of deaths in just a few months due to crime, illness and accident. We are on an on-call basis with other schools, if a favorite teacher becomes seriously ill or dies or if they are having problems with bullying or teasing behavior. We work with schools in many ways, providing support and education to children and youth, facilitating support groups or conducting memorials, and providing training and support to teachers and staff. We're in many schools now throughout the Bay Area and I still coordinate this program and work closely with Jimmy Pete, our Children & Youth Program Director. At present, I am actively involved facilitating weekly groups at Redwood High School. Its part of my job here. It's a big job.

Center Mission

The purpose of this Center is to build a community that cares for each other by mobilizing and training ordinary people to provide spiritual and emotional sup-port to those facing the challenges of illness, loss or other difficult circumstances. We emphasize service, and we believe in the extraordinary power of ordinary peo-ple to make a difference in each other lives. Mother Teresa once said, "If we do not feel peace, it is because we have forgotten that we belong to one another." This statement captures the heart of our work of building a peer support program that is fueled by volunteers. The spiritual aspect of the support we offer is not religious in any way or dogmatic in nature. Over the 27 years that we have been around, what we have seen is that Attitudinal Healing enhances people's religious or cultural beliefs and creates no conflict with it. This applies to those who are devoutly religious or atheists.

The Center exists to serve the local community of Marin County and the Bay Area and to serve as a model and training facility for similar centers around the world. There are 130 locations now worldwide.

A central part of our mission is to offer our direct services free of charge. We want to provide a place where anyone can walk in, take a look at our materials, and participate in our programs, without the worry of how to pay for it. So often, people coping with hard times such as illness, bereavement or other losses are facing real financial hardships and we do not want anyone to be turned away because of that. This establishes a kind of equality as well, in that no one need feel unwelcome or ashamed because of lack of financial resources.

Many of the people or families that come to the Center are facing the personal crisis of illness or loss. Many people are here because they are having what I would call a crisis of faith or, to say it another way, a complete breakdown of hope. They may be quite active in a church, synagogue or faith community and yet feel very separated and alone due to their difficult circumstances. Often, they feel they cannot face their own community, they may be ashamed or tired of giving only bad news or their community members may not be skilled at knowing how to offer support. The Center is a place where people can come for any reason, at no charge. Many are here because they want to be around people who are going through the same hard time and who will understand them. Many come to the Center for spiritual and emotional support while they work through a 'dark night of the soul.' Others simply feel lost, and the Center is perhaps a thread to a connection back to their own heart. Some people do consider the Center their church or their community while others see it as an enhancement to their spiritual path. I think the Center serves many people in healing their relationship with their God.

The Center also serves people who may be finding spiritual inspiration and values from many traditions and also want to be part of a place where they can find community and connection with others who want to strengthen their spiritual values. One of our programs, called Person-To-Person, consists of weekly group meetings that are open to any adult, for any reason. As with all of our groups, they are free of charge. People attend the Person-to-Person groups for a variety of reasons. Some begin to attend because they are coping with a significant life change or transition such as a divorce or job loss and then will continue in the group for years. Although we offer the groups as simply a place of safety where people can come and feel accepted and cared about, some participants have commented, "This is kind of like my church. This is where I go to connect with my higher self or my God.

As I've mentioned, we're based on a peer-support model of care and service and we utilize over 300 volunteers. Our approach to peer support is based on a kind of radical, conscious equality. One of our founding principles, which is read in each group or meeting, states "We are students and teachers to each other" regardless of age, education, or other differences. Therefore, we ask our volunteers to "leave their license at the door," as we do have many professionals who train and volunteer at the Center; including retired ministers, physicians, nurses, and teachers. Our peer-support model is distinctive because it includes a spiritual component. We emphasize the conscious practice of being fully present and honest, willing to listen with empathy, and practicing loving compassion with others. This practice, in and of itself, creates a very nurturing space that I personally think is holy, and is a healing atmosphere for everyone involved.

Center Philosophy

The Center's philosophy is based on the concept that we have the ability to choose our attitude regardless of circumstances. In other words, we all know that we often can't control circumstances, the people and events-around us or what may be happening to our own bodies but that we can choose our thoughts and attitudes about what is happening. We can make a commitment to peace of mind, and in that sense we can have a very high quality of inner life even in the midst of very difficult circumstances. The best examples of this concept are the people I meet every day at the Center who have been diagnosed with a life-threatening illness. They are going through, from the outside, horrific situations with their health and it is having an enormous impact on their family, relationships—every part of their life is changed. And yet, by facing death and through the Center's programs, so many seem to be able to live the life we all want, a life filled with loving compassion and inner peace. It is not unusual to hear people at the Center say "You know, I wouldn't have chosen this for myself, but I wouldn't change what I've learned through my illness and the spiritual growth I have attained through the process. It is not uncommon to hear someone that they feel more alive than we were before.

There are twelve principles of Attitudinal Healing that make up our philosophy. The first principle states that the essence of our being is love. This is a spiritual statement, inferring that we're much more than our bodies and larger than what happens to us. The essence of our being is love and what blocks our true nature or essence is fear. Draining, unhappy states such as anger, resentment, or judgment emerge from a field of fear and attitudinal healing is an invitation to develop awareness of our thoughts and attitudes, and discover we have the power to let go of fearful thoughts if we choose to do so. This is about taking responsibility for our thoughts and attitudes, gaining clarity and insight into what is motivating us, and exercising our amazing capacity to choose what it is we want to experience in each moment–peace or conflict. It is not about telling people what they should think or feel.

I think it is a wonderful thing to walk into a group at the Center; you haven't paid anyone, no one has any stake or claim about how you live your life or whether you get better or not, and you can just sit there and feel loving support from a roomful of people. This can be a very significant, powerful experience for some people. I've seen many people just walk in the door and start to weep because they've never had the opportunity to just be themselves, and to feel totally accepted as they are, with no strings attached and no agenda. I think this is a wonderful kind of community building in a world designed to create alienation.

There is a body of research behind our approach and philosophy of service. There are many current studies on the efficacy of a peer support model for those coping with stress or a life-threatening illness. Our approach is rooted in the work of Carl Rogers and his research on the "Healing Relationship" which is based on a relationship of equality as opposed to a relationship of 'expert vs. client.' Carl Roger's recipe for a healing relationship included congruence, empathy and unconditional positive regard. We've added spiritual values to these qualities; including defining health as inner peace and emphasizing forgiving rather than judging, and letting go of the past and future and living from the knowledge that now is the only time there is.

Carl Rogers proved many years ago that ordinary individuals could be of extraordinary help to each other. If you are simply being present with me, being honest, genuine, and empathic and you're caring about me, then I have the space and the ability to grow and tune in to my own inner wisdom and to find my way and to heal my life. That is what we're doing here–acknowledging and activating our profound ability to care, to help and to love each other.

Gerald Jampolsky, M.D, founded the Center for Attitudinal Healing in 1975. At that time, he was a Child Psychiatrist making rounds at U.C. Medical Center. He was visiting a young boy that had Leukemia and he left his briefcase in the boy's hospital room. When he returned to get it, an orderly was sitting on the edge of the bed of this child and they were having a conversation about what do you think happens when you die? He noticed that the boy's color had changed, that he was really engaged and in some ways seemed better, a lot better. He realized that children didn't have anywhere to go to really talk and to be listened to and he also realized that he needed to listen to what they had to say on their level—as an equal rather than as an authority.

Dr. Jampolsky decided to experiment and began an 8-week group meeting in his office with 8 to 10 children who were coping with life-threatening illnesses to see what would happen. The children designed the original format, which included dinner and was based on a peer support model with Jerry acting as a listener and an equal rather than the doctor/expert. There was nothing else like this at that time. The results were amazing and it was very successful. After the first 8 weeks, the children wanted the group to continue, and then the siblings and parents wanted a group. Jerry had written a book about this work, titled *Love Is Letting Go Of Fear*, and someone mentioned it on a TV talk show and that is when everything really mushroomed. The Center received a great deal of media attention for its work with children including Mr. Rogers, Phil Donahue Show, 60 Minutes and CNN. 28 years later, each Wednesday evening, the Center still has its children's and family groups with a free dinner, thanks to the generosity of many restaurants in the area. The Center has received many awards, and has applied the approach in many situations including war, political sectors, in prisons, the workplace and in all areas of health care.

Right now, we have a staff of 12. The staff exists to train and mentor over 300 volunteers who facilitate over 28 support groups each week or are matched with individuals throughout the Bay Area who are home-bound or hospitalized or coping with aging through our Home & Hospital Visiting Program. This program will serve over 300 families this year. We collaborate with many agencies and currently run programs with Whistlestop Senior Center, The Redwoods, San Quentin, Zen Hospice plus many public and private schools. We also work with most hospitals, home-health care agencies and hospice agencies.

I love the statement by Holocaust survivor and author, Victor Frankel: "The last of human freedoms is to choose one's attitude regardless of circumstances." I think that really summarizes our work, and it is such a hopeful message for people who feel victimized by the circumstances of their lives.

Louise Franklin is currently Chief Operating and Senior Development Officer for the Center for Attitudinal Healing.

Stacy Friedman Story

RABBI

History

When I was twelve years old, my family and I moved from New York to Salt Lake City, Utah. In New York we lived in a community where there were a lot of synagogues, a lot of Jewish people, and religion wasn't the central part of life, although we had a home that was richly Jewish.

When we moved to Utah, the first day of school I was in seventh grade and nobody knew who I was or where I was from. People would come up to me and they'd say, "Oh, what religion are you?" That was the very first question people asked. And this was from twelve-, thirteen-year-old kids, which you'd never find here and most other places, but religion was really the central identifying feature for people at the time in Utah.

When I told everybody who asked me throughout the day that I was Jewish, I got mixed reviews. Some people said, "Oh, I never saw a Jew before." Then at the end of the day, one little girl came up to me, said, "What religion are you?" I said, "I'm Jewish." She said, "So am I." And we became lifelong friends. But it was there that my Jewish identity really became central to me. I saw that Judaism was a wonderful way of life, capable of bringing me into people's lives, just as other religions are, but Judaism happened to be my religion.

I decided when I was about fifteen or sixteen that I wanted to be a rabbi. I remember telling a friend, "You know, I think I want to be a rabbi." And she looked at me and said, "How would you know?" At the time women were just starting to be ordained. I didn't even know women could be ordained. I had a lot of chutzpah to think that I would even think about being a rabbi.

I felt like I was called to the rabbinate, and so I spent the next years of my life learning more about Judaism, and learning more about our people and our tradition. I spent a year in Israel studying, and I went to Brandeis University, which is a Jewish university. The more I learned about Judaism, the more I found that all the things that a rabbi does I knew I would love to do. So I just kept following this path. Sometimes I rebelled against it. I took a few years off after college and I tried to do other things, because being a rabbi is not easy, and I was duly concerned, and rightly so, about the rabbinic life. But I haven't regretted it, and I love what I do. So it was really this unavoidable path.

Jews don't talk about being called in the same ways that I've heard my Christian colleagues and friends talk about.

I didn't apply to the seminary right out of college. But, they knew who I was, because I'd been in contact with admissions. I got a letter from the seminary. My family had moved around, so the letter came to my grandmother's house in Florida. She said, "Some rabbi's looking for you." They had to hunt me down, and said, "Come on back. We want you. Come and apply." I really ran away from it, like some of our reluctant prophets have. I'm no prophet, but I was reluctant.

I went to the Hebrew Union College Jewish Institute of Religion which has four branches. One is in Cincinnati; that's where I interviewed. One is in Jerusalem, where I went for my first year. One is in L.A., where I was for two years, and one was in New York; I went for the last two years.

The Difference Women Make

At Rodef Sholom I'm the third female clergy. There was a woman rabbi before me, and a woman cantor. So I didn't find that my issue was one of being a female rabbi. I don't speak, necessarily, about being a woman rabbi in my sermons. I do speak about women's issues, and I think that I am the second wave of women rabbis who can explore what women's leadership is about.

We're past the question of, can women be rabbis? That was the first wave. I think the second wave is everything else. And the reason why I say I'm in the second wave is because my class at rabbinical school was the first class that had more women than men. I remember we were in Israel our first year, and there was a woman chosen from our class to speak when we met with the president of Israel. In her speech, she mentioned something about our class having more women than men, and the dean of our school said, "You shouldn't say that." I feel that was a turning point.

I welcome the opportunity to talk about women's leadership in faith with other women leaders. Many women are choosing not to lead in traditional ways. I would imagine that's true in other denominations as well, because these roles were created to fit into men's lives. I think that there are some women who are finding that that doesn't work for them.

I consider myself a pioneer in that I've been a rabbi in this congregation for nine years. I have young children, and like others of my colleagues am finding having such a demanding job is difficult to reconcile with raising my family. I think it's not because there's something wrong with doing it both; I think that it's because there's something wrong with the construct of the way we perceived our rabbinic positions. So I consider myself a pioneer in wanting to change how that looks. It's happening in small ways around the country, as more and more women are entering leadership positions in congregations.

I think women are beginning to lead in different ways, and I think that when women are beginning to do it in different ways, it's giving our male colleagues permission to do it in different ways. And that, to me, is what's really important. It's not necessarily that women talk about only what it means for women. It's important that women and men talk about what it means for all of us. We haven't been very successful at restructuring yet. The conversations that I've been having with some of my women colleagues and with some of my male colleagues are ways to talk about having more balance, more fluidity in what we do.

I was talking with a female colleague the other day who served in two different congregations. She was saying that when she in one, when her daughter was on the bimah with her, somebody looked at her snidely and she took her daughter off the bimah. The bimah's the altar, the stage. And this person who was objecting said, "She shouldn't be here." Whereas when she was in a different congregation her kids were able to walk around while she was leading services.

That's what I find here. I'm really grateful that I am in Northern California, where we are a bit more informal, where my son feels comfortable coming on the altar, the bimah, or the stage with me. I think that that's important. I think as a wife and a mother, I can't pretend that my family doesn't exist, because they do exist and they're the most important thing for me. So to figure out a way to have them mingle is really the only way to do it.

I feel very fortunate that I'm also not a corporate person who works and lives in two different places, where those lives are very separate. My children go to school right here on this campus. I work in their schools as part of what I do. Being a rabbi or clergyperson, our families also are part of where we work, because they come here to worship, or they come here for religious school or to meetings, which is wonderful.

On the other hand, it also becomes insidious, because there are no boundaries. So I think that one needs to work hard to create those boundaries, but those boundaries need to have holes in them also. They need to allow for movement in both directions, because you also can't create a fortress around you.

I'm a woman, I preach in a different way, and I preach from a different part of myself, because I find that those issues are more important. For me, my heart is important. Emotions and a kind of non-intellectualism are important. I think that appeals to a lot of people, to women in particular. I think that that is something that I've brought to what I do.

Judaism is a very intellectual religion. We're called "the people of the book." And I think that that book needs to be translated to people in a way that makes them feel, not only in a way that makes them think. I think that Jews have been thinking for a long time, and I think that it's important to be able to feel and think simultaneously, or even independently. I'm also very emotional about Judaism and about life and about religion, and I think I've introduced that into what I do.

Our texts definitely are from a male perspective. But for years now women have begun approaching our ancient and sacred texts, most of which are written by men and are from a patriarchal point of view, with a different lens. We have a tradition called midrach, the word drach meaning to expound upon something, which we've had for hundreds and hundreds of years. But recently there's a movement towards creating contemporary midrach, or contemporary understandings of our texts.

So we can give voice to the women who didn't have voices. We can give voices to Leah and Rachel and all the women in the Torah. Men weren't listening to them at the time, or they were in two separate realms of life and nobody had a pen where they were standing. The guys were over there doing their work and listening to each other and writing down what they were saying, and not what the women were saying.

I think people who experience religion today and are able to separate their Jewish experience from the childhood, which might have been more patriarchal, and which might have excluded women to a greater extent, don't experience it as being patriarchal. We in our services make references to God gender-neutral. We've added references to women where there are references to men.

For example, in our prayer book, and it's not just in our synagogue but across the country, where we speak of the God of our fathers, Abraham, Isaac, and Jacob, we used to stop there. Now we've also added the God of our mothers, Sara, Rebecca, Rachel, and Leah. Where we talk about God as Lord, King, and He, our prayer book now makes the references to God gender-neutral, so we don't even say Lord, nor do we say Lady, but we keep it in Hebrew. We say Adonai, or we say the Eternal One, or God.

Spirituality

To me, having a spiritual life is recognizing God's divine presence in our lives, in people, in the world around us. So sometimes I'll stop during services if I don't feel like I'm doing that, and talk about it a little bit, because I feel if I'm having a hard time gaining that connection to a spiritual presence, then other people are also. So sometimes I'll stop in the middle of services.

There's a prayer in the beginning of our service about creation, and in the morning the prayer talks about thanking God for, and recognizing God for creating light and giving us life and breath. At night the same prayer in that place talks about bringing on the evening and the darkness and the stars. So sometimes I'll just take a moment and stop and ask everybody to look out the window and to make it real, as opposed to theoretical, on the page. I strive to make that real in my life.

I've had a daily prayer practice, and that ebbs and flows. I think that since I've had my children, a lot of my prayer practice is wrapped up in them, because for me there's no greater holiness or evidence of God's presence on this earth than my children. Part of my spiritual practice comes from being their mother and from loving them, and from working with them and praying with them at night before they go to sleep.

Our rabbis tell us that we are to say one hundred blessings a day. We say blessings over things in which we recognize God's presence. Eating a new fruit for the first time, there's a certain prayer for that, seeing a shooting star. I find that since I have two little kids, that so much of what they do they do for the first time, and so I have a lot of opportunities to say those blessings. So my own spiritual life really revolves around my kids and my home, and then the meditative and prayer practice I'm able to find for myself through our worship here.

Importance of Religion

I see that people are looking spirituality in all kinds of ways, and I think that religion is a wonderful anchor. It's a wonderful anchor for individuals, and it's a wonderful anchor for families. It's a wonderful way to not just find answers to questions, I think that's a limited aspect. But it's a wonderful way to find our place in life, and to elevate ourselves, and to put things into perspective. Hope and healing comes from this transcendent spirit and nature that religion can bring into our lives. Having an organized system for that makes it a lot easier.

There are a lot of people who don't believe in organized religion, or who can't find their place in it, and I respect that. I know it's sometimes hard to find our place in it. But the fact that it's organized brings unity to it, and I think that that unity is what is so profound about religion. Often we use that unity in that organization for evil and not for good. But I think that there's the most tremendous and powerful positive energy that can come from that unity. For me that's God, and that's one of the faces of God. But I think it's a power that is not as tapped to its full potential as it will be, and I think that people need it.

What Women Can Bring to Leadership

The directors of a lot of Jewish organizations are not women. A lot of the volunteers are women, and a lot of the attendees at religious services are women, and a lot of women bring their kids to religious school, but still the directors and heads of organizations are more men than women. And I would like to see more equity in that area.

I think for that to happen, people in leadership roles and on boards need to be able to appreciate the unique gifts that women can bring. It might be a different leadership style. They might not bang the gavel as strongly, or they might bang it more strongly. But I don't think we are ready to respect and appreciate and be open to the unique gifts that women can bring.

We have an organization called the Women's Rabbinic Network. When there are larger meetings of rabbis we get together in smaller groups. And we can connect to each other in ways that I don't think the men have done traditionally. The sharing and openness and collegiality and trust among the women is something that really benefits us. For example, when we get together, we talk about all sorts of personal and private issues. But we also talk about our professional lives. We talk about how much money we make; how many hours we work; how we deal with our boards; how we deal with our colleagues; how we make worship happen. We talk about these issues with great respect and great trust.

I think that that sharing is something that women can bring, because we're really good at relationship, and we're really good at openness and talking with each other, and learning from each other and leaning on each other. That, to me, has been a tremendous source of strength, and something that I think we need to spread to our male colleagues. I think that's a unique contribution that we bring to what we do.

Stacy Friedman is a Rabbi at Rodef Sholom in Marin County.

Renee Geiger Story

LUTHERAN MINISTER

From the Kitchen to the Pulpit

My father was a pastor; my uncle a bishop; my husband is a pastor. When I was growing up, my assumption was that that was not a place for women. I was from a conservative, almost a Fundamentalist background. Even so, in observing my husband in his work, I thought about how much I would love to do the work that he was doing.

I always loved the life of the church, but wistfully thought I would be the one who'd be making the coffee, serving the council and teaching Sunday school. But, I came to a point in my life when I was feeling aggressive restlessness. I felt I had something to do and to say, and I didn't know where to place this newfound energy.

In that two-year process of prayer and restlessness, I had a dramatic experience of being called to go to seminary, and to become a pastor. Some of these were almost mystical experiences. They were messages from other people who didn't know me, as well as my own experiences in prayer. I was terrified. I fought, knowing I was caught in this call and yet, feeling as though I was not capable. In that tumultuous time, I received a sense of graced confidence and an awareness of God's presence in going to seminary, to the extent where I felt that it was indeed done. All I needed to do was walk through it.

Before I went to the seminary I had difficulty in seeing myself as anything but a homemaker. I had been told that, and I just simply believed it. But one day, I was looking outside not really thinking about much of anything, and I almost audibly heard with such depth a deep sense of voice within my very soul, it was, "I want you to go to seminary and become a pastor." It was clear, and it put within me a deep, deep inner peace that it was right, and at the same time a deep sense of terror.

One night I was pacing the house because I was in such turmoil about this new venture. I was in the living room, sitting there in the dark, praying. A presence came and said, "You just wait." There was such a sense of joy in the room, that the room literally lit up, and the voice gently continued, "It is already accomplished. Just go."

From that day on, my confidence and inner peace were present. There were instances when friends of friends would say, "Do you have a friend named Renee? I want to tell her I had a dream," (I had never met them) "and I saw her walking down an aisle with robes on, and the voice said, 'Feed my sheep.'" And I had dreams of breaking open fresh bread, you know, the bread of life. I had people come up and want to pay for my education, folks that I hardly knew. There were just so many indications. Maybe God knew I needed that. I don't know.

When I got to seminary, it was like Disneyland for me. I couldn't decide what classes I could take first. I had all those books to read and a place where my voice was being heard. I absolutely changed in that process. My husband has said, "You are not the same woman I married, at all." He was extremely supportive, and I think understood before I did that this was my leading and my calling.

For me even to drive to Berkeley from San Jose was terrifying. I was so confined. I was so protected. I was probably the woman that most feminists would think didn't have a chance; yet, I completely transformed in the process. I received comments from professors saying that they appreciated what I said, and I thought, "You what? You mean you even wanted to hear what I had to say?" I could write a paper, and it was my paper, my thoughts. This was me, and so I really did discover myself in the process.

I have loved my work, and I can't imagine doing anything else at this point in time. It just took me a while. I was in my late thirties when I went to seminary.

Working in a Place When Religion Doesn't Come First

Being in Marin County I am confronted with the reality that a church life, religious life, is not important to over 90 percent of this community, and I'm very aware of that. I believe that religion is important because it gives an individual a foundation or a belief structure that offers them ground upon which they might traverse in their own spiritual journey.

I believe that attending a worship service and having some kind of doctrine, of having some kind of a holding tank for a religious experience, grants us a reminder of who we are in relationship with God. Concentration on relationship with God in community is very important. The teachings of the church of Christ are in many ways radically antithetical to what we find outside in the world. We need to be reminded of that and strengthened in that radical way of life, understanding how Jesus demonstrated the Dominion of God, what it means to be a child of God and how we are graced to live.

I think that that opportunity is very important. We need the support; we need the exposure to God's word; we need the power of the sacraments and the building of faith, the use of our gifts in a communal context where they can really make a difference in the world, in the name of God's presence in our lives.

I think we need the music, to have our emotions affected. And we need to have the conversation, "Really what is it that I believe?" I think we need to hone in specifically in one way of believing, for me it's Christianity. Obviously, that's how I've come to know God. And I think we could say, people have come to know God in different ways, through different faith structures, but I think that we can move so broad, so wide, that we don't go deeper. We can dabble in a whole lot of things and remain on the surface all of our lives.

What I say to folks who come here sometimes from nothing is that, "Let's go deep. Let's take a look at this God whom we have come to know through Jesus. Let's see what can happen in our spiritual lives together on this journey, to go deeper together." And there's somewhat of a holding of accountability in that journey, and a support for that. I mean, really getting down to hardcore questions and saying, "I need to wrestle with that. I need to wrestle with what that looks like in this world and in my life." Does it make any difference at all?

In our conversations we're talking about our faith. We're always asking, "How is my faith lived out? What is it that I believe? Where are the struggles in my journey? How can I help you? What is prayer, anyway? How does God truly affect my life? Do I care about some of the doctrinal things that could become so heavy? Does the sum of it really matter? Does it?"

I also try to hone in on the death and resurrection of Christ, the love of God who has come into our midst; at the same time, I hold the door open for where many people are. I don't close it down. I try not to, because people are coming from so many places, and if I verbalize it in a certain way and say, "You believe this, or you have no place in this church," they'll walk. And you know what? That's okay. I want people to struggle with their faith. I want them to be here with their questions. There are folks in my congregation who I would say are really not Christians, but they come every Sunday. They want to be here.

They want the community. They want to hear the sermons. They want to sing the music. They want to be in the community. It's a place of restoration for them. Some of them will not come for communion, because it doesn't feel appropriate for them, where they are faith-wise. That's fine. But they come, and I love that. And they teach me. They teach me about what it means to be here in this society today. "Tell me what you think, what you feel, where you are."

The Power of Words

There are those traditional Lutherans that don't want to change the language of liturgy and hymnody. That's their faith. That's how they came to know God. That's their sacred space. But there are other times when we do make changes through contemporary music and language. I try to be careful with my language when I preach, and with my storytelling, that I don't use words that have gone dry because they've been used so long, or are dead to people who are coming to the church and have no idea what they mean. I am careful of using the words sanctification, justification, redemption. Those are the kinds of words that do not have meaning for the majority of people. I try and stay as fresh as I can in my language.

This was very frustrating for some folks and received well by others. I don't change language just any time. I usually do not move into feminine language for God, but rather God-language that is neither male nor female. I would say I use more inclusive language than I do feminine language. I use other kinds of metaphor. Sometimes, I might say, "God, whom we may know as mother or father."

Some of my sisters are much more feminist about this and much more out front in changing language, and I have to say I'm more cautious. I'd say my language from the pulpit is feminine, so that I think they really do hear that. My way of presiding, my way of being with people is feminine; it just is.

I think that there are very few people who could be insensitive enough to say they don't have to watch language at all. I think there is a consciousness about paying attention to the language that we use. I would say that the strongly feminist women are still extremely frustrated by the language in the church. I know some that it just drives crazy. But it isn't something that gets me crazy; that's just who I am.

Examining What a Woman Brings

I draw from life in my preaching in a different way. I think they hear the feminine voice in my preaching, and administratively. As a woman, I want to get things talked through. I want to find common ground. I'm not very good at black and white, "I'm right, you're wrong."

I don't know if this is feminine, but I don't feel particularly competitive about having to be right or wrong. I feel like I want to seek out the truth, and so I wrestle within. It is important to see both sides. Consequently, I find myself in much more turmoil, holding the tension of two perspectives. How do we come together here?

I think I probably understand things at more of a feeling, intuitive place. Something feels right, it doesn't feel right, and I have to then move to logic, saying what it is that I'm really thinking, what I am really feeling, and get it more concrete in order to appeal to a more masculine way of understanding. But, then there comes the time when I know, the buck stops with me, and I need to make decisions. I realize that when I say something, it matters, so I try to be careful and thoughtful about what I say.

I think when people are looking for an experience of God, they want to be touched. They want their souls to be touched. They want to leave feeling different than when they came in. And they want to know that they're connected, that we are connected with one another; that we are connected with God. I think women can create a place where in worship there is heart. And there are men who can do this, too.

Women can bring something that is quieter, that is centered, that reaches the heart and the emotions, that speaks to unity, connectedness and that's not hierarchical. I think there is a lot in feminism and in the way women see things about how important relationship is; taking away fear, competition, winning and losing. Once again, I feel like I'm on fragile ground if I say that's only feminine, but that's how I'm seeing it.

One of the things that has been an issue in my own personal life, has been the balance of home and family and the church, especially when our daughters were home. I had dreams where the dining room was empty, but there was a tree sitting in the middle of it. I looked at the dining room, and I wept as though my heart would break, because so much of what my life was, was making that home around the dining room table, and I knew that there was a piece of that I would be giving up now. I stand at the table in another way now: at church, at the altar.

I want to do that nurturing, cooking thing, as well as this sixty-hour-a-week job. I wasn't the kind of person that just hated homemaking. I didn't. I just have to say that's a loss, and sometimes it's a hardship, because at Christmas the family wants to come home. And I do Christmas. You might ask, "Why doesn't your husband help?" Well, he does, but the bottom line is, I do the turkey and plan the meal. And, Christmas and Easter are when we're the most busy at the church.

At church you really do lay down your life in a lot of ways for people. You come in very close connection with them. But you've got a family that also wants that close connection from you. In the congregation, we know folks on a much fuller, broader basis as you see them in church. You laugh with them at potlucks. You're with them when they are dying or when they're very sick. You connect. And I value that connection very, very much.

Nevertheless, relationships can be really messy. The question becomes how do I keep boundaries here, and at the same time come as a representative of the church with deep, empathic connection. When folks see the collar, they think about God. We are somehow sacramental just being there, and so that puts a lot of responsibility on a pastor.

You want this holy ground to be a place where people can receive what they need, and you want to be present and let them know that you deeply care, that God cares, the church cares. If you have people who get angry with the pastor or the pastor screws up, that can really mess up people in a lot of ways around their relationship with God, their relationship with the church. I feel responsible. We carry something that we need to hold with great respect in how we serve and how we do ministry.

Work and Renewal

At the church we are going to be bringing in a special hymn writer; running a Sunday school program; starting up a book club; starting up a couples' club; and running three Bible study circles. In addition at the larger church level there is a Women of the Church group. I'm also going to be involved with the large synod women's gathering. I work on panels for interviewing seminarians at Pacific Lutheran Theological Seminary. I'm on the synod council, which is the council that works with the bishop.

Then there are the stewardship campaigns, and getting the newsletter together, and getting the council together, and fundraising, and our Marin Lutheran Children's Center and finally, facility growth; we're jammed. The multitude of questions to answer: We don't have room. How do we do that? How do we afford this? What do we do? What's the best way to build?

And I do retreats on the outside. I did a women's retreat with Jan West at St. John's Episcopal Church. Jan and I presided at the altar together, which was really thrilling. We did a healing station together, and that just felt very feminine in a very beautiful and strong way. I did a funeral at St. Sebastian's. Catholic Church I preached and I presided with their African American priest, which is huge, really, to be at the altar with him in a Catholic cathedral. I'm going to be preaching at an ordination at the Presbyterian seminary, as a Lutheran, I think that's thrilling in its ecumenicity.

I think pastors can be a little weak on taking care of themselves. There's a lot to do, a lot of places to be, a lot of nights gone, a lot of weekends that are filled up. It's very helpful for me to get away for two days in a row, and it's hard to do. I need to have quiet time, meditation time, stillness, to calm all the voices and all the needs that come. Just being in nature and reading poetry. God's voice comes to us in many ways. There are times when I can't look at one more Alban Institute book on church growth, you know. I need to put that away for a while, and then I need to just read Mary Oliver and just take in beauty and poetry and connect with God again.

Although I love getting together with women and men of like minds where conversation can be uplifting and stimulating, I'm an introvert. I lose my extrovert energy pretty fast and pretty radically, and I need to be alone. I don't mind being alone for extended periods of time.

Renee Geiger is currently the pastor of the Marin Lutheran Church in Marin County.

Veronica Goines Story

PRESBYTERIAN PASTOR

History

I am a woman who is the product of the black church tradition, even though I'm now serving in a multicultural congregation.

I was working as a graphic artist when I began to experience the call to ministry. There came a time when I found that I did not experience satisfaction in my work like I had before, but that there was a growing satisfaction and a growing sense of call to do the kind of work that I was doing within the context of the church.

At the time, I was twenty-nine years old and I was working with a group of young women around my age. And we began to feel that we needed to get our ministry out of the church building and out into our larger community.

We started a convalescent hospital ministry. We started a ministry with juveniles, at the Juvenile Hall in San Leandro. We worked primarily with young boys, preadolescent and teens. Working with these young men was important to me. There was something about just being there with them and helping them to look at their own lives and to recognize another source of strength that was available to them. We were helping some of them to develop a relationship with God and to have a focus in their life. But this work wasn't enough for me.

Over a three-year period, the call began to emerge, becoming more clear and focused over time. I knew that I was being called. In my spirit, I just kept hearing a whisper, "It's really time for you to prepare." And as I prayed about it, what came clear was that I needed to seek some formalized education. I had done tons of study on my own, through church groups, and Bible study. But I knew that the call was to something other than what I had ever done.

I talked to my pastor, and began to talk about some possibilities for graduate education. After checking a series of different schools I called San Francisco Theological Seminary on the phone, and I don't remember who I even talked to on the phone, but there was just this sense that that's where I was supposed to be. I felt like I had come home.

In my old church I had co-ministers who thought I was going to lose my religion by going to the Presbyterian seminary. I came to a point of having to look within and pray and listen and trust. I wasn't feeling the kind of support that I could see my brothers getting in their journeys, you know, just everybody rallying behind them and saying, "You know, that's right, that's right." I had to say to myself, "You know, I've got to be true to the one who has called me, even above any other voice that I'm comfortable following." I had to learn how to walk by faith, to walk by the spirit.

Self Maintenance

One of the greatest challenges in ministry is how we remain true to the One who calls us. That, to me, is the whole answer behind what we do to nurture ourselves, or what do we do to remain healthy and whole. What happens is that when we get into the seduction of ministry it can begin to take over our entire lives. It can claim all of our time, our energy, our focus, and it can even rob us of our relationship with God. It can become idolatrous.

A lot of people don't really know that, and there aren't a whole lot of ministers who will acknowledge and admit that out loud. But I will admit it, because it is something that I have to be consciously aware of. My call from God emerged over a three-year period when I just hunkered down and spent tremendous amounts of time praying. I remember eight-hour days that would go by and I'd been in prayer all day. That wasn't the norm, but four hours certainly wasn't unusual in a day's time.

So I had that intense one-on-one time in prayer, in getting clarity and direction, but then you get into the ministry and the demands are tremendous. Do we continue to set time aside to be with the One who loves us and fills us and calls us and empowers us? Because that is really first and foremost the way to be able to not only handle the challenges, but to be able to discern and make decisions about what it is that is needed.

But we have to make choices about what we do. And it is in prayer that I begin to get a real sense of what the priorities are, what has to be done and what can wait, and what maybe needs to be passed on to someone else to do. It's also in prayer that I get a real sense of what other ways I can nurture myself.

I set very clear boundaries for myself. I'm known for that here, by the congregation, because I can't teach and encourage in the members what I don't model.

I'm one of these strange pastors who takes her off days, who takes her vacation time, and I give it my all when I'm away. I hike frequently, I power-walk and I'm at the gym regularly. I do not spend my time focused on what's happening at the church. I am present to myself, I'm present to my own renewal process. When I come back here, I am focused and I'm clear and I'm rested. That is really important.

I am in spiritual direction monthly. That is, I sit with someone who listens to my journey and reflects it back to me, helps me to see myself, helps me to always keep in mind where God is in my life. I find that even when I go to my director with struggle around either a personal or work-related issue, and often it is work-related, I come out of there with a greater sense of clarity. Not that she's ever told me what to do. She's not one who gives advice, but she "listens me" into hearing myself and to hearing God's voice. That's been a really, really important part of taking care of myself.

In addition, I have a prayer partner I talk to monthly on the phone. We met about four years and we would literally spend time saying, "So, honestly, this is exactly where I am." And hearing each other, not correcting each other, not judging each other, but hearing those realities and those struggles inherent in ministry and family, and then we would pray. We would pray until we were encouraged and strengthened.

It's living in the tension honoring and recognizing the need for the boundaries and for some distance, and at the same time, acknowledging that with that does come a sense of separation. And so I have to be very intentional to be connected, in terms of friendships and relationships, where it is appropriate for me to pour my heart out and to be heard, and not do it in the context of the congregation.

Being A Pastor

The church designed a building that doesn't have a raised chancel area. And that is because it's a statement about ministers and the congregation all being called to be one. We're all called to be ministers of the gospel, so we don't elevate ourselves. It is a philosophical statement and a theological one that's in the structure of our building.

I am invited, as a pastor, into the holy of holies with families and individuals. I go into places with them where not everyone is invited to go, and I honor that. I hold that with the greatest respect and appreciation, and a sense of awe about the whole thing, to sit with someone in their last hours, or with their family, when someone is completely vulnerable in a hospital room. To see the humility and the honesty with which human beings can actually pour out themselves to one another, it's humbling.

There is this tremendous connection that happens in working with the congregation. I remember baptizing two children and holding them in my arms. I was looking at photographs of one of them just this past week. One, when I baptized him, snuggled his little head into my neck area and I didn't expect that. They're precious times, just precious, and you can't feel more connected than that, ever.

When I went to seminary I was resistant to consider a congregation, I was still thinking about prison ministry. I was not even willing to pray about it. So I had to ask what was the resistance about. My pastor thought that I would go into parish ministry, and he kept affirming that. But I didn't want to hear it from him, because I felt he had his own agenda. The entire congregation of my old church saw me as one of the pastors even though I was an unpaid volunteer.

Then I served for a year at a multicultural Presbyterian congregation, which was the first time I'd been in a Presbyterian congregation. I was commuting from Union City to Stockton, California and I was preaching every other Sunday, working with another woman pastor. She was an interim pastor, younger than myself. It was the first time I was able to work that closely with a woman in a pastoral role. Although, I was the one who was doing that in my own church context, I didn't have a model of someone who was actually working as a pastor.

I began to understand that a part of what I was opposed to in the pastorate was the model of pastoring that I'd known most of my life. It was always male, but it was also very authoritarian, and sometimes controlling. It was anything but who I was and I couldn't see myself in that role.

But I began working with this woman and watching her and I began to realize I could do this. And although I had been a Baptist all my life I also began to recognize that the Presbyterian structure fit my personality. I appreciated the relationship in the Presbyterian Church between pastor and session, that it has a kind of built-in checks and balances. The pastor is not just authoritarian, but the pastor is respected as a leader, and at the same time is working with empowered people around the table.

Now that I am pastor here at St. Andrew and gender is not the focus, I remember how people would say, "Well, why should women pastor?" Well, my goodness, I don't know who could be better equipped to pastor than women, to be honest with you. I don't know why it's such a marvel because I think it's what we do all the time. I don't think you can raise a household and not pastor and shepherd it.

But being a pastor of a church is multiplying what we do at home by a thousand. It is much bigger, but there are so many parallels, in the ways we extend ourselves within our family.

St. Andrews

Although St. Andrews is called a multicultural church I think the multiculturalism is not in languages or races. Everyone speaks English here no matter what culture they come from. Primarily, it's always been biracial, and I think the cultures are more in the socioeconomic range within this congregation. It's a beautiful thing to see everyone from CalWorks mothers to judges and attorneys and teachers and doctors and professionals. You see folks talking and sitting at table together and serving one another and working on ministries together. That is multicultural, because in our culture, in our nation, the socioeconomic range is where the lines get drawn.

In my first year here we had a church retreat for the elders, which is the governing board of the church. I said at that retreat that we're going to talk about the elephant on the table, and we've been talking about the elephant on the table since I've been here. The elephant is to be willing to acknowledge and to deal with inequities or things that we see happening that we might not be so comfortable about dealing with.

Sometimes these things have to do with race or they happen along racial lines. It's a not black-against-white thing. But what happens is there's a certain amount of privilege that I think members of the dominant race in our culture have. It's something that is almost innate. It's something that people don't necessarily have a lot of awareness about.

There's a sense in which they feel confidence in voicing their opinion. If you have black members in a black congregation they will speak up or not based on personalities. But when you have a mixture like we have, not everyone feels entitled to speak. I find that, as a pastor, I'm having to be a conscious person about making sure that both black and white voices get heard. That, for me, is probably the single biggest issue.

It's making sure that we have policy and we have structure, that we honor the policy that's already set, through our denomination, around inclusiveness and representation. And making sure that even around the board table every voice gets heard and every voice has weight. Sometimes it's a matter of someone having more education or status than another, but I don't care if it's Grandma Moses sitting over here if they've been called by the congregation and set aside for this leadership role, then we need to honor that voice.

I found that when I first came, there were certain voices that got heard and certain other ones that did not. I think it's because that's the way it happens in the world, and that we have to be real intentional about honoring diversity and making sure that we're not just saying we have it when we don't really honor it. It's recognizing all of that, and then trying to find a way to facilitate more evenness. You can't make somebody else less heard; it's just a matter of making sure everybody else is given voice.

Veronica Goines is currently the pastor at St. Andrew Presbyterian Church of Marin City in Marin County.

Jan Heglund Story

POLICE CHAPLAIN

The Call

I was a parishioner at St. John's in Ross, and at coffee hour a friend of mine who was going through school for deacons said to me, "Jan, you should take some classes. You would just love them." And there were two people standing one on each side of me, who leaned over, and said, "It's about time." So when I went home, I called them, and I said, "Don't say anything." I said, "I am just thinking about taking some classes."

Like most people who sense a call to ministry, I look back over my life and I can see that I was always interested in church, and was chaplain of the sorority that I was in at Oregon State College, and always seemed to end up in that role. I talked to the priest at St. John's about feeling a call. And I moaned and groaned. And I pushed it to the back of my mind, and I prayed about it.

I finally decided, "Okay, I will do this thing," I had to tell the priest, because a letter from the rector of your church is what opens your file at the diocese. So when I walked in and I said to Bart, "Okay, okay, okay, I'm going to do this," and he said, "Of course, you are. It's about time."

It was hard to go back to school. I hadn't been in school in a long time, although I'd been a great student in college, but that had been a long time ago. I think it's very intimidating for your ego. I'd be sitting there thinking, "Oh, please, dear Lord, don't call on me." That was hard. I had four kids at home, and I was working full-time at San Rafael High.

Then I had an epiphany moment, and it was great. I was driving down the Miracle Mile in San Rafael to San Rafael High School to work in the morning. In San Anselmo I got behind this car, and the license plate said "Happy Wife." Then I started this mental thing with myself, and I thought, "Why isn't that enough for you, Jan?" What I was doing was fine with my husband, and the kids thought it was great. I certainly had support. But it was a heavy moment, and I was tired of studying. And I kept staring at that license plate. I thought, "Why isn't it enough just to be home, baking cookies."

I thought to myself, "Okay, nobody's got a gun at your head." I could go home and write a letter to the dean of the school and say, "I thank you. I've changed my mind," and I could write a note to the bishop and say, "This was all some kind of mistake." And that's where the epiphany came, because all of a sudden there was sound, and there was this heightened awareness that came in a second, and it was "I don't want to go back to being what I was before I started on this path."

There was another great moment that I like to think back on. Dorothy Jones, who is archdeacon, I and Jan Cazden, were at her house. We were discussing what I'm going to be wearing at ordination. I had no idea about size and clergy shirts. Then they said, "Oh, you'll need a long-sleeve clergy shirt." And I said, "Okay, okay, okay." They said, "What size is your neck?" I said, "I have no clue." So they got Jan's clergy collar and put it on me. I looked in the mirror, and I looked at myself in this collar and the first thing I said was "This collar is too big." And later I thought "Touché." Later Michael Hanson, who's the assistant to the bishop said, "Jan, when you're ordained, even that day you're not going to have any idea of what it is." He said, "It's a role you grow into," and that was just right on the money.

Police Work

After I was ordained I didn't really know what I wanted to do. Then one day in the local paper, there's this little tiny thing that said, "San Rafael Police Department is starting a chaplaincy program." Again, I'm sure it was God. I looked at that and something just clicked. And, you know, I don't always read all the paper. So here I looked at it, this little tiny, tiny thing.

I came in the main building of the police station, and I sat down before Walt Kosta, who was the captain in charge of the chaplaincy program. The minute I sat in that chair. I thought, "This is me. It fits like a glove." That was in 1995 and I have been here for seven years. There are three of us right now that are the most active, and two people on reserve.

I belong to the umbrella national group called the International Conference of Police Chaplains, the ICPC. They have regional conferences once a year. They have classes, and that's how you sharpen your skills about the peculiarities of law enforcement. So you're really well educated and trained. One of their strong suggestions is you need to ride with a policeman eight hours a month which I like to do in two four hour shifts.

When I started I knew that trust is a big issue with law enforcement. And, they're not going to trust me until they know me, and there's no way they're going to know me unless I'm around. I just started being around all the time. So I'm always here. I usually drop in every day. Besides, I usually have a reason, to pick up something, or get mail. And that is where they get to know me enough to trust me, in the car, in the hall.

I've been out on domestic violence calls, on a fair number of suicides, on hostage negotiation situations. I've been out on everything now. A lot of ministry comes at those times, and a lot happens during the follow-up. But it's the little things that really are important. Because when I'm here at the station someone will say "Hey, Reverend Jan can I talk to you for just a second?" That happens all the time, and that is when we get the trust.

When I rode in the first car they said, "Expect it to take a while." You know, they're going to be wondering, "Who is this person, and why are they riding in my car?" A lot of credit goes to the captain who was in charge who sold it unthreateningly. I think also equal credit goes to the officers here for being willing to trust. But it came slow, as it should.

I've decided that ministering in a police department is just like ministering to a small church. They'll have concerns about another officer. They'll want to include me in discussions about how they're worried about that officer. And they will ask, "Do you think you can talk to him?" Their problems are not unique to law enforcement. Maybe they're having hard time in their marriage so they just need to talk. They need to talk to somebody that they can trust. I think it's vitally important that you are simply a pastoral presence where they are. So you had better be ecumenical. There isn't a place for coming in evangelizing.

In addition I've been asked to start chaplaincy programs for other police departments. At first some of the departments wanted me to be the chaplain but I said, "Oh, gosh. I'll find you somebody." So I did. So it's just great. Novato and the sheriff's department were first. They were some of the first people to have them. So more and more women, one of the two people that I got in Corte Madera's a woman, and one's an Episcopal priest, retired. Then the man I got in Mill Valley is a retired Episcopal priest. And they love it. There's something. It just gets in your bloodstream.

Stress

The police are under terrible stress. The divorce rate is something like 80 percent. And more officers are killed by their own gun, not enemy fire. These are statistics that come out of ICPC nationally. There is also a lot of domestic violence. They're under terrible pressure. They are doing things that nobody else wants to do. For example I saw a training video where I saw man who was talking about a terrible situation, and he said, "I thought to myself, 'This is interesting. Everyone is running out of this building, and I'm running in.'"

Another important program is critical incident stress debriefings. I'm on the North Bay Critical Incident Stress Management team. It's CISM. So there are defusings and debriefings. Defusion is a short, short period of time right after a critical incident. You gather people together that were affected, and you talk about it. But the debriefing is longer and it's best if it happens within seventy-two hours. Everybody that was connected with the incident should be at that debriefing.

There's a documented formula for doing it. One of the purposes is to correct invalid thoughts. It can take up to two hours. In some departments the people that go are ordered to go, and you can tell who they are. They're sitting there looking unhappy. If an ambulance was there and the ambulance person had to deal with this victim, that driver should be in that debriefing. Even if there was a citizen nearby and they had some connection with it, they should be there. The dispatchers are there and they often don't get to hear the outcome of the 9-1-1 calls even though they're the ones that hear the screaming on the 9-1-1 tape.

The first time around it's just facts. Who was the first there? Who was the first person? Who was the first responding officer? Who was the first one to walk in? What was it like? What happened? Just facts. So they go all around, and they'll say "Who was next." Then they'll go around a second time, and that's when you start talking about feelings. They will put it this way, "What happened for you when you said, 'Oh, shit.'? What was that like for you?" Well, that's where it gets really emotional, as you might imagine. And you can just see the value of talking.

Then they wrap it up with an educational part, and tell them what they can expect to happen to their body. They tell them about nightmares. They tell them all the things so that they say, "When this happens, if it's not already happening, you will know it's 100 percent normal, and that's what you need to know." They'll tell them what not to do. "Don't do anything different than you usually do. If you don't drink, don't go home and drink. These are numbers you can call." It's a wonderful process, and it works. It works.

So slowly those things are making a difference. Policemen are learning that they're not made of some kind of different fiber just because they're law enforcement. They're human beings, they are doing a job that they love and they're good at it. But they need to learn to deal with their feelings.

On-Site Academy

The On-Site Academy is a week-long intensive debriefing program. It is peer-driven and clinician-directed. In Massachusetts a woman gave her home and her property to this program. Men and women come who don't know each other. They come and they stay and they're fed and they sleep there the whole time. They're referred there. A department can say, "Officer Smith, we know you're coming apart at the seams. So here is a plane ticket to On-Site or you're fired." Now that word's getting out about the program, people will ask to come.

There's a family unit where they can talk about their family. Nothing is left uncovered. The clinician helps them connect the dots, and it just happens before your eyes. The clinician is very laid back. She's very casual. She's not obviously proactive at all. She just looks like she's sitting in on a real comfortable session, and she is a master, because this is for all emergency services personnel, ambulance, fire, police who are suffering from accumulated exposures to critical incidents, not just one. They're coming, they think, for this last incident. But, it's because it was the fifth in a row. But it's so wonderful to watch her.

I have helped to start our own academy in Marin County. We're putting on our fifth session in October, and it's so exciting. They come from all over the world. We had a London bobby come. We've been holding them in Episcopal retreat places. We had one at Silver Penny, which is in Petaluma. Our first one was at Dorothy's Rest, which is up by Sebastopol. Then we've had two at St. Columbus and Inverness, a retreat center. We've decided that one really fills our purpose the best, and the priest out there is a really good friend of mine. So we're doing it again there. It's probably the most exciting process in the world.

In the beginning I was the chaplain, and I did it all myself. I was out there all week long. The first session we put on, we had some of the staff from New York come. Now we have our own clinicians with their doctorates. We have really good professional people. At first we were scared. So we said to the people from New York, "You come, and you do it, and we'll watch you," and they said, "Contraire. You do it, and we'll watch you."

What happens in the sessions is confidential, and I wish it weren't. People will say, "Oh, the police and service people are just made differently." I want to line these people up and say, "You listen to their story and their thoughts of suicide and their divorce and the incidents they went through, and they shouldn't even be walking upright." They are human and are carrying a superhuman burden.

After the first session that we ran we thought, "We should debrief ourselves." I wish you could have seen us. After we'd worked from Sunday to Friday are went to the home of one of the team members in Sebastopol. We ordered pizza. Well, there were little kids there, and they had on cartoons. We all just watched the cartoons.

I said, "By the end of that week, the clients looked wonderful. We looked like the clients did when they came." We learned to give ourselves a week to recover before we debriefed.

What's been wonderful for me is to see the difference. I start and I end the week. When I come back on Friday, I cannot tell you how different the people going through the course look. They have developed camaraderie among themselves. They are laughing and they are kidding. Their body language is entirely different. It's like a miracle.

Woman

I am the only women in the chaplaincy program for the San Rafael Police Department. The other chaplains who are there now come from faith traditions where there are not women at the altar, and so that has been hard. And they didn't have experience with women as clergy. A couple of times I was quite discouraged, and I actually talked to our bishop about it, and I talked to clergy whose opinion I value.

Then I just decided, "Let go of that, Jan." I thought, "Okay. I know this is where God wants me. I know it with every part of my body. So that's what I'm going to concentrate on. I'm just going to worry about Jan and keep my own plate clean. I'll just pray." The minute I did that, of course, it started turning.

I think men come from a place of competition. I'm not competitive at all. I'm not in competition with them, and that is real clear. That sometimes elusive competitive thing is not there. So I am less of threat and seemingly more accessible, and that came as a surprise. I have some real advantages as a woman. It was pointed out to me by a male clergy person, I can hug them. And I'm a big hugger. So it's really ironic that some of the characteristics of a woman ended up not to be a liability but held me in really good stead.

Jan Heglund is a police chaplain with the San Rafael Police Department in Marin County.

Margaret Hough Story

BAHAI

Led by Her Daughter to the Bahá'í Faith

I always say my daughter is my spiritual mother—I'm a second-generation Bahá'í. But I must clarify that I am not a member of the clergy because the Bahá'í Faith does not have any clergy. I've just been an active member in whichever Bahá'í community I've lived.

I first became aware of the Bahá'í Faith in the late 1950s, when we lived in Winnetka, north of Chicago. There is a Bahá'í House of Worship near there, and we used to show our guests this beautiful temple. It's open to all people, all religions, and I was always impressed with the writings of Bahá'u'lláh, the Founder of the Bahá'í Faith.

In the mid-1970s my younger daughter dated a member of the Bahá'í Faith and at that time I read a lot about the religion because I wanted to know more about this guy. They broke up but then, in 1978, my older daughter became a Bahá'í. She became a totally committed believer, and I was impressed. One of the things she said was: "People make laws all the time, and they're always changing them, but God's laws are eternal." That made so much sense. I also liked the Bahá'í principle of the equality of men and women.

Growing Up in Another World and Time

When I was a child it wasn't possible for women to hold positions of leadership in religion. In fact, when I was born women still did not have the right to vote: women's suffrage in this country was still two years away. It's hard for young people to imagine the discrimination against women that existed in those days, and that was nowhere more obvious than in religion.

I was born to Catholic parents and attended parochial school for five years. Later I attended public schools and gradually grew away from the church. My father owned a small hotel so I was constantly meeting people. It was an interesting place to live; in fact, it was an interesting time to live. I have seen people change–I mean "the people, the public" change—as their legal rights and educational opportunities have been expanded.

I married an Episcopalian, and we raised our children in that Protestant tradition. My husband was on various church committees and I taught Sunday School classes. We also were both active in community affairs–the Parents-Teacher Association, Scouting, and so on. We were pretty involved in our five children until they grew up, and then we were more free to move on to different things. I began to paint, for example, and had a number of shows in the local galleries. I also got a part-time job working for New West magazine.

Emancipation From Others' Beliefs at Sixty

I was 60 years old when my older daughter became a Bahá'í. She had had a friend who had joined the Faith, and, after several years my daughter did too. I began to attend Bahá'í meetings and to read the books my daughter gave me. Like many people who are attracted to the Faith, I found myself in agreement with many of its concepts.

However, as I became more interested in Bahá'u'lláh, I started to feel a conflict. I felt that I was leaving Christ.

"When had I first believed in Christ?" I asked myself. And the answer was obvious: my father was a Catholic, so that's why I was a Catholic. There was no question. My husband was a Protestant so I was a Protestant. But by this time I was 63 years old, and I thought "Surely by now I can make my own decisions."

Later I realized that you can think of God as the Sun, and the Great Teachers as mirrors who reflect the attributes of God and who reveal the message of God for that age. And I realized that I did not have to give up Jesus: Bahá'u'lláh stated that Christ is the Son of God and that his message was true. It's just that I had to accept other Great Teachers as well.

I realized that I accepted the teachings of Bahá'u'lláh about there being only one God, about there being one family of mankind, and about the fundamental unity of the religions.

In fact, I realized that I accepted that Bahá'u'lláh is the Great Teacher of God for this age. I became a Bahá'í–a follower of Bahá'u'lláh. The date was May 9, 1982. I was 63 years old.

Life As A Bahá'í

One of the first things I learned to love about being a Bahá'í is reading the Bahá'í prayers. There is no ritual in the Bahá'í Faith–no elaborate set of religious rites–but we are enjoined to pray everyday and it is such a joy. "Create in me a pure heart, O my God, and renew a tranquil conscience within me, O my Hope!..." [Bahá'u'lláh] To me that just about says it all.

And we have beautiful prayers for children. The kind of prayer that I learned as a child was, "Now I lay me down to sleep, I pray the Lord my soul to keep. If I should die before I wake, I pray the Lord my soul to take." But the Bahá'í children say: "O God, guide me, protect me, make of me a shining lamp and a brilliant star. Thou art the Mighty and the Powerful." It's such a positive thing.

Another positive thing is our meditation each day. In the Bahá'í writings the manner of meditating is left entirely to the individual–as long as we guard against superstitious or foolish ideas creeping into the way we do it. So I have found a way to reflect on spiritual reality that's comfortable for me and I really find that meditating adds depth and beauty to my life.

On a daily basis, other than saying our prayers and meditating, Bahá'ís just try to "live the life." There are no dietary laws or dress codes or anything like that in the Bahá'í Faith, but we are enjoined to maintain a very high moral code in everything we do–the Ten Commandments and more. "Let deeds, not words, be your adorning," Bahá'u'lláh wrote. So, for example, we try to be constantly vigilant that our motives for any action are pure, that we are completely trustworthy, that we are well-wishers of all... The standards are very high.

There is a Bahá'í calendar–a solar calendar with 19 months of 19 days each year–and there are Bahá'í holy days. Once each Bahá'í month the local community gathers for worship, consultation and fellowship. I lived in the Del Mar area of San Diego when I became a Bahá'í, so I was registered as a member of the San Diego Bahá'í community.

In every location where there are nine or more adult Bahá'ís the community holds annual elections to democratically choose a local council to conduct the community's affairs for the year. These local tasks include registering births for Bahá'í families, holding children's classes, organizing youth activities, conducting weddings, providing counseling as requested, and officiating at funerals of Bahá'ís.

I had not been a Bahá'í very long before I was elected to the Local Spiritual Assembly of the Bahá'ís of San Diego.

Being a Leader

There were about 200 Bahá'ís in San Diego when I was elected to the Local Assembly (I'm told there are more than 800 Bahá'ís there now), and Bahá'í Assemblies only have nine members no matter how large the community, so it was tough. Remember that Assembly members are not clergy, they're just folks with jobs and families and other things to do. There is no honor or glory or financial reward for being an Assembly member, just work, and the way we tried to cover all of the things we were responsible for was to divide up the tasks. I was asked if I would do "external affairs"–that is, represent the Bahá'í Faith to the larger community–and this is why people got the idea that I was a "leader" of the Bahá'í community when, in fact, I was just one of nine Local Assembly members.

For example, the Assembly asked me to be the Bahá'í representative to the Interreligious Council of San Diego—and then I was selected as president of that organization for one year. It was an exciting time, because we wrote the group's first statement of purpose, and put together a book called Bridging Our Faiths, which was published by the Paulist Press.

I was asked to read Bahá'í prayers at the Mayor's inauguration ceremony, at the first interfaith ceremony in the Cathedral at the University of San Diego, and at the Soviet Art Festival Vesper Service. I spoke about the Bahá'í Faith at a Buddhist temple, a Catholic girls' high school, and at various retirement homes. And I read announcements of Bahá'í activities on the local television stations, so I started to become "known around town."

Bahá'ís are strong supporters of the United Nations, and I was elected to the Board of Directors of the local chapter of the United Nations Association. I also was a member of the La Jolla Peacemakers.

In 1986, the international governing body of the Bahá'í Faith, the Universal House of Justice, issued a letter to the people of the world called "The Promise of World Peace." It is eloquent, powerful, and inspired me to organize a series of talks at the Bahá'í Center on the subject of peace. We invited peace activists from many organizations to participate, and I ended up hosting 50 monthly programs with a total of 125 speakers. I also organized a series of Bahá'ís to speak about the "World in Transition."

This was a time when there were a lot of Southeast Asian refugees coming to the United States, and a certain number of them were Bahá'ís so I worked to try to help get them settled. I particularly worked with Hmong families, but also with Vietnamese and others. And of course the Bahá'ís had their Persian refugees, and I was made a member of the Persian-American Affairs Committee. So you can see that I was busy in these and other local activities.

In 1984, I went on a Bahá'í pilgrimage. This is a nine day program of visits to Bahá'í holy places in Haifa and Akka, Israel, and when I saw the Shrines and the gardens surrounding them I was deeply moved. It felt like all of the atoms surrounding the Bahá'í holy places were sparkling, sparkling, sparkling... It was indescribable. If I had had even one doubt about the truth of this religion before my pilgrimage it was entirely dispelled by that experience. This Faith is truly of God.

In 1986, I traveled to New Delhi to attend the dedication of the first Bahá'í House of Worship in India. There are only seven Bahá'í Temples so far—one on each continent—and the one in India is shaped like a lotus flower: it is stunningly beautiful. After the ceremonies, I traveled with my older daughter and her husband to visit Bahá'í social and economic development projects around the country. I had known people who had traveled to India and just seen poverty and despair, but as Bahá'ís we saw great hope and initiative in the Bahá'í schools, medical facilities, projects for women, environmental improvement, and so on.

I also went to China as a Bahá'í representative. That was quite a trip! We went to five cities in three weeks, and I was asked to talk about the relationship of the Bahá'í Faith and Buddhism. I enjoyed it, but you know—by the end I was tired. And I thought, why am I trying to keep this pace? I kept getting elected to the Local Assembly year after year, but there were lots of younger Bahá'ís who were very capable. So at one Assembly meeting I said: "Next month I will be seventy-seven years old. Do you want to be here when you're seventy-seven?" They looked at each other and said, "Not me," so agreed that it would be OK if I retired from the Assembly.

In 1996 I moved to Marin County and became a member of the San Rafael Bahá'í community. I was asked to represent the Bahá'í Faith on the Marin Interfaith Council and I came to know Rev. Kevin Tripp and others. But due to glaucoma I have become legally blind, so it's very hard for me to attend their meetings.

I still attend as many Bahá'í activities as I can, however: Sunday devotions, Nineteen Day Feasts, Holy Day celebrations, and whatever other programs they get together. I'm not on the Local Spiritual Assembly, but I do what I can. It's a way of life and I'm still active.

Margaret Hough is retired. But, she is still active in the Bahai faith. She lives in Marin County.

Carol Hovis Story

NON PROFIT CHAPLAIN

Seeking Depth And Diversity

The decision to go into the ministry was definitely not the first decision that got me on this journey. I grew up in a family that talked a lot about politics and history and social issues, and this was in the suburbs of Washington, D.C., in the sixties and seventies. My mother was a scientist, my father, a lawyer. My mom, in particular, loved to talk about the mysteries of the universe, and religion. All different religions were of interest to her, and, thus, to me.

When I entered the seminary I was seeking diversity in terms of ethnicity, because my college had been predominantly European American, and upper middle-class, and I wanted something really different, and Union in New York offered that. It was non-denominational, urban. It was devoted and committed to liberation theology, feminist theology, black liberation theology, gay/lesbian theology, and that's where I wanted to be. It was time for me to really be immersed.

After two years at the seminary I still had my doubts that I had chosen the right path. I had experienced a woman chaplain at my college, and I was raised to know that a woman could be and do anything she wanted to be and do. But my concern about becoming a minister was that I was afraid that I wouldn't be able to be part of who I am. I was concerned more about that kind of prudish, fundamentalist, southern Christian stereotype that I had been exposed to. My father's family is from the southern part of the United States and were pretty conservative, and I knew that wasn't who I was or am.

So I took a year off. I needed to be out in the world doing some things. I waitressed. I served for a year as a chaplain in a hospital in Washington. D.C. I could still wear big earrings if I wanted, or short skirts, or smoke a cigarette. Those were the kinds of things I was afraid I could not do, the kinds of things I had fears about. I just needed to work some of those things out.

I went back after that year and finished, and started the ordination process in the Presbyterian Church, USA. I finished at Union in New York, actually received my degree in May of '89, but I'd already started working in a church in Virginia the year before, and then was ordained in July of 1990. I then served a parish in Fairfax, Virginia, for a total of nine years—two years before I was ordained and then seven years ordained. I was an associate pastor in a church with seven to eight hundred members.

Finding A God Of Freedom

I began working as the spiritual director at the Canal Ministry three and one-half years ago. My title now is spiritual director, and the areas I cover are social justice advocacy, community outreach, interfaith community outreach, and staff and community chaplaincy. In some ways, one of the greatest joys about being at the Canal Ministry is that liberation, freedom, oppression are words that we use here all the time, and everybody knows what you're talking about. Justice and peace are just part of our language, whoever you are on staff. You can be the office manager, you can be the fund development director, you could be the bookkeeper, everyone understands that language, whereas in the church, that was not my experience. It is work that is closely aligned to the thesis of liberation theology.

Liberation theology began in the 1970s. It came out of base Christian community movements in South America and in Central America. The Hebrew texts of the Exodus tell the story of deliverance and the story of freedom the Jewish people experienced, leaving slavery in Egypt, and going into the Promised Land. This is an experience other peoples who have been enslaved, other peoples who have been oppressed continue to experience.

Liberation theology is the message of liberation and freedom you don't necessarily hear in many Christian churches. In the mainline Catholic, Protestant, and certainly in the Evangelical churches in this country, themes of liberation and justice are not the predominant themes happening in church. Once in a while there may be in a sermon or a prayer however they're not the drumbeat.

There's an interesting dialogue that we would talk about in seminary between Martin Luther King Jr., and Malcolm X. When is enough, enough, and when do people rise up and say, "I'm not going to take this anymore"?

Those of us who believe in liberation theology may be ordained, we may not be, we may have gone to seminary and chosen not to be ordained. Whatever our choices have been, there's a whole group of us—and I think it's a growing group—we believe in God. We believe that there is an incredible Spirit and force alive in the world. We believe in the goodness of people. We believe in compassion, and we want peace in the world. We want justice, and we don't really like the way, in a lot of ways, the institutional churches are participating in that. We're not walking away from our faith. We're not walking away from God or one another, but we're questioning a lot. We find each other, and that's who I found here, and we all know that there are lots of us across the country and around the world.

Applying My Beliefs

The Canal Ministry serves the Canal neighborhood in East San Rafael, California. The buildings were first built in the fifties and sixties as vacation rentals for people from San Francisco. In the seventies you had war and violence and devastation happening in countries like Vietnam, Guatemala, El Salvador, and Nicaragua. Some of that refugee immigrant influx arrived here. And the housing in this neighborhood was apartments and condos and the people—and this was mostly in the seventies—could afford it. Ever since then, it's been a neighborhood of incredible diversity, immigrants, refugees, as well as African American and European American folk who have been here for decades.

Twenty years ago, in 1982, people of faith in Marin started talking to one another, and said, "You know, we need to do something. We need to be something for these newly arrived folk." A couple of congregations got together and started the San Rafael Canal Ministry. We understand ourselves to be responding to the needs of the community. Twenty years ago those needs were around clothing, furniture, household items, as well as some English, teaching English. As the years went on, the ESL classes (English as a Second Language) became more important, so that part of our program grew more and more.

From its beginning, it's always had interfaith support and, therefore, spiritual understanding that we're doing this because our spiritual traditions say that this is the right thing to do. That you must take in the sojourner and the stranger and the children and the orphans and the women. You must pay attention to those who are being oppressed, those who are not experiencing freedom.

This neighborhood is cut off by the freeway and by the canals. There are no major grocery stores. There are no doctors or dentists. There are no banks. There are no freestanding congregations in this neighborhood, not one. There are a couple of storefront Pentecostal congregations, so out of fairness, they do exist, but there are no Buddhist temples, no Jewish synagogues, no Christian churches, as freestanding buildings.

I happen to be a Presbyterian Minister. But Canal Ministry is not a church. There is a group of mostly Latino folk who for years have been meeting in each other's homes once a month for Sunday worship. Most of them come from Catholic backgrounds. One of the beauties of Catholicism in Latin America that I've come to learn more about is they don't quite do it the same way that we do it here or the Roman Catholic Church does it in Europe. There's a lot of openness to mixing traditions and indigenous cultures. So it doesn't really matter to them that I'm a woman, that I'm European American, and that I'm Protestant.

So they came to me. They said, "We would like you to do this. Would you be willing?" And I said, "Yes." They wanted to have someone who could come and celebrate Eucharist with them, the Communion, and that's what I do.

It is a group of about twenty-five, thirty people. It's not huge. But I've been asked to perform weddings and quinceneros, which is a Mexican tradition of celebrating a fifteen-year-old girl's coming into adulthood, and that's wonderful. And I think they know I'm available when they need me, for example, a woman just lost her mother in Mexico and asked me to be with her, and I was there just being pastorally supportive. It allows me to really try to implement my beliefs.

Examining The State Of The Church

Since I moved to California for the last three and a half years I have been serving and working as a volunteer with lots of congregations. I continue to know firsthand the incredible pain and anguish that clergy are experiencing in their work, and the pain and anguish that congregations are going through, with one another and with the clergy.

The dependency and the passivity that I continue to experience in congregations is startling to me, remarkable, very, very sad, and maddening. There is the passivity and a dependency both in parishioners and leadership. It is as if people saying, "Well, I don't know how to do that. I can't do that". I know I'm generalizing. There's incredible leadership out there, but all of us, myself included, have just gotten way off track.

I don't think it's just Christianity, the institution, that is frustrating and in many ways failing the communities. I think other religious and faith traditions are in some of the same situations. I also know or believe that the way we're doing churches isn't really necessarily even responding to people's griefs and needs and struggles in the way that I think that God would want.

I think we've focused too much on professionalism in the clergy and professionalism in religious institutions. Studying and pondering and praying, that's all important, but we've created a group of people who are supposedly the experts on theology and religious matters and spiritual matters, and I have come to a point in my life where I really have a problem with that. I mean, at the core of my being, I don't believe that's what God intends.

It's one thing to be able to be an expert on the Bible and teach that. It's another thing when people say to me, "Oh, I don't need to do my spiritual work or my spiritual journey, because you're doing that for me." That just doesn't work. You know, I believe we're all here on this planet to do our own spiritual work and be on our journey. So my vision for what church looks like, what community looks like, is about people coming together and figuring out together all the different expertise we bring, and sharing that. It's much more of a team approach.

Some of us have talked about we would like to see. Instead of having one person be the pastor who works all the time and that's all he or she does, why not have three or four who come together. We may all have gone through seminary. We may all be ordained. But one of us may really love preaching, and another really may love teaching, and another one may really love pastoral care, and another one really may love administration.

I close my eyes and what I'm seeing and experiencing and feeling is that the institutional church has been for quite some time in many ways going off track, and I think it's continuing to go off track. I think the numbers are growing of people who are just simply not participating, not going, not affiliating. They've seen the institutional church and people will say, "It's not speaking to me. It's not relevant in my life. I can't understand what people are talking about. It's not meeting me where I'm at spiritually."

So you have a lot of people who just aren't affiliating at all, and yet there are also people, those who've been to seminary, and others in the church, members, parishioners who are saying, "Wait a minute. I don't want to be totally unaffiliated, but I don't like the way we're going off track and the way we've been going off track, so what can we do that's new and different?"

I guess where we're all at, those that are somewhat like myself, those of us who talk about this all the time, we're just going to keep attempting to do what we can do in our own small ways, and we don't really know exactly what's going to happen. My sense of history, human history, not just with religious institutions, but with governments and countries and peoples, is I think there's going to be some real falling apart. Things are going to, in some ways, get worse before they get better.

Carol Hovis is currently the Spiritual Advocate at the San Rafael Canal Ministry in Marin County.

Karyl Huntley Story

RELIGIOUS SCIENCE MINISTER

My Third Career

It's actually my third career. I was a high school teacher, and that was my shortest career. And then I was in college publishing. I was in sales and editing for a couple of different publishing houses for college textbooks, and that was my second-longest career. And now I've been in the ministry the longest. I've been thirteen years in the ministry.

I have been involved in my denomination, which is Religious Science, all of my adult life. I was very close to my minister fifteen years ago, and I took the first step in becoming a practitioner, which is like a spiritual counselor, and takes a number of years of training. I became a practitioner, and then I worked very closely with my minister in various staff positions and in charge of various projects.

It was a very natural next step to go to the School of Ministry. I had a conversation during a lunch with my minister about, "well, maybe sometime in the future, sometime, perhaps, could be, maybe," I'd like to go to the School of Ministry. And by the end of the lunch, I ended up planning to be his assistant after I had done the School of Ministry. So it was all organic and didn't have a big decision involved, just naturally went where it was supposed to go.

I went to the School of Ministry from this church, and then I began a church in the city. That was a small church. Then I was the assistant minister at a big church in Santa Rosa, and then from the assistant position, I became the senior minister here.

Becoming A Practitioner

I began my studies as a practitioner. Every minister must take practitioner training. And if you consider that most people that go to church are women, then the students of whatever classes are taught in that church are a lot women. And so the practitioners, moving through their class studies and practitioner studies, are mostly women. So, for women to make a big percentage of our worldwide ministry is no mystery.

A practitioner is someone who has taken a lot of classes in our philosophy, in science of mind. They know that in order for your life to change, that some internal change in you has to happen. In our belief structure we don't believe that God withholds anything. We believe that all has been given, and what we have to work on is our ability to accept. That's the crucial factor.

If people are unhappy or limited, if they feel that something is standing in the way of them achieving happiness or purpose in life, peace of mind or right livelihood, expression or creativity, it's not that there is something out there that is withholding it from them. It's not a capricious God that answers some prayers and not others. It is something within us that is standing in our own way.

A practitioner is trained to help other clients find inner clarity. So many people come to practitioners with the same issues that they would come to a therapist with, except we come at it from a spiritual perspective. As I said, God doesn't withhold, it is God's good pleasure to give us the kingdom, all has been given, and it is our work to move away anything that stands in the way of us accepting our good.

That doesn't mean more houses, more cars, more money, necessarily. It means genuine peace of mind and how, in the world, we can achieve genuine peace of mind and be in the world, be in our job, be in our families, be in our neighborhoods and cultures with peace, joy, lightness, love, connection.

What We Believe

Ernest Holmes, our founder, read widely in world religions, and you can see some threads in Religious Science from the Eastern traditions, as well as from Christianity. Many ministers quote every single week from the Judeo-Christian Bible, but the way I like to think about it is that we teach what Jesus taught, and that's how my relationship with traditional Christianity is. In fact, the person who's at the center of Christianity is also the greatest example of living well that we have, and so we go back to Jesus and what he said and what he taught, and we teach what Jesus taught.

We do not, however, believe that Jesus is inherently different than any of the rest of us. He said that "Greater things than these ye shall do" and "Right now you are the sons and daughters of God." One of the little aphorisms of Religious Science is that Jesus is the great example, not the great exception.

I think that religion shows us that there is something larger than the world of form. It shows us that there is an intelligence and a love that is literally holding everything together. When we honor and experience and court our relationship with the unseen—one of the things that I like to call God, is the pattern that connects—when we simply meditate on that which connects us to the larger, we cannot be against anyone. We cannot have an us and them if we go back to believing that we're all sons and daughters of the infinite presence.

I think that the high place of religion in a civil society is to draw us together. And the divisive place of religion is to say, "You don't believe what I believe, and so you're my enemy." We have just no place for that in our philosophy. In fact, the vision of my church is a world living in love. In order to co-create a world living in love, we cannot have factions that think that because the belief is different, that the essence of them is different. It doesn't compute in me at all. I don't know what I'd do if I didn't have this belief that we're all one, that we're all connected.

It's the fundamental principle of all of life, that we are connected, that we're one. And so you don't cheat anybody. You don't make an enemy of anyone. You walk a mile in your brother's shoes. You look for that which makes you similar, not what makes you different. You realize that we all love our children, and given somebody else's children, I would love them, too. So it is absolutely the basis of what I leave the house with every single day, and it's what I talk about all the time in my ministry.

People that just don't feel at home in some of the more traditional denominations come to us. People who have had negative religious experiences in the past, who really have a spiritual yearning, find us. We have a number of people who say, "I haven't set foot in a church in twenty years and vowed I never would again, and now I'm here and I love it." So those are the kinds of people that we normally appeal to.

We don't have a lot of dogma. We don't have a lot of rules. We don't have a lot of "You have to believe this way." What we do have is a philosophy of it's done unto you as you believe, that all life is the same holy life of God, the life that we're living, the life that's in the tree. The life that's in every life form is divine and is the same life, and that we are an aspect, a part of that one divine life. Oneness of all of life and the power of our mind to create.

We take that understanding and we apply it to our own desires, our own need, want, impulse to give and create. We apply that to community, whether it's a small community or the world. We honor everyone as the same life that we are, just in a different bag of skin, it makes it very easy to come from love instead of difference.

I've already said that the consciousness with which you look out onto the world is also the magnet that draws experiences to you. And our inner landscape, the beliefs that we grow up with, started very young, and most of them started in our family of origin, or neighborhood, or first years of school.

So when I'm in that high place of being very accepting and very forgiving, I can really see that every antic that anyone does, including terrorist acts, are the product of internal beliefs in separation, or beliefs that came into that person through hurt or separation or hatred or fear.

Outreach

We believe that we have the unifying philosophy that would appeal to Marinites, and, every Sunday, someone new will come and say, "My gosh, I never knew that somebody believed like I do." We are developing a marketing presence in Marin that will help people know that we're here, so that people can find us.

We have programs that help elderly people in Marin County. Twice a year we go out and do things like clean their yard and help them maintain fences and clean houses. We also have a sister community in Chikasi [phonetic], Ukraine, that we support financially, and also send people over there to assist the minister there.

The minister in the Ukraine has a little bit more of a challenge because she does not call herself a church. In the Ukraine she calls herself a teaching philosophy. But it is the same message as we teach here. Love is the foundational energy of the world and we have to live that love and give from that love and serve others, and love ourselves and each other.

We send money and we have sent two work parties over there and we're planning our third for October. She has a civil project that involves building a hothouse to grow vegetables for a school that serves children with spinal difficulties, and so we are building the hothouse. The people from Marin County go over there with their saws and hammers and build that hothouse.

The minister has a possibility of purchasing a big house, that would then be a retreat facility for Central Europe for ministers and practitioners who would like to have a sabbatical over there and help her teach. Religious Science has had a presence in Russia for a number of years, but she's really the first one who has moved to Ukraine to create a community there.

We have a table up every Sunday, where we have sold things like bumper stickers, we've sold things like purses that she's brought from a hand-crafted seamstress in Ukraine, to help her raise money. But mostly we send money and a couple of times a year we send people.

Women

Religious Science has a long history of women ministers. As a matter of fact, we came out of Christian Science, so Mary Baker Eddy is in our lineage. And then one of her students was Emma Curtis Hopkins. In fact, many, many of the students of Mary Baker Eddy were women, and she was teaching Christian Science to women at the time that the women got the vote, and it was really a part of that original women's movement that the whole metaphysical movement has its roots.

And so Emma Curtis Hopkins, one of her students, then broke away from Mary Baker Eddy and ended up teaching most of the metaphysical teachers that then started their own denominations. The Fillmores [phonetic] for Unity were her students, Ernest Holmes was a student of Emma's.

I tend to not want to generalize qualities that are women's qualities and qualities that are men's qualities, but for me personally, it is easy for me to be in my heart, and I think, in general, in this culture, it is easy for women to be in their heart. I don't care if I cry in public. I can tell touching stories and people don't think I'm corny or weak. And so I believe that my expression of my spirituality and my religion is heart-centered. That's not to say that all religious people have their power there. Some people are like the leaders of the parade. They are out there with this oratory, and they just froth people up and get them mobilized and get them going.

I can do it, but it's not my way. My way is to be in my heart and to model open-heartedness, model vulnerability, model teachability, and then I watch my people go there, too. They just open up, they cry on Sunday, they snuggle up, they hold the hand of the stranger next to them. I don't think that I could do that if I were a big, powerful man. I can't see that that style would work for most men. That's not true of all men, but that's how I use my gender in a very harmonious way with my delivery system. It works for me. This is the package I bring.

Karyl Huntley is currently the minister at the Golden Gate Center for Spiritual Living Church of Religious Science Center in Marin County.

Carolyn Kellogg Story

CATHOLIC CHANGE AGENT

Questioning

I'm a cradle Roman Catholic, born into it. And I followed that path well into probably the beginning part of my forties, although I had large reservations on the images of God that were being portrayed. Ever since I was a child, the God that I knew was a loving God. This God was not a vindictive God or a punishing God. I don't know where I got that from. It was just something that was an inward knowing of mine. I certainly didn't pick it up from anything I was taught.

My first shift off of basic religion was the Cursillo movement, which gave me a sense of God's love coming through others. Then I moved past that and got into my own recovery, through twelve-step programs, and in therapy for myself. I felt, "My goodness, I can have a God of any image I care to." The twelve-step gave me that permission. I didn't have to have the image that was fed to me. And that totally changed my life.

I went back to school, after raising five children with my husband. I went to John F. Kennedy in Orinda, and my major was transpersonal counseling psychology. I was exposed to religions other than Christian. That, again, opened up my life even more. I began a meditation practice. I looked and looked for something other than Buddhist meditation and eventually I did find something called "centering prayer" that was more God-based.

Then my mother died, and it's really interesting how this happens with people. After their parents die big spiritual things happen. That's what happened to me. I had a spiritual emergence experience that totally shifted everything for me. I had an experience of God's love, of divine love, of being loved, really and truly being loved. And everything blew open after that. I still went to church. I still was Roman Catholic. I still went to mass although I was constantly searching.

Eventually I just stopped going to church for quite a while. And then I found myself going back, because I had this thirst. It wasn't for what was told to me in church from the pulpit or anything else, but there was something about the ritual. I was absolutely drawn to Eucharist.

Feminist Spirituality

That's been my spiritual path, and since then I've really gotten into feminist spirituality. My definition of feminist is, everybody is equal. It's a discipleship of equals. It's not that women are better than men or men are better than women. Everybody is equal.

The first time I went to a feminist liturgy she did what we call agape, with the bread and the wine. And, to me it was Eucharist. I told her that, and she said, "That's right." I thought, "Oh, my God," literally, that this is possible, that some ordained man didn't have to do these magic things. I started looking around and talking to friends, and one friend said, "You know, I know about this group that meets. It's the women's ordination group that meets. Do you want to go to it?" I said, "Yes, I do."

I went, and that was in 1990. That was the first time I had gone to anything like that. They had the Eucharist there, and then we talked about things going on in the church and what the women were doing and how they were organizing and how they were trying to promote equality. I was blown away. I didn't know anything like that was going on. That's how I began and eventually I joined Women's Ordination Conference and Women Church.

I started organizing workshops and retreats on women in scripture. I got involved in the feminist side, the very left, barely hanging on by the fingernails kind of thing, with feminist Catholic women's groups like Women's Ordination Conference and Women Church. I was involved in Eucharistic celebrations that were done in homes that were just women. There were no ordained priests in sight anywhere, and we'd do our own Eucharists in our homes. That evolved into "A Critical Mass: Women Celebrating Eucharist," where we do it in public, and have been for five years, the third Sunday of every month.

A Critical Mass

I met Victoria Rue and she got the idea of doing "A Critical Mass." She happened to live in Oakland, and she got together with another friend of mine and they decided to do a public mass with women, and to deconstruct the Mass. That happened in Oakland five years ago, and we had 300 people there. That evolved into a monthly event. That's what I'm involved in now.

Deconstructing the mass was about changing language and male centered ritual. I had a friend who agreed to do this. He's a former priest. He had vestments on and he would start it and then he would be pulled back and we would do it in a feminist way. You deconstruct it once and then you have a feminist Mass, a feminist celebration. We changed the forms and added music and gestures and dance.

The words are very different. They're all-inclusive, and there's nobody who presides. Whoever is there is saying the words and invoking the spirit. And it is men and women, children, the homeless that live in the park there that we do it in, and whoever wants to join us. So it's very different from regular Catholic Mass.

Currently there are twenty, maybe, twenty-five people. But numbers are not the thing. It's that we're doing it. We're doing it in a park in Oakland. It used to be where the cathedral was, and the Loma Prieta earthquake knocked it down. They made a park where the cathedral was and gave it to the city, and so that's where we do it. The bishop's, residence, is right behind it. We didn't know that when we first started doing it.

The park is right across from the Greyhound bus depot. It's a homeless park. We go in there and we clean that park the third Sunday of every month, before we have our liturgy. We're in there with shovels and brooms and rakes, cleaning that park. The homeless would be there and they'd ask for food. So, we started bringing hard-boiled eggs and bananas and other food.

But two years ago a group of Franciscans came to our liturgy one time and saw us trying to feed the homeless, and said, "You know, we'll take that over. We'll do that." So now they make 150 bag lunches and bring them third Sunday of every month, and have them out. In the cold weather, they bring in blankets and coats and sleeping bags.

I would say that hundreds of groups of women are doing Eucharists in their homes now. Periodically, they will do it publicly. But there isn't any other group doing it publicly on an ongoing basis. We do it the third Sunday of every month. No matter where I go, if I mention Critical Mass, people know what it is, and they're really happy we're doing it.

On Being Catholic

That are splinter Catholic groups. In New York there is the Corpus Christi group. The priests just picked up and moved the whole parish over to someplace else and started their own church, and Mary Rommerman was ordained. She is a working priest there now. There are these splinter groups going on. But we are choosing to stay within the structure and trying to change it from inside. I mean, we're staying within the structure to an extent.

There was a big meeting of bishops down in Dallas recently. One of our people went. There was a lot of Women Church Convergence women, which is an umbrella group of thirty women's groups, of feminist women's groups in the Catholic church. A large group went. Women's Ordination Conference was there, Quixote was there. There were hundreds of people. Call to Action was there. Everybody was there.

They are pushing, pushing, pushing to get lay people to have some say in the church, and that's what we're pushing for. We are Roman Catholics. We're not old Catholics, we're not American Catholics, or this or that or the other thing. We're Roman Catholics, and we're pushing to have lay people, men and women, have more say, have women be equal. It's a very long-term effort. A lot of people don't want to put in the effort and they just leave, and they go do something else. That's fine. But there are a lot of us that don't want to do that.

I have tried other affiliations down the line and none of them fit. It's like I like to say, it's in my DNA and I really believe that. It's my church. That's what fits for me. I went to Episcopal church and it's fine, but it doesn't fit. And I've gone to other Protestant denominations, I've tried Buddhism, I've studied Hinduism. I've looked at all kinds of things. It's not like I haven't looked at them, and they all have something for me, but not what this does. And, you know, if I try to be logical about it, I can't be logical about it, but there's something and that's for me. So, I keep going. I don't ever go on Sunday.

One of my motivating factors of getting involved in trying to change the church is because of my family, We have a son and one granddaughter that live with us. She has come to Critical Mass a couple of times, and she says, "You know, this is really great. I feel a part of it." The other granddaughter is a practicing Catholic. The oldest daughter is a Buddhist, and so are her boys. The second daughter has just joined a church. It's Four Square Gospel Evangelical. And my youngest son married a Jewish girl. So I have two Jewish grandsons and two Buddhist grandsons. Which is okay with me. Everybody has their own path.

Women Do Things Differently

What we're working for is to change patriarchy. It has to be equality, a discipleship of equals. It's not going to work to add women and stir. For one thing, they won't let us in.

But when they are given the position and the power women do things differently. I was reading in the paper the other day that the women who are now in Congress are proposing all kinds of different legislation for the protection of children and health issues and all those things that men don't consider as important as women. So, you can see the changes going on in our government because there are more women involved.

The Need For Change

I think in this society organized religion is on the wane because it's losing its relevancy. It doesn't really fit for people. That is one reason I am doing what I'm doing, to help the religion become more relevant. Over the millennium, people have changes in consciousness, and there have been huge changes in consciousness, I think, over the last fifty years, and especially in the last twenty-five. Just large leaps of consciousness.

You look at the ecological movement, you look at all kinds of movements, and I think that the religions just have not kept up with that change in consciousness. They have not. What we do, just our little Critical Mass with twenty people, is raising consciousness. Without some kind of spirituality, without some kind of religion, people, they shift to worshipping other idols. They worship money, they worship power. They worship the big house and the SUV. They just shift their allegiance to something else when the religion becomes not relevant in their lives and doesn't fit for them.

What Jesus had to offer is really beautiful, and what Christianity has done to it is not so beautiful. But if somehow we could get back to that basic message of love and compassion, love and compassion, if we could bring it back, and that means love and compassion for everybody. Jesus didn't discriminate against anyone. He accepted everybody. If we could get back to that again, maybe, who knows what would happen.

Carolyn Kellogg is a counselor in private practice and works with the group A Critical Mass.

Theresa Kime Story

UNITARIAN UNIVERSALIST MINISTER

Early Disillusionment

I was raised as a Methodist and I really always loved going to church. My parents didn't go, but I went. They took me to Sunday school as a child, but when I was old enough in high school and could go on my own, I went to the regular church services and sang in the choir.

Then when I went to college, and I started really becoming aware of the gap between what we hear and feel in church and how we then take that out into the world and live it. It seemed to me that there was a large gap between what was said in church about how we are to treat each other and our world and how people were actually treating each other and our world. And in addition to that, it seemed that religion had been used largely to separate people, as a weapon, rather than as a way to draw people together.

Now looking back on that, I think that that sharp awareness really broke my heart, because I saw religion as being something so incredible and beautiful. I saw religion as having the potential of being something so glorious in its ability to connect people and call forth their best, that it was really heartbreaking for me at that time to realize that wasn't really happening.

So, I didn't have anything to do with organized religion. I became one of those people that kind of makes jokes about it, and I was sarcastic about it. I went into the Unitarian Universalist congregation in San Francisco it was because I had ended a long-term relationship and was re-discovering who I was, and I found I wanted something spiritual in my life.

I wasn't sure how I could find spirituality given what I was thinking about organized religion. But the bus that I took to work went by the Unitarian Universalist congregation, and they had these wonderful sayings out every time I would ride by. They had quotes from Emerson and Thoreau, and other authors of wonderful, inclusive, big, broadminded ideas. And I thought, "I'll give them a try. I really think the chances are about zero, but I'll go. I'll sit in the back, and I will leave the minute I'm offended."

Finding Unitarian Universalism

And so I went. This was in the early eighties, late seventies. I discovered first thing from their order of service that they had taken the sexism out of their hymns—had Xeroxed them from the hymnal and made them inclusive. I was impressed they had made that effort. And they had two sayings printed on the wall that I really liked, Biblical quotes: "What dost the Lord require of thee but to love, do justice, love, mercy, and walk humbly with your God." And the other one was, "The kingdom of God is within you."

And then, there was a woman minister. It was the first woman minister I'd ever seen, and while I was looking at her this incredible thought popped into my head out of nowhere: maybe that's something I should be doing–be a minister.

I didn't find anything that offended me in that service, but still distrustful, I went to their library afterwards, and I was sure I'd find something in their belief system that I would say, "Ha! I knew they were too good to be true," and I could leave. But I never found that thing, and those little voices about becoming a minister started and didn't go away.

I thought, "this is such a joke." I mean, this is the biggest joke going, that I would become a minister after all the ways I've pushed religion away. It just seemed really funny. I think the Holy One definitely has a sense of humor. But it was one of those things that didn't go away, and I just kept following it. I just said, "Okay, I'll take the next step, and then I'll take the next step and see what happens." And step by step the path just kept opening up and being there for me.

I went to Starr King School for Ministry in Berkeley. It's part of the Graduate Theological Union. It's one of the specific Unitarian Universalist schools for the ministry. Then after school we have a rigorous credentialing process where we go before a panel, called the Ministerial Fellowship Committee, consisting of ministers and lay people from across the country, to be "tested," in a manner of speaking. It we get their tentative approval (your ministry is evaluated three years before final approval is given), we can then enter what's called a search process. Each of our congregations govern themselves, and so they call their own minister. Our association headquarters, which are in Boston, is the place that connects ministers with churches that are looking. So I joined that process, and my first congregation that called me was in Erie, Pennsylvania, and I was there for twelve years. Then I came to Marin two years ago.

Defining Religious Beliefs

I think at its best, religion calls forth the compassion and wisdom of the people who believe in that particular faith. It makes them more loving and more compassionate to everyone, not just the particular people in their faith tradition, and that at its best, it can call people to reach out to one another to make sure that everyone lives in a world where they feel blessed and where they can bring their blessings to the world.

It becomes important that as people of faith, we make sure that there's justice in the world, and there's peace, and no one goes hungry and everyone gets an education. It's important that we really work on trying to become the best people we can be, in terms of compassion and care for one another.

How we particularly image the holy is important, but I would hope that that's not a barrier to us, that we can still reach out to one another despite our differing ideas about what the holy looks like for us. I try to help folks in my congregation know the different ways that people understand the holy, and to encourage them to find that source and connection within themselves, and then to understand it in the context of our faith tradition.

We Unitarian Universalists have what are called our guiding principles, and they define for us, or help us articulate how we think a religious person lives out their life in the world. It starts with honoring the inherent worth and dignity of every person, and promoting justice, equity, and compassion in human relations, encouraging spiritual growth, and acceptance of one another. We also honor the right of each individual's conscience and foster the use of democratic process and the goal of world community with peace, liberty, and justice for all, as well as respect for the interdependent web of existence of which we are a part.

We are unusual in terms of our definition of religion, in that we start more with how we think living out a religious life helps you be in the world, and we leave it to each person to discern how the holy speaks to them and encourages and supports their living such a life.

So one person might really find that Jesus is the path that speaks to them. Another person might find Buddha. Another person might find nature speaks to them about what is good and true about life. Our assumption is that it's fine to have different images, but we still all come together and make the world a place that is welcoming for everyone.

Interfaith Beliefs

I'm very much drawn to Buddhism, although there's also a lot that I like about Christianity and feel connected to, and it was the tradition I was raised in. I have a lot of respect for all traditions, and I believe they each have something very important and beautiful to give to the world.

Our congregations govern themselves, and members are active in a variety of ways. We have an active social concerns committee that explores and supports issues and informs the rest of the congregation about them, and I participate in that at different times. I do classes on different spiritual disciplines, so that hopefully people will find the one that speaks to them, and that they can stay with and learn from.

I'm particularly drawn to interfaith work, so I participate in a local interfaith clergy group, which I really enjoy. We've done several interfaith services together. We did a Thanksgiving service together, and then on September 11th, after the terrorist attacks, we came together and did a service that evening. It seemed so right for me, that at such a time we should be reaching out to one another and across interfaith lines, coming together as interfaith communities to care for and grieve together.

Self Nourishment

Self-care is one of the trickiest things for ministers to do. I think this is across all faith tradition lines. Over the years, I've learned different things at different times that help me. Right now one of the things I do is first thing in the morning take some quiet time, doing reading that I find nourishing, and then meditating to start my day.

I'm doing more and more little things throughout the day like lighting a candle when I get to work, and thinking about how I want to orient myself to the day, and being grateful for my many blessings and opportunities. I ring the gong occasionally and let that sound bring me back to what's important. Just to have a moment of stillness can be refreshing, and, I think, help me be more centered and present to the work I'm doing.

And over the years I've come to understand the more I'm doing something that feels joyful and that's calling out my creativity and my excitement, then the more energy I have to give, and the more things don't seem so burdensome; they seem like adventures. The more I can develop my curiosity, the more that happens.

It's easy to get pulled into things that maybe don't feel so nourishing, or to lose track of what the main thing is that I need to bring forth each year–what it is that's going to excite me and bring me alive in my ministry. I think that's really a key thing, to ask myself about that, and then to keep returning to it, because it's easy to get distracted.

This year I've been going to a class at Spirit Rock Meditation Center (Buddhist) at least a couple of times a month, and try to do daylong retreats there, since all of these things are nourishing for me. When I was in Pennsylvania I lived near a Trappist monastery and I would go there at least once a year for a silent weeklong retreat with the monks doing the liturgy of the hours and chanting the psalms.

Self care means finding those things that nourish you and then reminding yourself that it's important to keep doing them, and to not let yourself say, "Oh, you know, I really need that time to get this project done." And then the next time it comes up that it's time for you to go do that nourishing thing, it's just easier to say, "No, I'm not going to do it." And then before you know it, you're not doing anything to nourish your soul, and then that's really the route to burnout. And it's real hard not to take that route.

Women's Gifts

Women do bring certain gifts to the ministry, perhaps partially because of the way we're socialized. Women are often taught to be more nurturing and compassionate, to develop the ability of listening more than many men who have not had a chance to develop those qualities, I think largely because of our social conditioning. And given that, I think often many women have natural gifts for the ministry, which does ask for the ability to listen carefully, to be present to others in their struggles, and to walk with people in all aspects of their life.

There are many men that are compassionate and wise and they make excellent ministers. And, of course, there are women who haven't developed these qualities. There are many ways to do ministry. But I think overall at this point in our history and our society, women have been taught to develop those qualities more, and are more likely to bring those qualities to this the ministry in a way that's very useful.

At one point in our clergy association, male ministers were talking about how female ministers had changed our ministry. They said before many women became ministers, often at ministers' meetings they would just sit around and sort of compare notes about who had the biggest church, and who was doing the most this or that. There was an element of, you know, who's doing the best. It was hard for them to share their struggles. And since ministry can be a very isolating profession that kind of sharing is important. When we get together with colleagues we need to have the chance to be completely human, sharing our struggles as well as the joys and our triumphs. Men have commented that women ministers made this possible now at our collegial gatherings. It is so important and helpful for the health of our whole ministry to be able to speak to the struggles and to say, "Hey, we're all human. What are you finding difficult right now?" and, "No, I'm not really doing real great at this particular thing," as well as, "I'm having a lot of fun with this, and I'm enjoying that"

I think the real trick for us as clergy is remembering that we stepped into a role. It's an important role. But, it's not all of who we are, and of course we're not going to do it all right all the time. I think there is a certain seduction to its power, and that's why we need one another, to say, "Let's be real clear that we are all human here. And let's face up to whatever is going on with us." And that is part of what women bring that has been so important for the well being of all clergy.

Theresa Kime is currently the pastor of the Unitarian Universalist Congragation of Marin in Marin County.

Carolyn Logan Story

LICENSED MISSIONARY

Born in the Church

The denomination that I'm in is Church of God in Christ, a Pentecostal denomination. I've been in this denomination ever since I was born. I often say I was born in the church. So I grew up in the church, and it just became my lifestyle. Then later on, when I was about eighteen years old, although I worked in the church and went to church on a regular basis, it was when I was eighteen years old that I accepted Jesus Christ as my personal savior, and began to develop a personal relationship.

I've always sung in choirs. I began playing the piano when I was perhaps about eight years old. My father's a musician. My mother's a musician, and my father sings. I'm from a singing background, so as long as I can remember, my brothers and sisters, we all sang together. I sang in the church choir. I played the piano for the church, beginning at about age eight, so I've grown up doing that.

I'm the minister of music here at Cornerstone. Currently we have three choirs. We have our Children and Praise, and then we have our youth choir and adult choir. So I'm responsible for rehearsing them, preparing the music, and then I play while we sing on Sunday mornings.

My own son plays the drums, and another young boy that's about eleven is beginning to play the organ. So I work with them to develop their skills and to help raise them up so that they begin to minister. Other young people direct the choir, and I'm responsible for training them, so it keeps me quite busy doing that.

The bottom line to music in the church is that in the Old Testament we see where the Bible talks about sending the tribe of Judah first, and I'm just making this short, but there were twelve tribes, and so one was the tribe of Judah. The tribe of Judah was the tribe of praise, so whenever the Israelites went into battle, they sent the praisers first, and they would go praising the Lord and singing and ministering unto the Lord. So when the Israelites had to go into battle, they said, "Send Judah first, and then we will win the battle."

So we believe our singing sets the tone for the rest of the service. Therefore, those that sing and lead worship, they are ministers because they're setting the tone for worship for everyone that will come behind.

Helping the Community

We've had people come to our church who are on welfare and don't have much of anything. We'll help them by feeding them, but we're also going to be encouraging them to go back to school, to be able to get a better job, and to raise themselves up. So we watch our congregation move from being on welfare to having their own homes, and having well-paying jobs. Then we know that they'll be able to take care of themselves and their families. So you start off with just trying to help people for a minute, but the ultimate goal is to have them become self-sufficient.

People come to us. They know the church is here and they come, it keeps us so busy that we don't really have to advertise. Sometimes we aren't able to help. You feel it in your heart. You want to, but sometimes you just can't, you know, you can't meet all of the needs, because there's so many. But as we get people to come into the church, we try to raise them up. Like the Chinese proverb that says, "Give a man a fish, he'll eat one day. But teach him to fish, and he'll eat forever." But as they join the church, then we're able to help them more and more.

Licensed Missionary

In our church denomination, Church of God in Christ, women are allowed to expound the word of God, or to share the word of God, with the idea of getting people to commit themselves to the Lord, and to receive salvation, receive Jesus Christ into their hearts. They can become a licensed missionary, that's what I do. It's similar to a preacher. But in our denomination we do not ordain women as preachers.

You can start as an aspiring missionary, which means you only work in your local church. And then you become a deaconess missionary, and then once you become a licensed evangelist missionary, that means you're free to travel over the country, and other churches of the same denomination will welcome you to come in and minister there.

I teach in my own church and I travel. I travel over the state of California, and I can travel outside of the state of California, sharing the word of God with people, and compelling them and instructing them on how to receive Jesus as their savior and Lord. And that's the responsibility of a licensed missionary. Some licensed missionaries travel into the foreign field. Others are just here on the home territory. I've never traveled to the foreign field, but I do support other missionaries financially and in prayer.

Basically my ministry has been just here in California, and so I've ministered in San Francisco, different churches in San Francisco, Vallejo, again, here in my local church, Santa Rosa, Oakland, San Jose, all over the northern part of California. I have a group of ladies that are in prayer, whenever I need to minister I have them in prayer before I go. So they pray with me, and then they travel with me when I'm going to different churches.

People may call me to come and minister when they're maybe having some type of women's function, or a pastor may just feel like I could help his church by sharing the word. A lot of people know me and they've heard my ministry, so then they'll call me to come and help. It's by recommendation. Someone has heard me, and they'll recommend to a pastor or a pastor's wife to have me to come, and then I'll go.

Just recently I had an appointment in San Francisco, and the lady called that wanted me to come. She says, "I need you to come on this date." It happened to be July the 21st. She said, "I need you to come," and it was for pastors' and ministers' wives. So she said, "You're a pastor's wife, and I feel like you have something that you could share with these women that will encourage them and build them up."

Do the Work, Don't Worry About the Title

I tell women that God has ordained us. He's given us all a purpose in life, and titles do not determine what your purpose is. I don't call myself a preacher, but I feel like the Lord has put his words in my mouth, and I'm supposed to share those with people.

So my denomination says I'm not a preacher, per se. But does that stop me from preaching? No. And so that's the way I feel about it. You know, the title placed upon you does not make a difference. If they want me to be a licensed missionary, I have no problem with that, as long as I can share what the Lord has put in my heart. Too many times women will fight about the title instead of just sharing their ministry, and then they are doing the world a disservice.

I would much rather, you can just call me Carolyn. I'm going to go to the prison, and I'll preach when I get a chance. I go to the prison; I'll go to the convalescent hospital and preach. They don't ever have to call me a preacher, but I make myself available to share the Lord with people. And to me, that's what's most important. You know what the Lord has put in your heart to do, and you just do it. It's not about entitlement. Sometimes that bothers me, because I do see women spending too much time trying to get people to say, "You're this," and, "You're that," instead of just doing the work. That's my opinion.

When I run into women that are concerned about titles, I tell them. "Don't worry about entitlement. Just do the job," because if you're out there sharing and doing what God put in your heart to do, doors will open for you. Room will be made for you, and you don't have to fight. You know, don't fight about that."

The Women's Retreat

I sponsor a women's retreat in February. Last year we had eighty women who came to the retreat. I have people that come from all different denominations, different walks of life, and we just get together for a weekend, it starts officially on Friday. Some people come in early just for a day of rest on Thursday. But Friday, Saturday, and then Sundays we head back to our own church.

But it's just a time to be refreshed. We get together. We pray together. We share the word. Sometimes I minister the word. Sometimes I invite other people in to minister the word. But it's just a time of refreshing. Other licensed missionaries are there. Some women who are in other denominations, and even women ministers from other denominations come. We just share and minister to the needs of women.

The needs of women are different in that women are called upon to be nurturers. And I personally believe that because of that, women give out more than men. They're responsible to their family, their husband, their children, if they have husbands and children. Generally if they don't have a husband and children, they'll have a parent that has to be taken care of, an aunt or an uncle or someone.

Somehow or another, they're always giving out, and the focus of my retreat is, "Come away to a designated place to meet Jesus, where you leave your focus of your children and your husband. You leave them all at home, and this is a place you come to be refreshed." Do men have that need? Yes, but not as much, because they're generally not the homemakers or the ones that take care of parents. Even if it's their parents, their wives are usually the ones responsible to take care of them if they're disabled or need assistance.

So I believe that a woman's needs are different, because she needs someone just to give her a little space, to pamper her a little bit, to recognize that yes, the life you're living can be overwhelming, because so many people are calling upon you. So that's the purpose of the retreat, to give women a chance to step away, and to take care of herself and be refreshed and renewed.

Women's Leadership

I believe it's important for women to be in spiritual leadership, and that leadership is at different levels within different churches. But women are needed. They have a place. In my particular area, I am a licensed missionary here at the church. I'm director of women's ministry, and I'm the music director.

It's important for women to be free to do what God has placed within them to do. I believe that that's what's most important. You need to know what your assignment is, and you need to be free to do that. When women do, when they support the ministry, when they support people spiritually because of the nurturing that's in them, it helps to grow the church. It helps to grow people in a way that a man could not do that on his own.

I believe women's role in ministry is similar to a mother in a relationship with a father. It takes both to get the job done, and it doesn't really matter what your title is, as long as you do it, as you do the job that's in your heart to do. It's very, very important. And I'm not one to let obstacles, you know, or hindrances stop me from doing it. I feel like I'm doing what I'm called to do. I'm called to serve alongside of my husband, but then in my own right, I'm free to do what I believe I'm supposed to do.

Importance of Religion

I feel that religion has a great deal of work to do to help the society we live in. A lot of people that are into drug addiction, alcoholism, immorality, those type of things, I believe they do that because in each of us God created a part of us that's just for him. And when he is not a part of our lives, people spend their lives looking for him, even though they don't understand that what they're looking for is that God part of them, that spiritual part of them.

So they'll look for it, and they look in all the wrong places, trying to find it. So religion, and I like to use the word relationship, because when I think about religion I'm looking at more of man's attempt to get to God, but relationship is God's attempt to get to man, and he did that through his son Jesus. So I believe everyone needs to get to know Jesus, and the more that they know Jesus, the more he helps them to put their lives together.

A lot of the issues that we see, like I said, alcoholism, drug addiction, mental illnesses could all be changed. The world could be so much different. There wouldn't be as many killing and as much violence if people would find a relationship with God.

When I see people hurting and looking for something, I love to tell them, "You need to come to church. That's the part you're missing. You've gone to school. You have a good job. You have a family. You have all of this, but you're still empty. You're still searching, but this is the part you're missing. This is Jesus." And I tell them, "Come. Try it. And if it doesn't work, you haven't lost a thing. But come and try. This is one part of your life that you're missing." So I love it. I encourage people to do that.

Carolyn Logan is the Women's Ministry Director at the Cornerstone Community Church of God in Christ in Marin County.

Susannah Malarkey, O.P.

SANTA SABINA CENTER

Anyone who comes here steps into holy ground and finds nourishment for their own path.

Harriet Hope Berman and I run the center together. The center as it is today is a result of our joint vision which is also co-created by our excellent staff who share the vision. This sharing of vision and work is of great importance to me, it is so important to understand that one does not create all by oneself. Harriet is an artist and the importance of beauty at Santa Sabina is very much her work.

The center was built in the 1930's as the novitiate house for the Dominican Sisters. In 1970 the novitiate moved and the building was established as a retreat center. Since 1983 we have opened our programs to the wider spiritual community.

The Santa Sabina philosophy is to provide a place for peace, oneness and acceptance. It is a place to feel safe to be yourself. It is a deep contemplative center, a place to find the sense of mystery at the root of our being that goes beyond denomination.

I feel blessed to have been able to spend my years as a Dominican Sister expanding the opportunities of people to experience the divine. The Santa Sabina Center has become a central place for retreats in the Bay Area. We are proud to provide a place for the contemplative way of being held in a space that is uniquely beautiful.

Sister Susannah Malarkey is a Dominican nun and the Co-Director of the Santa Sabina Center.

Mary Neill, O.P., Story

SPIRITUAL DIRECTOR

(Sister Mary Neill did a short interview which follows. She has allowed us to supplement her interview with and exert from her book, *The Woman's Tale: A Journal of Inner Exploration.*)

Interview

Catholic Church leadership for women is often behind the scenes.

I know I don't always act as people would expect a nun to act. A lot of people when they met me say, "You seem really far out. Why are you still in the church?" I say, "Well, it's my church." A Navajo story says that some people go on a journey and they're told to go home a different way, and others are told to go home the way they came, and I felt told to go home the way I came. The communists call it "boring from within." You go within the institution and you try to change it from within. So I have stayed a nun working within both myself and the structures.

In many ways, religious life as we know it seems dying, and I don't think that's a bad thing. I'm experiencing people who are truly searching for a deep spiritual life who are not in religious life. I have many Protestants who are coming for spiritual direction. We learned as nuns about the interior life and the cultivation of the interior life. The people who are coming for spiritual direction want that interior life, and they want it badly. I feel that it's a good thing that the structures are creaking and groaning, leaving gaps for new life.

There have been great changes since I became a nun. The nuns were told to renew at Vatican II. The nuns were told, "You've got to look at those terrible clothes you're wearing. You've got to look at all these robes you're wearing, and you've got to go back and look at the origins of your founder, and find out what religious life is like." So we did it with a vengeance, with pain. But we have examined and continue to examine what religious life means and what it means to renew that life. And we continue to make changes.

The idea that religion is just about good citizenship is wrong. Religion is really about transcendence. It isn't that the ethical is unimportant. It is very important. You've got to be a good teacher, a good preacher, a good nun, a good person. You've got to do that, but if you don't really remain in contact with the mystical transcendence of something larger then you are missing the essence of religion.

Book Exert

The Cinderella Tale from her book *The Woman's Tale: A Journal of Inner Exploration*. Harper and Row, New York, 1980.

When Ronda and I divided up the fairy tales prior to writing this workbook, I had no trouble "giving" her Cinderella for major treatment it's too obvious, too popular, too saccharine. But my hand and eye thought differently from my head, and "by mistake" I did this one, instead of the one assigned.

So my response to Cinderella is not response, but full-blown re-flection. Cinderella wanted me, even if I didn't want her. Willful girl that one.

I have come to trust such mistakes; to listen to them-to honor that my hand and heart know better than my head what needs to be done. "Pity that the head is slow to learn, what the swift heart beholds at every turn" is my rewording of St. Vincent Millay's sonnet line. Have you ever made mistakes such as this, which consume extra time and throw you off of plan? Do you trust this? How do you deal with it?

Cinderella is the most popular and ubiquitous of all fairy tales found all over Europe, Africa, and Asia. One scholar produced a study of 345 versions. A central theme, however, is common to all the versions: a young woman once held in high esteem falls from favor into degradation and then is given an exalted role in the end. She is recognized despite her tatters because of a slipper which fits only her foot.

The Grimms' version I will comment on contains these additional details: the gift she asks of her father (a hazel branch she plants beside her mother's grave which provides her with the clothes for the ball; Cinderella's triple flight from it; the lost shoe; the shoe test; the sisters' mutilation of their feet to win acceptance; the warning of the birds; the vengeance on the wicked stepsisters by the birds who pluck out their eyes.

The version used by Disney, based on that of Perrault, seems to me rather too cleansed from violence; Cinderella far too passive to the abuse showered on her. The Grimms' Cinderella has more spunk and I like her better since feistiness in the face of abuse seems to me an important moral virtue.

The Cinderella tale strikes this central chord in me: the necessity of the endurance of loss of respect, of aloneness, of alienation and hard work in our soul's journey-the suffering each of us encounters because we are not confirmed and seen in our true worth by those who should-those we live with.

The hearth that should give us warmth and sustenance is the scene of our tattered clothes and ashes. We are left without an outer advocate. We feed as the scriptures say, on dust and ashes like those Babylonian exiles, we cannot sing, but sit and weep in nostalgia for all the nurturing mother-love that once sustained us, but is no more. Like Cinderella, we weep on our mother's grave without protection.

If we are lucky, we weep. For it seems to me that the tears feed the reality of the longing and so move us to search for that which is lost. All experience this loss; but not all can weep and they are the worse for it. In memory of her mother's love, Cinderella plants a tree (a tree of life) to grow from death. This tree later supplies her with the clothes for the ball, the dance, the marriage feast. Losing and weeping are prelude to finding and keeping. Before Easter, when the tree of death becomes a tree of life, comes the forty days of fasting, sackcloth, and ashes, the weeping for the sins which make the kingdom lost to us.

The Cinderella story reminds us that we are always under attack-the powers of loss, decay, selfishness eat at the goodness we have. To live means daily confrontation with loss and lack of love.

To be a heroine is to fight to regain what is lost, to confirm oneself in love, so that we must search, leave our hearth in order to find our love-to risk being found by him not only at the ball, a shining dancer, but in the ashes, a drone who wears tatters and is not by outer appearances but by what we stand on—our foot which fits a lost slipper. Such a prince, inner and outer, is not found without courageous searching and many tasks.

And what are the tasks that Cinderella performs which help in her transformation from rags to gold? (We may be degraded by accident, but in the spiritual kingdom we are not elevated by accident. Once graced with a wedding invitation, we must weave a wedding garment, or be thrown out in the darkness, as Jesus warns.)

Her first task was to remember what had once been. Faith, as Newman noted, is not to deny in the dark what one has seen in the light. She remembers and ritualizes her mother's nurturing love; thereby internalizing it, so that she could learn to do for herself what once her mother had done. Her fleshly mother gone, she had to live gladly, internally through her god mother. And Cinderella honored this memory not only by weeping, but by planting. Remembering is central to faith, as we hear the command at Eucharist: "Do this in remembrance of me." We are a people who remember Jesus and so become planters of life where death has been sown.

Secondly, she does all the annoying tasks set to her-helping the ungrateful sisters get ready for the ball, sorting out the lentils her stepmother twice throws in the ashes. She is patient, as the psalmist promises: "In patience, you shall possess your souls."

Thirdly, she not only is unafraid to cry, to live with aloneness-she is not afraid to ask for help. She asks her father for a gift; her godmother tree for clothes; the birds to help her sort the grain from the ashes. Though she is alone and harassed, she knows that she cannot make it alone; she must do all she can and also call for help, from nature itself.

Often, when I am sorrowing, I will not ask for comfort. So I am moved by the account of Christ's agony in the garden when he was not ashamed three times to ask for help. When his disciples fail him, he prays and an angel comes to comfort him. Have you not sometime experienced comfort from nature, from inner consolation (the work of angels) when no friend outside stood by? Faith is also believing that we have a right to receive help and that if we ask extravagantly, even impudently, it will come.

Fourthly, she risks being happy again. She doesn't cling to her sadness, to her identification with ashes and humiliation. She works hard to get to the ball; she goes three times and dances until dawn (only Perrault presses her to midnight return). She lets herself laugh and dance and be beautiful and vulnerable, even careless in the loss of her shoe.

We often cling to unhappiness as to an old identity it gives us. The danger of suffering is that we may take it as our inheritance and not as a season. Cinderella, though patient, is not passive. She believes that she can find what was lost; she believes that she was made to dance and to love-to be a finder and a keeper, and not, in the end, a loser and a weeper.

Fifthly, she lets herself be found by love, as she is-part dancer part drone; part honored, part despised. Unlike her sisters, she mutilates no part of herself to fit someone else's shoe. In the Grimms' version, the sisters are blinded by the bird to live in darkness. They obeyed only their fleshly mother-accepted only the identity she gave them. Hence they are thrown into perpetual darkness. They created a hell for Cinderella. They are put in their own hell.

Perrault's version does not punish the wicked sisters-to gruesome a detail for our violent age, which has rejected the law of retribution, "an eye for an eye, a tooth for a tooth." But psychologically understood, when we are evil, our psyche does make us pay. We do not achieve inner harmony. We are blinded to reality. We live in darkness. Our eyes for seeing the transcendent world are ultimately plucked out. Cinderella could see and hope in her darkness and she came to her kingdom. The wicked sisters would not see inner values. They mutilated themselves through obedience to greedy worldly standards and so they are cast out into darkness.

I trust the "hard saying" of the Grimms' version, as Jesus asked his disciples to trust his hard sayings. Should children be protected from such hard versions, such hard sayings? Emphatically not. They experience many hard things, loss, separation, rejection, rivalry, wounding. Cinderella assures them that a way can be found out of the hard things–a hard way, but one where what they do, or don't do, makes all the difference.

One of the loveliest parts of the story to me is that the happy ending finds her. She searches for the prince and flees; he searches and finds her. I have learned to trust such a pattern of activity and passivity, of doing and of waiting, of withdrawal and return. So, with God, it seems that we pray and seek and knock and do, and then we know we are searched for; we are awakened by love.

When the Prince, who has seen Cinderella first in golden robes, puts the glass slipper on her foot amid the ashes, then has their union solid foundation in the marriage of opposites; rags and silks have honored one another; poor and rich, female and male, "for better or for worse, in sickness and in health."

Of all the things that the Cinderella story urges me to do in my spiritual struggle, to remember, to work patiently, not to cling to sadness, not to mutilate my identity, to let myself be found by love, I find the last one the hardest. For it means letting go of how and when and with what face love shall meet me. I find that once I have my active energies up, I don't want to pull back, be passive, and wait. Maybe I am not sure I will be found—or that anyone is searching. Darkness is seductive.

Sister Mary Neill is a Dominican nun. She has recently retired from teaching theology at University of San Francisco and now does spiritual counseling.

Aline O'Brien Story

PAGAN AMBASSADOR

Finding My Faith

The faith traditions in which I was brought up didn't answer my spiritual needs, nor did they offer a feminine image of the divine. And all of those things came together around the same time. I was religionless for a number of years, because what I had presented to me didn't resonate, and I hadn't found anything else. I didn't decide in a hurry; I nosed around.

In those days Witches were very discreet, and so it was hard to find them, even if you were looking. But I did find some in 1971, and then in 1975 I went to a workshop. It was called Women and Spirituality, or Feminist Spirituality. I went with a friend, and there was one other person there beside her and the leader who gave the workshop. The woman was a person who called herself Starhawk. It was at a little occult store, downtown San Francisco, on Sutter Street. We became friends and I went as a guest to some rituals, and it just unfolded after that.

Witches are very diverse, but we do have a lot of community. But we have been hidden, and so have women. So in that sense, I think we're a little bit parallel as a movement, as a religious movement. And I do consider it what I call an ancient-future religion. We draw upon ancient heritage, but most of what we do is reconstruction or experimentation. There are certain things that bind us. There are certain things we share in common.

What Are Witches

I don't use the term Wicca. The broad inclusive term would be Pagan. That includes all kinds of other Pagans as well. Probably the most numerous group of Pagans are Witches. Wicca itself is British-derived. It has a system. There are systems of elevations. There are male and female divinities who are called into circle every time. They're hierarchically structured. They're much more formal, much more structured. They're all Witches, but Wicca is a particular subset. It's like Catholics are Christians, but they're not Baptists. They're all Christians. The Baptists and the Catholics are both Christians.

The oldest and largest organization of Witches, nondenominational, which is in the United States, is called COG, Covenant of the Goddess. It was founded in 1975, right here in the Bay Area. I have been very involved in that since around '80 or '81. I've been involved on a national level, too, and it's been through that organization that I've been exposed to lots of other Witches.

That's been the primary place that I have been exposed to other Witches and other ways of doing magic and other ways of looking at things. I do find that it's very regionally oriented, because as an earth-based spirituality, the people who live in the plains use imagery that comes from the plains in their rituals, and they feel very connected to the plains. And the people in the Rockies feel that way about the Rockies, and we out here on the Franciscan complex experience the earth upon we walk in a unique way, that's unique to this bioregion.

I wouldn't say that Paganism is totally devoid of sexism. It's very woman oriented, and statistically there are more women who practice it than men. It certainly isn't limited to women, but there are more women. The goddess is primary in almost all of Craft. I think probably in all.

What Witches Believe And How They Practice

You can't really speak to what Witches believe, because we're all so different, even within the same working group. Even within the same coven, we're very independent-minded. It's very experiential, and I think what binds us is our practices and our values, more than our actual theology.

We all work in a circle, for instance. We create a sacred space that is circular. We honor the four quarters and four elements. The elements are the same, but the descriptions might change. In my tradition, air in the East; fire is in the South; water's in the West; and earth is in the North. That's the most common, but sometimes they shift around. We all invoke deity, in one way or another. Some of us do spellwork, and some of us don't. And some of us sometimes do spellwork.

We all celebrate the turning of the wheel in the form of eight Sabbat, which are four quarters and four cross-quarters, the quarters being the equinoxes and the solstices. And the cross-quarters are agriculture-based times of celebration that are in between those, and they may or may not be associated with particular deities. But they're generally the same, for instance the one that I call Lughnasad but a lot of people call Lammas is the first harvest. That's August 1st or August 2nd.

Personally, if I get depressed or discouraged about the state of the world, I find that reenacting certain rituals and doing certain things—gestures, words, song, breathing, reciting certain liturgy—is restorative, and it makes me feel good enough to not be totally pessimistic. And it helps me to live life and enjoy the world, and try to live as lightly as I can on the earth, and not be sucking up an unfair portion of the resources, as we are prone to do in this country. So it helps me to keep on course, and it also reawakens the sense of joy, of being alive, of this glorious world. We don't look for escape from it. We don't look for getting off of the wretched wheel of Samsara, or salvation in another world. We live here.

I feel that the more I do ritually that can reawaken that awareness in me of our interconnectedness, the more I feel satisfied, balanced, renewed, and restorated. Because it's really easy to get depressed, when you look at what's going on in the world, especially after 9/11. We've been very sheltered, very protected. We live in incredible privilege here. The poorest American is more privileged than most of the humans on this planet, and we forget that.

Intuition, An Important Gateway to Practice

In a rational world, we tend to look at only the quantifiable things that we can label and tangible things that we can feel, and we don't necessarily value it in the same way other qualities, other experiences. Intuition is certainly part of it. And intuition can itself be either abused or misinterpreted. For instance, I think that some people credit to intuition what may be desire or fantasy—and there are ways to learn to distinguish. Because it's really easy, if you want the world to be a certain way, to say, well, I see such and such. It's really easy to kid yourself, particularly because it isn't something you could measure.

I certainly think that little signs, if you're alert to them, can come up in your daily life, that are giving you a clue about something that you're grappling with. And I think you can start to look for that under every rock, and they're not always genuine. I don't know exactly how I could say how you could filter them. But some seem genuine and some don't, and sometimes one gets so obsessed with something, you see it everywhere, even if it's not necessarily there. And you also may see it everywhere because you're so ripe for it, you're so open to it, you're so ready.

There are techniques, and they aren't limited to Pagans by any means. I think that everybody has those gifts, some more than others. But I think that anyone can have it awakened in them, to some degree. Some people are more—well, maybe less—filtered than others. But I think everybody has those senses. It's sixth sense, I suppose, and not just in the context of Craft.

The Heritage of Secrecy

Our rituals and use of intuition have seemed to separate us in the past from people who have reacted out of fear with persecution toward Witches. A lot of Pagans fear the kind of persecution that has happened in the past. I don't. I'll give you my little rap about secrecy, which has played a big role in Craft. You don't ever tell anybody what your name is, or who your friends are, or where you meet. There were reasons, I think, to keep that confidential. But there's a difference between secrecy and confidentiality and privacy.

Witchcraft is a mystery religion and a lot of the experiences we have are mystical experiences. And they cannot be told. The secret cannot be revealed, because it needs to be experienced. It can be approximated through the arts, through poetry, dance, painting, and music. But it can't really be told, because it doesn't lend itself to narrative description. So in that sense, there are no secrets. There are mysteries. There are reasons to be confidential because we work in small, intimate, bonded groups. There are issues of privacy and confidentiality. The whole world doesn't need to know what a certain individual or group experienced. So in that sense, confidentiality and privacy are to be respected.

But secrecy for secrecy's sake, in my opinion, is just a breeding ground for dysfunction. That's how abusive families and domestic abuse perpetuates itself. That's how alcoholism, incest continue. Look at the Catholic church right now. Secret.

Searching For Contact With Other Faiths

Pagans didn't even know each other in 1975. But now secrecy is not as strong. In COG membership the members were coven members, and you didn't necessarily know, even if you were a member of the covenant, who was in an individual coven. Now we do. One of the main things that COG has done that I think has been really beneficial, really remarkable, is working with the media and working with law enforcement and the government, just generally educational outreach, and public information. As a result of that we got involved in international interfaith work.

Back in the eighties COG, the local group, was involved in the Berkeley Area Interfaith Assembly. But in 1993 in Chicago there was a second-ever Parliament of World Religions. And in 1993, we had several delegations go there. COG had a delegation. EarthSpirit Community in Massachusetts, who are COG members, had a delegation. The Circle people in Wisconsin had people there, and there were a few others. And we made a big hit, and we were very active and very, very involved.

Now since 1981COG has local councils in other parts of the country. There are lots of people, for instance, who are very active in interfaith down in Lancaster, California. They recently had a big to-do with a Christian minister who was harassing them and screaming doom and gloom and was very disrespectful. There were several other Christians who said, "No, wait a minute. These guys are fine. We know them. They're just citizens like you and me, and have a belief system." It was alarming, but it was also very affirming.

Personal Calling To Work With Death and Dying

I also have a calling to work with the dying and I do workshops around the country. That's not the only thing that I do workshops on, but I do workshops with Pagans on death and dying. Because I think it's a great privilege to be with the dying. I feel that any death that can be made more spiritual, meaningful and easier. If anything that I bring to people in terms of insights helps them move through their own grief, address their own dying, or work with the people they love who are dying, or other people who they don't love, it is a good thing.

You take all your cues from the dying person. You don't ever go in there with an agenda. So it depends what she's receptive to, what she's interested in, what she seems. That's a place where intuition can come into play very strongly, because there might not be something that's articulated, that's an opening of a way that you should proceed with working with this person. But you may pick it up from other kinds of signals, and move in that direction if you're called to.

And there are some things that Pagans can do with a dying person that aren't necessarily religious-connected, but may be very spiritual for that individual. For instance, the book that we have out called *The Pagan Book of Living and Dying*. We have several suggested meditations in there to do with dying people, that really come out of our tradition, but they're not limited to that. For instance, a meditation on forgiveness, and who in your life you might have things you want to resolve with or have some closure with or some clearance.

They might end up saying, "I really need to talk to my ex-husband, and I want to have that cleaned up before I leave." They may do something like that. My ex-husband did that with me, and I'm eternally grateful, because I didn't feel that I should intrude when he was dying, without his invitation, which I did get, and we're all, I think, better for it.

Our Place In The Ecosystem

I do stuff that in the mundane world would be considered leadership roles, I suppose, in the sense of being a representative to various other non-Pagan groups. For instance, the Biodiversity Project Spirituality Working Group; the Sacred Dying Foundation; Marin Interfaith Council.

So even though I'm white, I'm European stock, I'm American, I'm middle class, I'm female and all those things, and it's easy to get boxed in and say, "Well, you're an educated white woman who's never been hungry". I think it's important for us to reach beyond ourselves and become more aware of how many of us there are and how different we all are.

I think the culture does things—I'm not talking about myself now, but it is myself, too—does things to mask that or make us forget that we are that different and dependent on the ecosystem. I'm very upset, for instance, about monocultures in agriculture, agribusiness. I think we're all weakened by that. Diversity is essential, and again, diversity in biology and in botany has its parallel in faith traditions and in humanity.

I feel that we are very much a part of the world, as opposed to being elevated or separate or top of the food chain. We are the top of the food chain but so are some other mammals. But I think we lose sight of our interdependence and our immersion in the world, the breeze that we can feel on our skin, the warmth of the sun that's filtering through the trees, the smells of the plants around us, and at times, animals around us. We're very dependent on all that and every breath we take is filled with life, and our bodies are filled with other life forms. There are flora and fauna in our bodies that make them work the way they do.

Bridget's Cross, Current Symbol Of Work

I wear a Bridget's cross, and that's because I've currently been working a lot with the goddess Bridget. Bridget's cross is made of reeds. It's a traditional thing in Ireland and other places where she is worshipped. Her time is in the early spring, February 1st or 2nd, which is also called Candlemas or Imbolc. I tend to not use the terms that have a "mas" suffix, because it implies a mass, which is a little more formal than I am. Imbolc means something like "in the belly," or the lambing season. It's when they're born.

She is a goddess, a triple goddess, of the forge and of the healing waters and of the flame of inspiration. And all of those are qualities I would like to foster in my life. I'd like to be inspired to write things that are eloquent and say things that are eloquent, which I am challenged to do a lot. I don't feel that I'm that great at that. She is the goddess of smiths, handcrafts and things that you do make, and the forging and the tempering of metal. We are very often put in a forge and hammered away at, to reshape ourselves.

And then she's a goddess of healing waters, and soothing, healing things. We can always use that, and we can always share it. I mean, we can use our own healing, and we can, in my situation, call upon her or draw her in to do work that we couldn't do without that influence of her. Our hands, if we're using our hands in a healing way, are more likely to be efficacious, in my experience, if I'm very conscious of her, that I'm doing her work, or that she is guiding me. So she's outside; she's inside, and all around. And that's just one manifestation of one deity who happens to be very strong in my life right now.

Need For Faith

When people are unwilling to look at the need for faith, they are depriving themselves of several dimensions of being alive. I need it. I would have been a suicide or an addict or a drunk or something if I didn't have some of these methods and techniques and people, community, to practice my spirituality with. I just would have been too despairing.

It's not that I totally buy into the "Religion is the opiate of the people" thing that Marx propounded, but religion is comforting. But not comforting in a sense that it makes the world go away, and if you just follow these rules you'll be taken care of. It's not comforting in that sense, and certainly Craft is not that way. You really do, you're met with challenges all the time, but it's comforting in terms of, I think we all need to feel we belong, and I do feel like I belong to something that's comprised of people, as well as the world in the bigger sense.

Aline O'Brien is a priestess and witch. She has written the *Pagan Book of Living and Dying* and gives workshops around the country.

Betty Pagett Story

HOUSING ADVOCATE

History

I grew up in an active Methodist family. My mother was a minister's daughter. I'd never met a woman in an ordained ministry, but I saw how my mother worked in the community and in the church. I started out to go to seminary to be an educator, and my first degree in seminary was in education. It was only later that I decided that the only way that I could really make a difference in planning and leading was to be ordained.

The church was a place where I felt my gifts could be used to make a difference in people's lives and in creating community. I believe the transforming aspect of individuals and groups comes when you create communities that nurture whole people then you begin to change structures. So it seemed to me like the church was one place for that to happen, and that's where I decided to put my energies. And in order to do that, I felt ordination was necessary.

People were very empowering to me and I never really questioned whether I could become a minister or not. It was something that I chose, and my leadership had been recognized and I felt a deep affirmation of my calling through my faith. There were lots of funny stories I collected as people encountered me as the first woman in ministry that they'd met. Once I was asked to preach at a large interfaith Thanksgiving service and told, "we've always had the great preachers but this year we'd like a woman." When I left my first parish, a leader was heard to say, 'she's better than any minister we ever had.'

I never really experienced great limitations in my work among lay people. Reception came as people found someone who could relate to and serve them and bring gifts that make a difference in their lives. I don't think that I ever experienced real discrimination from lay people, but I did from hierarchy within the church.

Student and Parish Work

When I graduated from seminary I went to Paris to work for the London Methodist Missionary Society with international students. They had a church there, and I lived in the church and ran a student hostel there and worked in Paris. This was 1965, so it was just as the Vietnam War was being escalated. It was a very interesting time to be an American in the international community.

My students were from Africa and Europe, and it was an absolutely wonderful experience of ministry. I led the Sunday evening service. There were two other just-recent seminary graduates studying French in Paris, and together we had a collegiality and a very stimulating mentoring that we were able to do for each other in our first year out of seminary. So we actually had the work with the students, but we also had a parish.

I came back to New York and worked with students through the United Methodist Board of Global Ministries and the Church Center for the UN. My job included setting up the conferences at the UN and in Washington, D.C. I set up programs during the January interim months, providing urban learning experiences for the mostly smaller colleges throughout the Midwest and New England that had January interim study months. Students were in the frontline of thinking about women's liberation, student organization or urban renewal, international development.

International development was the emerging term for what was becoming known as the "third world," as we began to think beyond cold war definitions of the world. I worked with parishes around the country as well as with students and was part of creating a variety of innovative educational tools. Then for one year I was an Auburn Fellow at Union Theological Seminary in New York, working with a peer group on the impact of the Judeo-Christian Tradition on Women. I stayed on as a lecturer at Union for one more year, then knew that where I wanted to be was in a local community-centered ministry.

I was in parish ministry for twenty years, three and a half years on the East Coast before we moved back to California, which was my home. I grew up in California and went to college in California, so we came back in '78. I stayed in parish ministry then doing seminary teaching on the side until 1991 when I began with Ecumenical Association for Housing. I served churches in White Plains and Bedford, New York, and in East Oakland, Concord and San Rafael.

I was assigned to Marin in 1981 to be the minister at First Methodist Church in San Rafael, so I was there ten years. During those rich and full years, one of the issues that was prevalent among my own parishioners and the homeless people coming to my door was the issue of housing.

Housing

I began, as many clergy did, affiliating with Ecumenical Association for Housing, which worked with the congregations that had started it, and was offered the position of education and advocacy director in '91. At first I turned it down because I thought it was administrative and I never saw myself as primarily an administrator. I wanted to be involved in programmatic and advocacy work. When I became convinced that was possible here, it seemed like a good move for me at that point in my life. I could stay close to my family here instead of being transferred somewhere else the way the Methodists do it. So I stayed here and now, eleven years later, I'm still here.

Housing is a challenge, but it's one of the essential pieces of community, and there's great consistency that I'm still concerned about how we create community that nurtures whole people and whole structures. And as Marin's housing crisis has developed over the years, it's really shattered any possibility of community. When the people who work here can't live here, and when people can't grow old here, and people can't be close to families, such as the young people who grow up, or the older people, we lose so much of the essence of who we are as a people. I just never realized how hard working for affordable housing would be or I might never have tried. And, it doesn't get any easier.

As I've worked on the housing issue in all our communities I've met a lot of very wonderful people who care about creating housing. Even though they don't need it themselves, they realize how important this is.

But I've also watched the people who try to block the housing. When I look at that, and I look at the way those blocks are embodied in our community policies, I see a spiritual crisis, because it shows people separating themselves from other human beings. They're saying that the people who teach my children, or take care of me when I'm sick, or serve me in a restaurant, don't deserve to live here if they don't earn enough money. They are saying that their property values are more important. Many conversations that take place in the public arena show no identification with other people's humanity.

I guess that's the hardest thing that I deal with, finding that people don't have any way of relating to someone who happens to become disabled and on permanent disability and can't afford a high amount of rent. Or they cannot see that you might grow old and at that time have an income of only $1,000 a month.

You know, these are all very human experiences, but so many times people separate themselves from those human experiences. So to me that's a real spiritual crisis.

Minister at Large

I have a deep concern for the most vulnerable people, children and frail elderly. My work really is a spiritual challenge. I have found many people in the community with spiritual questions. Marin County tends to have many unaffiliated people," people who feel like they aren't spiritually fed, and that's led me to a do some spiritual nurturing as part of my job, to be available occasionally for pastoral care. In a sense, I'm a pastor in the midst of being an advocate.

So many times I'll be having a meeting with somebody who works actively in the community. The real issue they want to talk about is not just the town's housing proposal, but when it gets down to it, they have personal concerns. They might have a child who is mentally ill and homeless, or there will be personal questions or family questions. There will also be the issues of burnout, and how do you keep going.

One young woman, who's the executive director of one of our nonprofits, asked the other day out of the blue as we walked along meeting on business matters, "I don't think that I know how to pray anymore." By being available, I find people in the midst of life and death and birth and a range of life choices. So in a sense, Marin is my parish. And I'm available to people and hopefully connecting them to faith communities where they can continue to grow.

I'm very much interested in how we nurture lay people to do their jobs, because they're in ministry in what they do Monday through Friday. How do we nurture families that are just so stressed, because both the mother and the father are working? How do we have a nurturing presence in the community out of which will come people the energy and vision and support to care about the wider community?

Many times we sort of have our own churchy agenda on Sunday morning, and we don't feed people. We act like the only thing they do that is important is taking a church office or being on a church committee. Yet to me the most important thing they can do is to think about how they live with their families everyday, how they do their weekly 9 to 5 jobs.

There are ethical issues involved in our world of work. There are struggles. There are opportunities. We have in Marin County some incredibly talented, wise, and educated people. How do we mobilize that, so that they understand themselves in ministry? They are the laity who allow the work of the church. So I'm very interested in how that works, in a different way than I might have been when I was in the parish. I think I have a kind of different thought about worship since working Monday through Friday in a day job. I re-think who we are as a church and what we offer on Sunday morning to nurture people.

Retreats

I always have thought retreats were important. I had two a year in my congregation, plus some day retreats with women or with men. We need to get away and have a little bigger space of time to think and reflect. It gives us the opportunity to try things we might not try if we were sitting in our building in Marin County. It gives people an opportunity to play together, and play and worship are very related.

Most of my retreats have been intergenerational. This will be my third year for Mt. Tam United Methodist. It has been transforming to have the children part of it, because the children help the adults learn in a different way than they might otherwise. We can use story, we can do other ways of learning and worship that we might not do inside our sanctuary.

The planning of the retreat is really restorative to me, because I don't have study time in my schedule, like I did when I was in a parish. But when I have a specific retreat to plan it is like study time, just that I do it after work. Our retreat in 2003 will be soon after the anniversary of September 11, and the committee would like to reflect on faith themes raised by that experience. I listen to their questions, and then design a way to approach that. We'll be thinking about vulnerability and safety, fear and trust, interdependence, and the presence and transformation of evil.

When I've planned retreats for women I've found inspiration in the Native American idea that women don't need vision quests, they need the healing quest, because they give, and give, and give. So this is a time to be nurtured. It is a time when somebody takes care of your children, and you can go apart. You have healthy food, create, meditate, study uninterrupted, rest and be in a nurturing surrounding.

Women's Self Care

Taking care of myself is something that's evolved over time, and probably like many women of my generation, it took a long time because we never learned how to give ourselves spiritual care. I was asked to speak on passing values on to the next generation. I talked to my daughter about the values she felt she learned from her growing up. One of the things my daughter said was, "If you want women to respect themselves, you have to take care of yourself."

I knew the things that nourished me, but they didn't necessarily fit what I had been taught. So I thought, well, they must not be the right things, because they weren't the way men did it. I was asked to write a chapter for women clergy in a book on clergy continuing education It was cut out of the book because I suggested women's life patterns and styles of learning and restoration might vary from the traditional male model. For me, I have found that it is very important for me to schedule long walks and being outdoors, and being alone. I was with people all the time, and I needed to draw on my inner resources. I just needed time away and I needed it not just occasionally on a retreat, but every day.

So I do try to do that, to have that walk, to have that peace, so that I'm restored, because there's a lot that destroys it in this work. Lots of meetings feel very toxic so restoration is very important to me.

On the other hand family and friends are crucial. I have been incredibly blessed by loving family and friends. They make me laugh, they keep life in perspective. And a lot of young people both when I was in the parish as well as in recent years keep me human and alive and thinking about the fullness of life. They help me play.

I think my prayer and spiritual life is particularly nurtured in my walking time, because I need to be moving. I've done enough sitting, so that's how I deal with my personal time in the presence of the Holy. I am fed by worshipping with my faith community, and by the time around the table at home.

Women's Spirituality

I suddenly realized in a course on Jeremiah in seminary (1963 was before feminist consciousness was revived) that all the paintings around the room were men. And all the professors and all the people that we were studying were men. The only exception was the harlot image in Jeremiah's writings. Over and over that image would come to me as I looked around. I identified with the harlot!

There's always been a women's spirituality. We don't know exactly what it was in ancient Israel, but we know it kind of pops up with a little word or a poem here or there. Like Miriam and the women dancing with the tambourine. I love that story, because you know, they didn't just do that once at the Red Sea. That was part of some tradition we know is there.

I believe part of the history of women's spirituality is taking care of others. I feel like somebody needs to tend to the nurturing and practical love needs of our community. Hopefully it's not just women, but I'm not going to not do it, because I'm a woman [minister]. So I've been one to think about practical expressions of caring, like food and children's care and who's going to take food to that family, and who's going to help that elderly person when she comes home from the hospital. Maybe that is one way that I've been different. It has added a great richness to my life as well!

My own spirituality is practical. I feel that my job as an advocate, an educator, is to help people find a vision and bring it to fruition in very specific ways. I want to help people use legislation for housing opportunities, to help people understand what the needs are, what the opportunities are and what it takes to do help those who need the housing.

Betty Pagett is an ordained Methodist minister. She is currently the Director of Education and Advocacy at EAH in Marin County.

Lama Palden Story

SUKHASIDDHI FOUNDATION

Finding My Teacher

I've always been extremely interested in religion and spirituality, and I was a devout Episcopalian growing up in Marin. But it didn't go far enough for me. From the time I was about thirteen, I felt a strong pull to do practice. I was in the Episcopalian church and I felt like, when do we do the part where we go to the desert? I felt that it wasn't enough that Jesus did it. I felt like I had to do something and it wasn't going to happen by only going to church every Sunday.

I became very interested in all religions and started studying. From middle school on, I studied and loved comparative religion. In high school and college I studied both on my own and in academic situations in various traditions. As a young adult I did yoga and practiced Zen, which, of course, was Buddhist, but I didn't see myself as a Buddhist at that time; I was also studying and practicing Christianity, and later Sufism. During this process, I started a daily meditation practice as well as a daily yoga practice, and I began to really pray.

My family has lived near Dominican College since the turn of the century, and I used to go to a garden there with a Mary statue in it. In the old days nobody ever took care of it. It was all run down. I used to go there and pray by this Mary statue. I was praying to meet my true teacher.

It turned out he was a Buddhist. In the seventies in San Francisco, a friend dragged me off to see this old Tibetan master, I knew within five minutes that he was my teacher. I'd been studying with other teachers, but I'd never had that feeling. He was Tibetan Buddhist and had been the first Tibetan to establish three-year retreat centers outside of Tibet. He had educated people from all the Tibetan Buddhist lineages because he was so highly regarded. Shortly after I met him I went to Darjeeling in India, in the Himalayan foothills, and studied with him.

A lot of people say "Tibetan" Buddhism, but it's really inaccurate, because the real term is Vajrayana, which is a Sanskrit term. Basically, yana means vehicle.

170

Vajrayana is part of the greater Mahayana which Zen is also part of. Maha means great, the greater vehicle, and vajra means indestructible or diamond. It's not translatable in one word. So technically it's really Vajrayana Buddhism because it spread to places beside Tibet. But, of course, that's where it was preserved the most strongly.

There are four main lineages of Vajrayana Buddhism in Tibet, with some other smaller sublineages. There's a lot of cross-pollination between lineages and they take teachings from each other. My teacher was actually a teacher of the Dalai Lama, but from a different lineage. Each lineage has its own head. The Dalai Lama is head of the Gelukpa lineage. And my lineage is Kagyu.

Being a Lama

After I found my teacher and visited him in India, I continued my studies with him by attending one of his retreat centers for three years. It was in British Columbia, on top of a mountain on an island, when I was there it was pretty primitive. We had no electricity; we had outhouses. I used to wonder how I always got myself in these situations where there was no hot water and no bathtubs.

In the Vajrayana tradition, there are meditation practices, which form a graduated path, and there's a lot of variety within each stage or level. A person studies and practices a combination of meditation, philosophical study, and ethical study. This is pretty complex and takes years for a thorough training. The three year retreat was the best thing I have ever done with my time in this life. It was the hardest thing I've ever done. It's a very intensive experience. You're faced with your own mind and your own habitual patterns, and the reworking of all of that. You are purifying the mind, speech and actions. The scheduling is very intense, up at four a.m. and meditating until breakfast. You get a half-hour break for breakfast and then back to meditation and intensive yoga practice. Then you get a longer break for lunch, where you would study. Then you meditate all afternoon. In the morning and afternoon, we'd do services together. Then dinner, followed by meditation in our own rooms. So we spent most of the time by ourselves in our own room.

The practices are designed for purification and for unifying yourself with the divine, with true nature, true reality in prayer and meditation. Tibetans are the masters of prayers. They have more and longer prayers than anybody you've ever heard of. You pray for everybody under the sun you could ever have imagined in this universe and other universes.

Three year retreat is very challenging for westerners, because, first of all, we weren't raised as monks or nuns, so we hadn't grown up with the discipline of meditating and praying. We had two half-days off a year on Christmas and New Year's. We had a relatively small compound, so you couldn't walk very far. You have to be suited for that kind of life and know how to work with what comes up and turn it into part of your spiritual path. Whatever would be going on inside yourself psychologically, emotionally, or physically you needed to turn that to the path.

For example you might see how your mind tends to have very negative thoughts about people. Maybe somebody's doing something minor and it is irritating to you. It reminds me of a passage from The Little Flower of Saint Theresa where she talks about one nun who drove her nuts because she was coughing all the time. St. Theresa finally did a practice of really loving this one very irritating nun, and that totally turned it around in Saint Theresa's own mind.

That practice is similar to many of the practices we do. We work with what's arising and turn it into the path, turn it into loving kindness. Maybe you're seeing a lot of anger come up in your own mind and projecting it out onto other people and you try to learn to turn that into loving kindness.

When I was finished with the three years I became a lama. I find it interesting that the word lama means highest mother—ma, is mother, in Tibetan, and la means highest. In Tibet a lama is a priest and teacher and most lamas function as kind of a parish priest. But, in the West we do a lot of teaching as well.

One great misunderstanding about Buddhism in the West is that the people who do retreats in caves are isolationists which is far from the case. My own teacher actually spent twenty-five years in retreat, thirteen in a cave. Then he came out to work in the world. And they're all like that, all these great masters from the Himalayas. They come out and they're very active in educating young and old people, maintaining or establishing monasteries, nunneries, schools, hospitals, etc. They even help settle wars and disputes.

Tibet

In Tibet, there were a lot of people who were completely uneducated. In fact, almost all the education was in the monasteries. They didn't have a public education system or even a private school education system. A lot of the lay people weren't trained but they had a tremendous amount of faith.

What was different in Tibet was that so many people had a lot of realization. There were so many practitioners: yogis and yoginis, that almost everybody I met in the Himalayas had an uncle or an aunt or a cousin or a grandpa or somebody down the street in the village who actually became very highly realized.

That's very common among Tibetans and I was surprised when I was in my twenties and visiting. For the Tibetan people, I think that ordinary life is quite different, because being around these people is very different than being around ordinary people. Most people notice that kind of difference around the Dalai Lama. It's not like being with an ordinary person.

Many of the Tibetans that were tortured by the Chinese and imprisoned for a long period of time, and even the people that weren't in prison, but escaped and had many of their family members slaughtered, had compassion and loving kindness and forgiveness, and the ability to heal, and to go on with their lives. There's that profound sorrow that doesn't go away, and the experience of suffering, but they were not destroyed by it like other refugee peoples. I've talked with a lot of these people that had great emotional resiliency even without having done meditation practice.

Sukhasiddhi Center

Five years ago I started the Sukhasiddhi Center. I wanted to be able to reach out to people that might not come to a Tibetan teacher because of the big cultural gap. Originally it was not my idea to devote my life in this way, but I felt somebody needed to do it. So after so many years, I decided I should, and asked a friend of mine who was also doing some teaching, and who was a student of the same teacher, to co-teach with me.

We started having classes, and we ended up getting this space. We've moved very, very slowly, and the emphasis has been on people who want to do serious, deep spiritual work. That's really what the center is about. Which is what our lineage is about. Most of the people who come to the center are people who've probably been meditating between five and twenty years, although we also love to have beginners come. The basis of our tradition is the wish to awaken for benefit of all beings.

We're trying to integrate spiritual realities and an ancient lineage with Western culture and psyche. We're in the process of trying to create new systems of organizing. I can't teach the same way my teachers taught. It wouldn't really feel right because it's not me. My way of doing things, which I feel has more of a feminine quality to it, is to let things grow very organically and slowly.

For example, in Tibet there would be a whole hierarchical system in a monastery, similar to the Catholic Church. There would be an abbot who would be involved in a combination of religious and administrative duties, and then people under him. The decisions would be made only at the highest level. The monks don't vote on what's going to happen. Here, the other teacher and I don't make all the decisions except in terms of real spiritual matters and how we're going to teach. But in terms of how we're running the center we involve people at the community level.

We now are working with the council system, where certain people from our community step forward on their own volition to be on a council that helps determine policy and helps run the center. They consult with me or the other teacher. We're trying to have a more organic, grassroots structure. And it has been working well. It's much slower but it seems to be coming along and it feels in harmony.

We have started our own three year retreat. I have two women that I'm training right now in a three-year retreat that are up in the mountains near Tahoe. It is a huge project for me. There is a huge amount of teaching involved. As far as we've heard, this is the first center in the United States to start and run a three-year retreat by a woman. But my teachers, all of whom are male, have been incredibly supportive. We're renting a place for this retreat, but we'd like to be able to establish our own retreat center for short-and long-term retreats on our own land.

Women

One of my teachers said, when I went to see him recently in India, that he felt that women should be the leaders now in spiritual groups, in religious groups, and in world groups. Men have been doing it for so long that it's an entrenched system that has gone corrupt. There's all these ways that men have of working together that basically need to be revamped, but it's very hard to revamp a structure and a system that's so ingrained. It's not that women are inherently better. But women would bring a whole new fresh perspective without all these old-boy networks in place.

We haven't been in positions of leadership or power and we are more relationally based. It's not true for all women, but in general I think we're more concerned with the group than personal achievement. It's an asset.

I also feel that men, in our culture, in order to be psychologically healthy, need to achieve something in their life, and they need to come into their own place in society. At least in their own eyes, they need to come up to their own standards of how they fit in the structure of things. And I think as women, that's not something that's so important to us. Our psychological identity issues and the health of our own psychological identity is not so much based on rank or position or what we've achieved.

In the Tibetan tradition, they say that the wisdom aspect is the feminine aspect. So maybe there is natural intuitive wisdom that also is a little bit easier to access for women. I have a lot of male friends, both Western and Eastern, who are Buddhist colleagues. I probably have many more male colleagues than I have female. Many of them are much brighter than I am, some extremely brilliant. But quite a few of them have told me that they don't have the intuitive sense of the practice or the inner knowingness about doing the inner work that I have. And I think that is more of the female forte.

In the whole women's movement, a lot of women, especially in the beginning, just mimicked the men and did it in a male way. Nobody knew how to do it different, and they were trying to crash the barriers. But I think the feminine way is actually a different way of going about life, and so I've been trying to explore that and open myself to the divine feminine for many years. I feel like it's a big gift to be a woman.

Lama Palden teaches Tibetan Buddhism through the Sukhasiddhi Foundation in Marin County.

Carol Saysette Story

PASTORAL COUNSELING

Called To Be A Midwife Of Souls

In the mid 1970's I was asking what I meant to do and be. I started having two dream series. In one of them, I was in a tower, and I could smell the moss and dampness in the room. I was sitting at a wooden table, reading a Bible. It was a very large Bible. I looked down at my arms, and I had on a robe, a dark-colored robe. And I had that dream three or four times a week for a number of months. I would wake up incredibly happy from reading the scriptures.

I had been out of the church for quite a while. I hadn't attended a church in at least ten years. I'd been wandering through the wilderness, you might say. That dream reminded me of how much I had loved those biblical studies classes I had had in college, and so I started reading the Bible again and asking the big questions of what am I meant to do in my life.

The other set of dreams, there were only about three of those. They had different story lines, but they ended with the words, "Be a midwife for souls." And I thought to myself, well, I'm learning how to be a therapist, but is that soul work? I wasn't sure about that.

One day in 1976, I remembered that the seminary was in San Anselmo. Oddly the seminary had been my first thought when I learned we were moving to Marin in 1967. In one of those spontaneous bursts, I called the seminary and talked to the Admissions Department. There was one week before the deadline for applications for the following Fall. The process went smoothly. When I entered San Francisco Theological Seminary I wasn't one of the first women but I was in the beginning of the first big wave. If you look at who the graduates are five years before me, four years before me, there would be three or four women in the whole class. And my class, I we had maybe ten women, even one who had a baby halfway through seminary and sat there in Christology nursing this baby. It was quite wonderful.

The Challenge Of Being A Pastor

After graduating I was a pastor for 12 years. The pastorate is challenging beyond belief. I have never had a hard time keeping a good calendar, except for the years when I was full-time ministry as a pastor. You very nicely arrange your week in what appears to be a very sane way, and then three people die, or somebody gets a cancer diagnosis, or you know, a member's best friend's son just commits suicide. And you've got lots of counseling and/or a memorial service, and you've got to do those memorial services, you know. Most people don't want to wait till it's a convenient time for the pastor.

So especially with a really busy parish, which our parish was, I mean, we got up to 650 members. So we had four services every Sunday, and lots of weddings and all the rest that goes with all that, classes and counseling and crises.

It's the kind of job where you have many, many bosses. Each lay person who's in charge of a committee, for instance, is aware of what you do relating to that particular part of what the church organization is doing. But that person isn't aware of the counseling you just did with the couple that's probably going to get a divorce, and the fact that the maintenance crew has just decided that they're quitting just as the toilets are overflowing. It's like nobody in the church sees everything you do. They don't see the phone calls at home. They don't see all the meetings that are required on a denominational level, plus the Marin Interfaith Council, plus any other things.

But the rewards are so great. I had one of my clergy directees today say, with joy just radiating out of her, "What a privilege to be part of people's lives as they heal and transform, and to know that the body of the church is facilitating that transformation." It is awesome, just awesome. I don't know a better job to have to really know what people are about and to see God working. It's sometimes just quite breathtaking.

Being a Woman in Parish Ministry

And it was actually kind of a hoot, because I'd walk out to officiate for a wedding, and I could see people's jaws drop, you know. It was really fun. It was like I've always had a piece of me that's been a real feminist, but I've been the kind who just does it. And this was like the great example of just doing it.

Some of the first women in ministry did it as though they were men. They copied a very male style of preaching, of leading worship. They wore the black robes. I decided that if I'd been called and I was who I was, I was going to do it as a woman, which didn't mean I didn't do a lot of the more masculine things, like biblical research. In fact, I did more of that than my co-pastor. But I was a mother. I had three children. I'd use sermon illustrations about cooking I did it as a woman, and it was lots of fun to do that.

The Practice Of Pastoral Counseling

I had always been interested in pastoral counseling and in 1992 after 12 years at Community Congregational Church in Tiburon I entered the training program at the Lloyd Center at SFTS to become a pastoral counselor. I left the church in July of 1993, and continued my training at the Lloyd Center, and also began a Ph.D. in Clinical Psychology. I wrote my dissertation for the D. Min. at SFTS that same summer.

There are lots of people that call themselves pastoral counselors, so I'm going to confine what I say to the group that I am certified by, which is the American Association of Pastoral Counselors. It spun out of the chaplaincy group, the Association of Clinical Pastoral Education, and we're the American Association of Pastoral Counselors. So it's AAPC and ACPE.

It is a national organization that I believe started in the East, and some of the founders wanted to be the best therapists anywhere. They wanted to be even better than clinical psychologists or psychiatrists. So it had a very strong theoretical base, very rigorous training, and I would say that that is still true. If you're a pastoral counselor, some states will license you. California doesn't. We are only certified.

But the training is very rigorous. You do many hours, hundreds of hours of supervised counseling. You have to go through a training program. They have ways that you move up this ladder of steps, where first you are a counselor in training, then you become what's called a Member Associate, then you become a Fellow, and once you're a Fellow, you can supervise other people. Then the last step, for very accomplished people, is Diplomate.

So if you're a Pastoral Counselor, you work with anybody, not just pastors. My doctoral studies were in Jungian psychology, so for some of my clients I use that. For some I use more object-relations theory-type modalities. You have to be an ordained person in a religious group in order to become a certified pastoral counselor.

In the Christian tradition, there is accountability in being part of a group. So to be a pastoral counselor, you can't just set up an office all by yourself. You have to work for a seminary, or you can start a counseling center, a nonprofit. There are lots of different models, but no matter how long you've been a Pastoral Counselor, you have to be supervised. Even Diplomates are supervised. And you are held accountable by other members of the organization.

I've benefited a lot from Jungian work. One of my analysts was an Episcopal priest. Now, the training I did in my clinical psych doctorate was basically Jungian training. By the end of the training, I realized that being a Jungian wasn't my religion, that I'm Christian.

Jungians come in a lot of flavors. There are Christian Jungians and Jewish Jungians and mythological Jungians. If we look at the Jungian world, most people who gravitate toward Jungian analysis, as I did myself when I was in the seminary, have had a flood of dreams that they know are incredibly useful, powerful. They don't know what to make of them. They tend to be people who do think mythologically somehow. Maybe one out of fifty people that have come to me have dream imagery and it is usually a seminarian who wants spiritual direction. I ask them, "Well, tell me about your call," and they'll tell me about their dreams. And I say, "Oh, you're a dreamer. I'm interested in dream work." And then as I work with that person they bring in their dreams.

The Importance Of Spiritual Directors

I do spiritual direction as well as pastoral counseling. In fact, I was doing spiritual direction first. I was trained as a spiritual director in the early eighties. I started in '81 when I got my full-time call at the church.

Spiritual direction has existed for centuries in many areas, probably most prominently in the Catholic Church. But I think rabbis did it before Jesus was born, and you know, wise men in Asia do it, and there's lots of kinds of spiritual direction. But the kind that Protestants do these days is based on the principles of a centuries-old discipline. It used to happen mostly in convents and monasteries where the abbot or the abbess were directors.

There is a simple little recipe for spiritual direction. The director and the directee prayerfully look together at the way the Spirit is directing the directee. It isn't the director directing the directee; it's the two of them noticing how the Spirit is moving in that person's life.

It would be nice if all ministers had spiritual directors, but they don't. Some denominations encourage it. The San Francisco Presbytery really likes it when their people in care, have spiritual directors. A lot of Episcopal diocese really like it when their in-care people, their postulates, are in spiritual direction.

Spiritual direction's usually only once a month, unless you're starting to get to know each other, or one or the other is out of town, or the directee is in some kind of a life crisis, and then you can step it up a little. And it goes on a long time. It can be a lifetime relationship, or a very long relationship.

There are many ways to find a spiritual director. There is a group called Spiritual Directors International, the most recent director has lived in San Francisco. People will call San Francisco Theological Seminary because they've trained so many people, and they'll say, "I'd like some names of a director." There are three of us on the Lloyd Center staff at this point, who do spiritual direction. And in Berkeley there's a plethora of them, a lot of Catholic ones, Episcopal ones.

It's really, really grown in the last twenty years among Protestants. We didn't use to have Protestant spiritual directors. Boy, I sure could have used one myself in my thirties.

Taking Care Of Myself In Order To Take Care Of Others

To keep myself centered to be able to do the counseling that I love I do a number of things. I get up really early. I get up at 5:30, usually, and I sit and pray. I do a number of different kinds of prayer. I do usually some centering prayer, and then I do what I call kind of mulling prayer. I just let people or concerns come to me, and I try to hold it all prayerfully. I believe prayer is a two-way thing. It isn't just saying a bunch of words; it's also listening. I find questions running through my heard how to best meet with a directee, or what do I need to do on a given day, or praying for people I know who need prayer, or for the world.

An important part of my life has been in being part of the founding Staff of the Pacific Center for Spiritual Formation. We as a group, and the retreats and groups we lead, are all focused on the contemplative life, prayer and meditation.

And I love to read, and I love being in nature, friendships, children, grandchildren, going to church. I love silent retreats. And the work I do is very, very nourishing. Hearing people's stories and how God is working in their lives increases my faith. Well, I'm very, very grateful that I have chosen this path. Yes, I feel I could die tomorrow and feel my life was very full.

Religion As A Model For Community

At its best, religion holds up the best of what it is to be human. I think there's a very common thread through all the great religions of the world, for compassion and kindness and understanding. I think we all need reminders of being called to our highest selves. I think religious institutions can provide community in a way that nothing else I've ever experienced can.

I can remember working really, really hard for the PTA in a number of different positions when my children were at Old Mill School, and as soon as they graduated, I was no longer a member of that community. With religious institutions, it's intergenerational. I don't know another facet of society that provides a stable, ongoing place for meaningful community, where values are lifted up and people can prayerfully open to the divine.

We're back to kind of where the church was before Constantine. And you know when you go to church that the people who are there really want to be there, and want to worship God. I don't know a better institution for helping to promote a positive change in the world.

I believe the church will continue to exist. I'm really grateful that I'm part of the church. Doing hospital work, for instance, I found out how lonely a lot of people are. You know, there was a distinct difference in what it was like for a patient in the hospitals I served, if they were the members of a church or synagogue or sanga, compared to those who weren't. I find myself feeling sad for the people who aren't. I don't know a better place for real community.

Carol Saysette is a pastoral counselor. She works through the Lloyd Center of the San Francisco Theological Seminary in Marin County.

Fu Schroeder Story

BUDDHIST TEACHER

Finding My Tribe

Before beginning this practice I was a traditional American child, raised in a suburb of San Francisco, and exposed to the world through television. I went to public schools and state college and planned to be a teacher. I had a fairly confident and narrow expectation of life, myself, and what the possibilities were.

By the time I was in my college years, the world around me had more or less collapsed into what we now call the sixties. My college, San Francisco State, changed from being a teachers college to a very radical political event, and I changed with it. I became a political science major. I was pretty radicalized by what was going on during the Vietnam War.

I was quite lost and confused in those years and did the various drug things that were available, had remarkable experiences of the supernatural realm and the mystical realm which even made it all the more confusing. Where am I? What am I supposed to be doing? What's happening to my culture? Where's my culture? I think one of the questions that was leading me after college was the question, "Where's my tribe? Where'd they go?"

Trying to find answers I actually made an appointment with an Episcopal priest. I'd grown up as an Episcopalian, thinking perhaps I could re-hook whatever this deep burn was, and maybe that this person could help me. I wrote a paper in preparation for that visit, asking the question, "What is God?"

I remember the priest as being nice and charming, but he made some mistakes with me. He asked me things about my social life, "Do you have a boyfriend?" I felt trivialized by his meeting me. I really wanted to know about God, and what I concluded after that meeting was that he didn't know. Which may have been the case.

Finally, one night I was invited to come for dinner at the Zen Center. I remember thinking when I walked in the door, "There they are." They were my tribe. They were mostly dressed in black, but they were my age. They looked interesting, and some of them had shaved heads, but I could tell that I belonged here. This is the place I'd been looking for, and my conviction hasn't ever changed.

I respect and trust the people I have worked with since then. Studying the Buddhist teachings and creating community was a good thing to do. I've seen such tremendous benefit in myself, and in people who come here, by taking up meditation practice and beginning to question their lives in a deep and sustained way.

Zen Center

When I came to the Zen Center in San Francisco we were doing so much and it was very exciting. The Tassajara Bakery made the first all-organic, handmade, hand-rolled croissant. All the things we did were done really well, and the bakery was a lovely bakery. Fresh flowers every day were set out, and coffee was good, and the line was around the block. And that was my experience of Zen Center for many, many years. Everything we touched was wanted and valued and new and not available out there.

When we started Greens restaurant I went over there. I was waiting tables there for several years, and eventually I was the buyer. We always crank up responsibilities. As people stay, they go from washing dishes to teaching other people how to wash dishes, to cooking, and finally running the kitchen. Someone once said each time you take a new responsibility, you are asked to make a 70 percent improvement in what's required of you. So we do try to grow people's confidence and their skills in and through work.

The real emphasis is not on the product. It's about enthusiasm, how much you are willing to engage with the tasks. I think I was pretty enthusiastic, so I've always looked forward to the next 70 percent. It's been exciting for me to receive more responsibility.

So at Greens that was good. In those years there was such a growth of the entrepreneurial enterprises of the Zen Center, that that's where the juice was. I was happy to stay in the city, live in the city and get up early in the morning, work late at night and wash piles of dishes.

Tassajara

At some point there was this request that's made of all of our students here to "Get thee to the monastery." So although life in the city was really to my liking, it was clear that if I wanted to remain in the community, I needed to spend time at Tassajara. I had a tremendous resistance to doing that. Tassajara is a serious monastery. It's cold in the winter; it's hot in the summer. There's no electricity, and you live a very simple life. You eat what's served, and you sit a lot of meditation. It's very daunting by contrast to what I was used to and what I had been exposed to. I didn't know what the discomfort would be like. So it was a big deal for me to go to Tassajara.

The entry into Tassajara is what's called tangaryo. It's a tradition from Asia that as the monks traveled around, when they wanted to study with a certain teacher, they would approach the monastery. There was a monk's waiting area, and you would spend any number of days sitting in that waiting room, to show your sincerity before entering the temple. So our tradition here is that it's five days of waiting at your seat in the zendo before being admitted. It's an initiation, but it's an initiation that's really different than the one we did in Girl Scouts, where we walk over a bridge. There's a real serious physical challenge involved, like mountain-climbing or something. So I had been worried about my ability to do this dongario.

I finally ran out of excuses, and I went to Tassajara. It took about a year for me to arrive there psychologically. I had to cut all of the various attachments that I had with friends. They're still my friends. But to be at Tassajara, I needed to actually let go of the maintenance of those relationships for a while. It took a year for me to do that, to actually be in that valley with those people doing those things that we did together.

But once that happened, I felt like the next great gift of my life occurred, which was to find my place, and my seat, and my abdomen, and my breath, and my amazing body that can do just fine when it's cold and just fine when it's hot. I learned so much about living, what it is to be a living being, through these simple basic elements of what we require. Warm food in the winter is invaluable, a big bowl of hot beans for breakfast. There's a kind of knowing that I could never have read about or studied, that came from knowing my own physical body in that way. It was a whole different culture. I was there about three years altogether.

Green Gulch

After 10 years at San Francisco Zen Center and Tassajara I was invited to come to Green Gulch, to be the head cook, and I wanted to do that. It seemed like a good next step. So I came here and joined staff and was the Tenzo, the head of kitchen. Since then I've done pretty much all of the monastic offices.

I've been the head of the meditation hall which is to be the representative of practice for the folks who are coming to do practice period for the first time. You have a very new group of people, and then you have someone who's a role model of the practice, and that's the position you take after ordination. At ordination you are involved in a rather large initiatory ceremony where everyone in the community asks you a question publicly, and you answer. It's called the shuso ceremony. So that was a big watershed in my training. It's the first time people really hear you express your understanding.

After I was shusoed I was the head of the meditation hall. Then I was invited to be my teacher's assistant for a while. And then I was invited to be director of Green Gulch, which I did. I had written a little list of things I'd like to do for my own training, which included becoming director.

Now that I am the Tanto which is the head of practice I think what I'm supposed to do is to be aware of the people who are here and how they're doing, how it's going. I meet with people who come here. When they first come, I meet with them privately and I'll encourage them to bring up anything they want and to bring up any concerns or fears, or whatever they want to talk about. I think my role as Tanto is about developing intimacy with the people who are here, both the old-timers, who've blocked off certain parts of themselves that they don't allow you to access, and the young ones who are just trying to figure out what's going on, and whether they can trust us or not. So I think my job is to be friendly and welcoming, and also a little strict.

Child

Although I had learned and grown in my years here, my most profound transformation took place when a child came into my life. I got a phone call from a friend, saying, "Would you be interested in hearing about a baby?" Social Services had taken the child from the mother who was drug-addicted. That's when I heard about Sabrina. She was pretty ill when she was born, and wasn't expected to live very long. She was very tiny and premature and struggling. She does have mild cerebral palsy as a result of her birth trauma some other things. That changed everything.

I was the director of Green Gulch. I was planning to go to Japan and study tea ceremony in Kyoto. I'd made another path for myself that was going to be very career-driven and dharma-driven. And then three weeks later we brought home this one-month-old baby girl. In some ways I could say that practice began with the arrival of Sabrina in my life, and that all of what I wanted to do became quite secondary to her and what she needed. I mean, it was the first time I experienced a foreground shift, where I was no longer the foreground element, that there was somebody else where I had always been. And it was a shock, to say the least.

Over a period of many months, and through many dreams I was having those first months she was in my life, of panicking and not knowing where she was, and trying to find her in the blankets, I felt like something in my psyche was restructuring me for motherhood. I didn't have the instincts of a mother, and I didn't go through pregnancy but something worked me over, because by the end of that phase of those dreams, I was very attentive and very tuned in to her. And that hasn't changed at all. I feel like I'm a doting mother.

My story sort of takes this turn toward the PTA at this point. It really is a big shift in direction. Sabrina's health improved. She went from really fragile to doing pretty well, and she continues to do pretty well. She takes medicine daily. I don't know where it will all go. I guess we don't know with anybody. But I used to think she was only going to be in my life for a little while, and now I have given up thinking like that. I have no idea what's going to happen. I wasn't expecting her to talk or to sass me back, or go to school, and now she's looking like she's going to be a teenager. She's getting very teenage behavior, and it's just been a miracle.

As we speak, I'm in the process of reading parenting books. I'm doing a lot of trying to learn what it is to be a good parent for her. I've actually been invited this summer to teach a class on parenting, which stopped me for a bit. I thought, "What am I going to say?"

But, gratefully, I've been working for many years, since Sabrina came into my life, with a wonderful therapist who is a child, adolescent, and adult psychiatrist. He had offered pro bono work for people working with fragile children in Marin, and so I had signed up with him way back when. He's been a constant companion of my effort to learn how to be a parent.

He's gotten me turned on now to Rudolf Dreikur's theories of childrearing, this whole stunning approach to letting children learn the hard way. And it's so fun. I'm having such a great time. Now I feel like I have something to say at the parenting conference, because it's just been great successes in allowing Sabrina to develop. Because of her cerebral palsy, she walks with a walker, or runs with a walker, mostly. I think both Grace and I had a tendency to be slaves to her. Out of some good intention, of course, but clearly, now that I'm beginning to learn more about this, it's clearly not what you want to do. You don't create these monster children and turn yourself into a slave. That now has been reversed, and I've learned to say over and over again, "You can do that." And she can, and she does. And she's so clearly proud of herself for all the things she can do.

Learning Compassion

I think one of the first observations I made about myself in my dealing with an infant was that as I said in one of my talks that she was the "flowering of my heart." Along with this background-foreground shift, there was also a visible lovingness coming out of me that I had not experienced before. I'd had a guarded lovingness available on a limited basis, to a limited number of people. But this other feeling was the source of what I consider my compassion for the world.

I really think I came to understand what compassion was by accepting, by saying yes to this relationship with Sabrina. Without that, I have a fear, and I don't know that this fear would have been realized, but I was headed down a pretty cold path of perfecting forms, perfecting intellectual knowledge. I was very interested in philosophy, and considered going to graduate school in Buddhism and becoming a scholar, and really investing my affections for the teachings in a more scholastic vein.

And now I'm interested in the children's program. I'm really interested in making this a place where everybody feels welcome, where noise is not only okay, it's required. There has to be a feeling of flexibility in our presentation to the world and what we're doing. It's not about making anyone feel uncomfortable, unwelcome. I certainly had been saying something quite the opposite as a young monk. I had a lot of very strict views about what's required for practice, including silence. You know, "Children, sorry, they're very nice, but we don't have them in a monastery." I mean, I was really not sympathetic to the mess of human life.

The experience one has of the quality of one's own life, and how to help someone get in touch with that quality in their own life that brings them peace and that brings them joy, is really all we're about here. We want to help people to open out to their own deepest wishes and their own desires to be helpful to others. It's inviting people to come into themselves and be as much as they can be.

Fu Schroeder is currently the Tanto, or head of practice, at Green Gulch center for Zen Buddhism in Marin County.

Sue Severin Story

QUAKER ACTIVIST

Looking for Peace and Justice

As a child I was sent to whichever Protestant church was closest. The very first one I ever went to as a little girl was Episcopal, and then it was Methodist, and then, finally, Presbyterian. It was mainly something my parents could send us to on Sunday morning, so they did not have to deal with us.

When I started college and took Western Civ, I realized all of this religion stuff is nonsense. I mean, the birth of Christ exists in various different religions, and it's nothing special, and Christianity isn't anything special. And so I became an atheist, and for years I was perfectly comfortable being an atheist.

Then during the sixties, when I was back in California and going to graduate school, I became a hippie. As part of that, I got into meditation and a certain kind of spirituality, incense and gongs and all of that. Also, during that time, I got very involved in social justice issues, and was protesting first the Vietnam War and then various things. So I was a meditating, social justice activist, but I had no religion at all.

But then I had my son, Ezra. I remember thinking, "I'm going to have to find some way to introduce him to our Judeo-Christian cultural system," but there weren't any churches I wanted to take him to. By chance I went to visit a friend of mine who was teaching at Princeton. We'd been medievalists together at UC. She was on the faculty of Princeton, and she said, "Would you like to go to Quaker meeting tomorrow morning?"

We went to the Quaker meeting in this wonderful old meeting house, almost like a log cabin, sitting on benches with a fire going, and I sat down waiting for it to begin. And after a while I realize it's begun, and everybody's meditating. I go into meditation, and then darned if somebody doesn't get up and say something that spoke to my social justice issue. It was like, wow. It was absolutely amazing to me to see the combination of meditation and social justice issues.

That was in about November of '74. I came home, and in January there was a little article in the paper saying that the Marin County Quaker Meeting was moving to a new place not very far away from here in Kentfield. I took Ezra to the Quaker meeting, and I didn't miss a meeting for the next year. I was so completely ensconced by it, because here I was meditating and concerned and speaking out about social justice issues. It didn't come from my background at all. It came from my reality as I grew up and became a responsible adult.

Quaker Values

There are a number of Quaker values that I try to live by. One is worth for value, value for worth. I didn't like the idea of gambling, and after I had become a Quaker, I discovered Quakers don't gamble. I remember in college, at a blackjack table up in Reno when we were skiing in the Sierras one time, my boyfriend and I had ten silver dollars. We put one silver dollar out, and a woman sitting next to us was throwing out hundred-dollar bills at the same rate we were putting out single dollars. And I remember being horrified at what I call misuse of money.

Speaking truth to power is another Quaker value. The value is to have a single standard of truth. That, to me, is so important. You say the same thing to everybody, not one thing to one person and something else to another. And then speaking truth to power is absolutely vital. That's the only way to get changes sometimes.

Speaking truth to power means telling your boss when what he or she is doing is wrong, or telling the government. Not putting up with something just because the power has it. Being willing to put yourself out there and say, "This is wrong. I will not continue this way. We cannot continue this way." Even though you might be put in jail, or even killed. I haven't been in a situation where I've been threatened with being killed, but I certainly have brought up unpopular ideas in work situations. I will be honest in situations where those in charge would rather I keep my mouth shut about something.

Another Quaker value is simple living. The saying is "live simply so others may simply live." It is about using resources effectively and not wasting them. I learned a lot about living simply in Central America, where we had nothing, I mean, paper to write on? I remember saving the piece of paper that came out of a little Kleenex pack, because there wasn't any paper around. Or one day I found a paper clip on the ground. It was a treasure. Paper clips didn't exist, I mean things we take so for granted here. So for me, living in Central America in the Witness for Peace program really helped me to winnow down that simple living, and realize what it is I really need, and what I can do without. It helped me in living simply back here in the States.

Witness for Peace

The point of Witness for Peace was to go to Nicaragua and to report on the impact U.S. aid to the Contra was having on the Nicaraguans themselves.

My job in Witness for Peace was, first of all, to live with and as a Nicaraguan, so I could see for myself their reality; secondly, to arrange for delegations. Delegations would come down, and then I would take them out into the war zones, into the areas where I lived, so those people could see for themselves and come back and report. And third, to document Contra attacks against civilians, so that I could report back exactly where my government's money was going in another country, and the destruction that our money was doing in another country, and to counteract the propaganda that was coming out from the Reagan government.

And again, to me, speaking truth to power and documenting what needed to be shown, that was a very Quaker thing to do. Some of the people who started Witness were Quaker, but most of them serving when I was there were Catholic or other Protestant religions. But it fit in very well with Quaker values.

While I was there I started working with people doing childbirth education, because I had done that myself after my child was born. I realized that was a real way to get involved with people, and that some of the most active social change agents were health brigadista. They went into the communities and helped mothers understand that their kids were getting diarrhea because of the dirty water. And helped them to find ways to get clean water. The people who were being helped were then transformed into social justice activists.

As a Quaker, I don't usually use God language. But when I was living in the war zones of Nicaragua, and a potentially dangerous situation occurred, I felt that I was in the hand of God; not that I was safe, not that I wouldn't get hurt, but that I was where I was supposed to be, doing what I was supposed to be doing. It was a wonderful feeling, to have that sense. Instead of fear or terror I felt utter calmness and a sense of being centered. As it turned out, the situations that I have been in haven't ever resulted in any damage to me, but I now know that I can count on becoming centered and calm in a time of danger. Quaker centering helps me to do that.

Observing Elections

From having lived in Nicaragua I started getting asked to help set up delegations to do electoral observation, because I knew how to go into a community. I'd make contacts and set things up, and then take delegations of people. So I was asked to do that, which fit right into my previous life, because my BA was in Poly Sci, and I had worked for the US government.

I was very interested in politics, and I'd gotten very involved in local politics here. So going to observe an election was great fun for me. We were always invited in by a nongovernmental organization from the country involved. You never just go and barge in. You're asked to come, to observe, with the point of it being to help keep elections honest and fair and clean.

We have to be certified by a governmental organization to be officially allowed to be there. Again, it's a Quaker value. We're trying to keep people honest, and my job is not to push one side or another. My job is to be impartial and neutral, and all I can do is document any misuse, and perhaps point it out to the head of the particular place where I am, the head of that precinct. But I can't step in the way; I can't change anything. It's simply shining my light on it, saying, "Wait a minute. It looks like such and such is happening here."

If there is abuse and they do nothing about it, there's nothing I can do at the time. I document what I see and then report on it afterwards, so that there's a sense of whether the election was free and fair, or not. My job is simply to try to help people be honest and clean and fair. So, frequently, people are very pleased that they have observers there, because they know that will help to keep things on the up and up. And if not, the abuse will be reported and then changes will happen afterwards.

Quaker Queries

Quakers have questions called queries that relate to Quaker values. One might be, "Do you come to meeting prepared for a spiritual time?" The Quaker book that list the queries is Faith in Practice. All of the queries bring up individual Quaker values. They make you ask yourself, "Are you aware of these Quaker values? Are you living according to the Quaker values?"

One of the queries I ask myself is do I live in such a way as to remove the occasion of violence from my life and the life of those around me? And I'll remember that when I'm speeding down the highway and somebody's about to cut in, and I think, "Wait a minute. If I back off, I'm removing an occasion of violence." Or letting somebody in on a crowded road. Some of these are little things that I can do which can remove an occasion of violence from somebody else, that I'll never know and that I'll never talk to. Maybe they're in a hurry and then they realize that they can get in, or maybe I opened the door for them when they're carrying a bunch of boxes. It's a way to soften their situation a little bit, so they'll feel less likely to become violent.

So that's a query that I try to remember a lot, because I'm not going to say that I don't ever get angry or mad or whatever. But when I do, if I can remember that query, then I can back off.

Rule by consensus is another Quaker value. In Quaker meetings we have no minister but a clerk who is chosen by consensus. We don't vote in Quakers. You do everything by consensus, and if you don't have consensus, then you don't move forward. In other words, it's not majority rule. One person can stop the meeting moving forward on something by saying, "I do not agree with this." Then if it's an issue that we've brought up, and we haven't reached consensus, and it's put aside for another time, and then can be brought up at a later time to see if we've reached consensus.

I remember having to teach the people on the Witness for Peace team about consensus decision-making, because you have to be much more responsible than you are in a democratic process, where it's a vote. Because when you vote on an issue you can show that you disagree with it, but know it's going to pass anyway. So you can afford to vote against it to show that you really don't agree with it, but you'll let it happen.

With consensus decision making you have to really evaluate what's going on and be very responsible about how you come down on an issue. You know, are you really willing to stop something for the whole meeting because of some little quibble on your behalf? Is that really worth stopping it for everybody? Now, if it was a vote you could say no for your quibble, and it might not make a difference anyway, but it gives you a chance to get your quibble out for others to see. But with consensus you have to decide is this quibble of mine worthy enough to stop our moving forward on this particular issue.

God In Everyone

It took me some years to be able to say, "that of God." I could say, "Holy light, divine light, divine spark." Now I can say, "that of God." When you truly believe there is that of God in everyone, then how can you do anything else but follow

Quaker principles, i.e. how can you kill somebody else? How can you cheat them? How can you treat them unequally?

I have to admit sometimes it's hard to find that of God in people. In fact, Phil Drath has a wonderful commentary about that. Somebody once said to him, "Phil, I know that we're supposed to be looking for that of God in everybody, but, boy, it's hard." And Phil said, "We're supposed to look for it, not necessarily find it." And I know for me during the eighties, trying to remember that about Ronald Reagan, when he was doing all this Contra stuff, was very hard, but it was valuable for me to remember to focus on that, because some place in him there is that of God.

My goal is to appeal to that of God in everyone, to try to find that, to try to appeal, to try to connect with that. And frequently, that's what can make the difference. Instead of coming on in an aggressive way, you come on in a much more gentle way, and it's there. Everybody was a baby; everybody was little; everybody had those sweet things in them, no matter where they are now, and it's a matter of connecting with them. So that, to me, is the basic Quaker value from which everything else follows.

Women Quakers

All the way along for Quakers women have played an equal role with men. There were times when women sat on one side of the meeting hall and men sat on the other side, but they were all there. The early feminists were all Quakers; Susan B. Anthony, Amalia Bloomer, Elizabeth Cady Stanton. And that's because these were women who were used to being treated as equals and seen as equals, and they realized all women should have that opportunity. I became a feminist long before I became a Quaker, and I remember one day after I'd become a Quaker somebody telling me, "Oh yeah, it's all those Quaker ladies who did it." After I'd become a Quaker, I thought, "Really!" and I went back and checked up, and sure enough, yes, Susan B. Anthony, Elizabeth Cady Stanton were all Quakers. In fact in Seneca Falls, the first feminist meetings were held in a Quaker meeting house, because that's a place where women could be treated equally.

Do you know the story about bloomers? Well, women used to wear skirts all the time, even when they had to go out and work in the garden. Well, skirts, you know, they're a drag. So Amalia Bloomer created this sort of fluffy thing out of underskirts. She made pant-leg things that women could then wear when they're out working, instead of these skirts that got in the way. So they were called bloomers. That's how we got the name bloomer, and pants have gone a long way since then, but I love that thought.

Empowering People

I came to maturity before the woman's movement started, and I was so frustrated by my inability to do what I wanted to do, because I was a woman. I really felt the unfairness of that. So when the women's movement hit, for me I was very much an activist, because finally we were going to have some power in the world and have equality.

Because of that, I think, I'm really aware of how important it is that everybody in the world has enough food, security, health care, education, not just a few very rich people, or people who have the power. That's what I'm continually working on. What I prefer doing is training the local people, not being the one who comes in, the expert, but rather, helping people to empower themselves. Not shaking my finger at them, but helping them to understand what they already know, and then empowering them to enlarge upon this and empower other people.

It started with me wanting to empower myself as a woman, to be able to have equality to men, but now I want to help all people to empower themselves, to have a life that's worth living, that's comfortable for them. Maybe they have to work hard and the life is not luxurious, but everybody needs to have access to the necessities. That's why I go down to Central America or Colombia.

Politically it's about our government putting its nose in where it doesn't belong, and my job is to try to get our government to stop, and doing that by letting all sorts of other people know what is wrong, so that we can put pressure on them. Whether it's contacting my representative or my senators, or whether it's out protesting on the street, or signing petitions, or working with candidates, it's all part of helping to empower people, helping people to empower themselves.

Sue Severin is a full time advocate and volunteer who travels frequently to Central America as teacher, witness and observer.

Janie Spahr Story

LESBIAN ACTIVIST

An Early Call

I knew I was called when I was thirteen or fourteen years old. It was absolutely clear to me. I knew that I was to go into ministry, and almost at the same time, I began to see that I was lesbian. I hid my lesbian feelings because I didn't know what they were. I just knew that my deepest feelings were for my friends. I began to hide from myself. And it was horrendous for me until I broke free.

From the age of fourteen onward, I had a light that went through me, this incredible experience that's like, "Okay. Okay, okay, I hear you. I hear you." So I always had a wonderful relationship with God. I think my early relationship with God had something to do with being a twin. When you're a twin, you have total communication with another. I felt very in touch with God.

When I went to college I took religious studies. I went to Penn State and there were only three of us in religious studies out of 20,000 students. Luther Harshburger was great. He was a Lutheran, but he brought in Hindus, Buddhists too. I had an incredible experience in college hearing all the ways that God comes to us.

I'd gotten married to this wonderful man, told him all my feelings about sexuality, but we didn't know what that meant. We had two beautiful sons. But my feelings did not change. People have said, "Well, you'll get over those feelings." Well, you can't get over yourself.

Coming Out

I was ordained in 1974 to the Hazelwood Presbyterian Ministry. My associate was Wanda Graham Harris, mentor and friend. It was the first time they ever put two women together in that presbytery, working together. It was an amazing experience.

From there, I went to First Presbyterian Church, San Rafael. Served wonderful years. We had amazing youth groups, college, high school, and junior high school youth. It was an experience I'll never forget, and they helped me love me. We talked about sexuality; we'd talk about every kind of thing. They just opened their hearts to me, and the more they did that, the more I knew I had to face myself.

I was at First Presbyterian in San Rafael and the Presbyterian Church was doing a study on homosexuality. I was asked to speak about the oppression of women, and what that has to do with the oppression of lesbian, gay, bisexual, transgender people. It was there that I met Bill Johnson and Ellen Barrett. Bill Johnson is UCC, openly gay, and Ellen Barrett, the first Episcopal lesbian minister.

I heard their story, and I came running home to Jimmy, and I said, "Jimmy, that's my story." He had left the book around for a whole year called Loving Someone Gay. He said to me, "You ought to read this, Janie."

So when I said to him, "Jimmy, I think I am a lesbian," he said, "I know. I've been waiting for you to tell me for a year."

That's the wonderful story. We sat down at the dinner table that night. We cried out of relief. Because when you love someone and you're not exactly meeting each other it is sad and frustrating. So we sat at the dinner table, and Jim said to my two little wonderful little boys, "Mommy, tell the boys the wonderful thing you have learned about yourself."

I always tell the story that I was crying and Jimmy said, "Oh, mommy, you love people. That's what is most important." And he then began to cry with me, and I looked at Chetty. Chetty said, "Oh, Mommy, you found you," and, "Let's go tell the church. Isn't this wonderful?" See, because I'd raised them in the church. But we said to Chetty, "We know, honey, the church won't be as excited as we are."

From that time onward I came to know me. Finally I left San Rafael I went to the Oakland Council of Presbyterian Churches. We worked with African American, Asian American, European American, and predominantly Chinese American youth. I was just getting my feet wet there and I was coming out. I had moved over there with my partner. It was there that the council brought me in and said, "Well, Janie, we want to talk to you about your lifestyle."

I just remember being so stunned. Then it hit the papers and I thought, "I wonder if I'll ever be able to do ministry again, as long as I live?" I was so called to it from childhood and couldn't imagine what life would be without being in a ministry. But I left the job in Oakland and I went and worked at a little nursing home over here in San Rafael, and bathed the older people, and loved on them, and cleaned their rooms.

Beginning My Ministry

It was Jimmy Spahr, my former husband, who called Metropolitan Community Church in San Francisco and said, "You ought to hear Janie Spahr preach." I hadn't preached in six months, I was feeling all this angst at not doing what I loved to do. My children were there. My partner was there. We all were there. Jimmy, my former husband was there.

Just before I preached I said, "I want to introduce you to my family," and my sons and Jim, and the wonderful person I was with and her children were all there. The entire congregation stood and clapped for five minutes. Can you imagine my boys? I looked at the congregation and thought, they're me and I'm them. It's so hard when you've been told you were bad and wrong all your life to find people who really love and appreciate you. And there was a sea of people looking at me and clapping. I was there for two years, and I became their minister of pastoral care.

That's when AIDS hit. The bars in San Francisco raised the money for the LWBT churches, because other places wouldn't do it. But it was this integration of community that came together, and I fell in love with what it means to be lesbian, and what it means to have my faith. I learned about a lesbian, gay, bisexual, transgender community that has been so misrepresented. I saw, I felt God everywhere.

The AIDS epidemic hit so many young people. It was like being with my children. They used to come into the church, and they had spots. It was Kaposi's sarcoma. "Look at this, Janie. What is this?" they would say. So what happened to me during this time was a deepening of my own spirituality, but most of all a compassion for my own community and a passion for justice!

When I came back here we developed the Marin AIDS Project. We had parents' groups and therapy groups. It was called Ministry of Light at first, and after ten years we named it Spectrum. I buried friends of mine who were the most incredible community activists here in Marin. But they taught me all about God and all the ways that God will show herself, and opened me so much.

There were parents' groups and a speakers' bureau and all these things just happened from the community. The community just opened and opened and opened. We had family camps and kids, and they just happened to have two mommies, two daddies. They said the only way that you could tell that it might be a lesbian, gay, bisexual, transgender camp is that the women played softball and the men watched the children when the women played softball. We laughed and hooted and cried with our kids.

We started a women's spirituality group in which we had women from all faith traditions. We met in people's homes rather than churches, because lesbian women felt unsafe in the churches. Women began to trust and to listen and to come out about not only their sexuality, but their spirituality. Sacred stuff, whether it be the goddess or whether it be Jewish or Christian, we were able to share our deepest parts of ourselves.

Those ten years I'll never forget as long as I live. We had youth groups that were just incredible. We met with therapists throughout Marin County, to have therapists that our people could go to. And I thought, "God, I love this so much." And as soon as I said that I knew that something was going to change. Because as Wanda my associate from Pittsburg, PA said, "Once you get the hedges fixed, then you just hop over." So I knew I would be on to another challenge.

Being Lesbian

I say to people, "The reason why I'm a lesbian is because of God." Because I feel like God keeps coaxing us into our freedom, keeps coaxing us to dare to be who we are. This is especially hard for women in a patriarchal society, and as a lesbian woman who says that she doesn't need men, she just loves them. It's a dissonance for patriarchy.

In this county women work together on all kinds of issues, from abortion to social issues, the law, anything that we did together as women. We don't have to do it alone. Look what we had to do and how we helped each other. The Iroquois women helped Elizabeth Cady Stanton and Susan B. Anthony. We are fighting a patriarchal system that says, "Women are less than." We're seeing it in the world still. There's still horrendous abuse. Look at what's happened in Afghanistan. To be a woman is to be political. To be a lesbian woman is to be more political.

I'm afraid for the church that it will be damaged if it doesn't open its doors to us. The spirit of God is about yearning for freedom and for justice. It's like I'm almost looking over my shoulder, saying, "Come on. Come on, we've got work to do. We can do this together. Come on. Don't keep saying we are not allowed to serve, we are God's people." We're all God's people. Some of us have been terribly wounded. Some of us have been very hurt and have spent a lot of time helping other people through their woundedness.

That All May Freely Serve

So after ten years of the most incredible experiences of my life, I opened myself to do the work of another organization called That All May Freely Serve. We're doing our work on racism and classism. It's a movement of love and justice because the church has to open its doors to its children, or God help it.

It is a spiritual movement, which is sexuality and spiritual all together, it's a movement of love and justice for freedom. It's to liberate people, so that they can become who they are and serve the world and serve the community. When people aren't free and they're hidden, then they can't serve with all of themselves, and that's what these churches are doing by keeping us from our freedom. And God will set us free. Systems must be broken open.

We take van trips, just like the old circuit riders. Get in a van, here we come. We went into one church and when we said, "Being lesbian, gay, is a gift from God. Being lesbian, gay, bisexual, transgender is a gift, just like heterosexuality, just like our sexuality is a gift." And then you knew who was queer right then. Tears were rolling down their faces. Nobody had ever said out loud to them, "You are good for who you are."

We went to the University of Vermont. We said to the youth that were there, "You can come out as lesbian, gay, bisexual or transgender." They said, "Well, Janie, you know, we don't only want to come out as lesbian, gay, bisexual, transgender. We want to come out in our faith tradition. So I'm lesbian and my name's so-and-so, I'm lesbian and I'm Jewish, and I am gay and I am Roman Catholic." We set up a door which we had them walk through as a symbol of coming out. Then they talked about their faith as well as their sexuality. Then we took the door and made it a table. And we said, "Now come to the table. Everybody's welcome." It was fabulous.

Universities now have safe zones and signs on teacher's doors. Because you've got many gay, lesbian, bisexual and transgender organizations doing incredible work. We have developed a safety sticker, which is displayed by professors or teachers, that means it is will be safe for people to talk to them about lesbian, gay, bisexual, transgender.

It is important to create safety. Unfortunately the church is still the greatest perpetrator of violence against lesbian, gay, bisexual, transgender people. There are still so many churches who label us as evil, as bad. I've had people spit on me. Yell "Get her out of here." I've had death threats.

But I know I will be safe. When I first started to go out to do the work of That All May Freely Serve, I came home one day and checked my phone messages.

There was a message that said, "Jane Spahr, you will never be hurt, because you have a cloud of witnesses of people on the other side that are with you. So don't worry ever." I have never worried, because I know it's true.

I'm sixty this year. And a lot of the work that I'm doing now is for and with younger friends. I am hoping that the work I do will give them a chance to serve in the church. Right now the policy is one cannot speak the truth of one's life and serve in the church. The faith community says, "Speak the truth." Then when we do speak the truth we are rejected. I have seen so many young people who have been called and who cannot serve in the Presbyterian Church.

My Hope For Change

I say dialogue is to be between equals. And right now the Presbyterian Church says that if our people speak the truth of our lives, we can never serve. There is nothing equal. We don't have voice or vote on presbytery floors, when voting comes. That's not equal when you can't share power. So we're here to invite people into mutuality and to share power, into justice. That means changing a patriarchal system.

We are asking for shared leadership. It is inviting those in power to let go of some power and share it. It's inviting people to change a system of inequality to equality. It is a huge task. As a woman, it was a huge task and still is. As a lesbian woman, it becomes a bigger task. Because you're fighting a system that says, "These are the rules and this is how it is." We say, "No." Because if we don't have equality then there really is not love. And love without justice is not love at all. We're going for a just, loving society. That means people sharing their power.

Some of my friends ask why I don't transfer to a church that will allow us to serve like the United Church of Christ. But, I was raised in this church. I'm Presbyterian-stamped even though I've been with Buddhists and Hindus and all different faith traditions. And I say, "Wow. Anyway you want to come to your spiritual path is just fine with me." It's in one's heart, it's in us, this wonderful accessibility to God. I respect other traditions and this is my faith tradition. This church has got to stretch and do what's right and just. It's just got to because it is the right thing to do, so that All May Freely Serve.

Janie Spahr heads the national campaign "That All May Freely Serve." She lives in Marin County but travels widely in her work.

Kelly Thomas Story

CHOIR DIRECTOR

Women Leaders in the African American Church

In the African American church, women were more in leadership roles in terms of becoming missionaries and evangelists, and often work with music ministry and children. Now a lot of women are becoming ordained ministers. I'm from a Pentecostal persuasion, I don't know of a whole lot of women who are ordained.

It's something that's going to happen more often, and women are starting to take those roles. But I don't think it's about, "Well, I'm a woman and I can do just as good as a man can do," but I think it has to do with the call a woman feels she has on her life, and that we have been called to preach, we have been called to evangelize.

The call in my life is that of an evangelist missionary, and I know that, and it comes out in my work. It doesn't come out just as music. It has to be the whole thing put together where it's about winning souls and bringing people to Christ, and introducing them to something better than what's going on and in another way.

What I'm trying to do through the ministry of music, through being able to evangelize through music and art is to be able to feed the spiritual needs of people, so that spiritual part gets stronger and begins to dominate. Then the old part, which is created after the flesh, will have to lie down, and people will always then be able to do the things that are right, the things that make for good, the things that make for peace.

I believe that that's what it's going to take to turn our communities around, to turn our world around, overall, and if God is going to use women to do it, I'm all for it. God is not a respecter of person. He's looking for a willing heart, and that's how I like to look at it. I try not to get into the thing about, "Oh, you can't preach, or you shouldn't be teaching because you're a woman." I don't even want to get caught up in that mindset, because then I'll fail God.

Leadership Skills From The Beginning

From the time that I can remember, I was always a leader. I was never really a follower, and my parents would always say, if my sisters and I got into trouble, it wasn't because we were following somebody else, that it was because we were doing what we wanted to do, and I really believe that.

Leaders are not always born, but they're made, and I've had some really good leadership in my life. My parents were good role models, provided the kind of leadership that we needed, and because of that, I think I had the tools of what God could use, even early on as a child. I was always the child that, when my friends fell down, scraped their knees, I was ministering to them.

Singing In Childhood

I started singing at a very early age, just around my home, sitting next to a stereo. My dad was big on entertaining and he always had company over or would be going to parties. My sisters and I would sing together, and we would entertain at all of his parties, and sometimes we would be invited to go and sing at some of the parties of his friends, and so that's how I got started.

As I grew older, I started participating in talent shows. At age ten I became a part of a group called the Concerned Citizens for Marin City. We put on benefit dinners and shows to raise money for the children in the Marin City community who wanted to go on to college or vocational training.

Singing with my family went on for a long time. I got saved when I was ten years old, not understanding what salvation really meant, but I knew that Christ had died for my sins, and I had accepted Him into my heart. But I continued to sing secular music, I guess, because that was what was going on. I didn't do a lot of it. I limited myself to just the group that I was singing in, the Concerned Citizens for Marin City, and that was something positive. I love singing, and it really gave me an opportunity to develop my style of singing, also to learn stage presence. I didn't have enough money to take voice lessons so that was my place of being taught.

I sang with that group until I was nineteen, that was the last performance that I did with them. I had gone through a lot of things in my life, drugs, abusive relationships, not physical but emotional. I lost my brother when I was a junior in high school, and that was a hard blow because he was the first person that had been that close to me, that we had lost.

From Secular To Sacred Music

I never was social because I didn't drink. I didn't really party. I was pretty much in the house with my mom until I was about fifteen, sixteen, so a lot of the things that came into my life, I don't think I was prepared for, because I was sheltered. But God brought me through, out of my love for Him and being so grateful that He had given me another opportunity. He could have taken the gift, the voice could have gone, but He was gracious to me. And when I gave my life to Him, it wasn't a thing that I thought about and said, "Well, okay, now I'm going to sing secular music." It was just part of the conversion process.

Once I gave my life to the Lord, then I started singing in choirs, and I got out of the secular scene and really started devoting my ministry of music to the Lord and dedicating the gift that He had given me back to Him.

I think the first choir that I sang in was the Marin County Community Choir. Since then, I've gone on to found a Marin City Youth Choir. I've always worked with young people, and having children of my own and realizing their gifts and the their talents in music and acting, drama, arts, I figured who better to do something?

I had been injured on my job back in '96, and I had all this time with nothing to do. It was a way for me to still stay plugged into the community and also have something that I could do that made me feel good about being able to get up every morning and focus my attention on doing something positive.

Starting The Youth Choir

I started the youth choir about four years ago. We started off with just my daughters, my nieces, just to get it going, and then before you knew it, we had kids from Tam, from Martin Luther King, and even a few Baysiders. We had to break it off after a bit because we had mixing in ages, and the attention spans were off with the older kids wanting to sing more complex songs. Now I'm working on getting two choirs going, one a children's choir and the other a teenage choir.

I'm going to probably combine the five-year-olds up until about eleven or twelve, depending on their abilities, because some of the younger ones could actually sing the songs, but the ones who couldn't I need to give them opportunities to have someplace to grow into.

The choir is not affiliated with any church. It's a community project and in choir, and when I say community, it's not limited to Marin City, because some people work here and they want their children to be a part of, but they live in the surrounding communities so it's open to anybody who wants to come in and sing. There's no denomination tag on it at all. I'm excited. I'm really excited. I feel like this is a legacy that I'm able to carry on even with more meaning from what I used to do when I was singing.

My vision is a choir of choirs. I know my church, Cornerstone Community Church, has a youth choir. I would like to see the children, if not all of them from that choir, come and be a part of the community choir same with First Missionary, Village Baptist, Church of God, Presbyterian, and Gospel Fellowship. I think of it as a community choir, and that then we would be open to anybody else who wanted to join.

The Need To Minister With Music

I would say that what I've learned from my pastors, what I've learned from people who have taught me, I can take that with me and go on and to perfect the gifts that God has given me. But definitely I believe that it's a vision that God has given me to minister to young people, so that they don't have to bow down to things that are ungodly. They can say no to things that they need to say no to. They can stand up for what is right. Because some people have a problem standing up for what's right, so what I tend to do in my ministry is deal with issues of self-respect, self-esteem, confrontations, communication, being able to relate to other people. It's real-life stuff, stuff that happens every day.

One of the things that I've realized just dealing with young people; they don't know how to communicate, or they believe that your opinion or your impression of them is one thing, because of maybe how you act or how you speak or respond to them, and so they'll completely shut down, and they'll have an attitude. So a lot of it is just breaking through barriers and teaching them how to deal with life on life's terms, because that's why people get into drugs and alcohol and gangs and things. If we can teach people early on how to cope in life, because life is not always easy, life is not always fair, but you have to make right choices and good decisions, regardless. So that's kind of what my ministry is about, I believe.

I often tell people it doesn't matter what you're singing about, it's going to minister, be it good or be it something bad. I can see how the music in today's world, particularly secular, when you get into the hard rock, when you get into the rap, it's really degrading and really demeaning. People don't realize that it's speaking to your spirit, and at a time when you're least thinking about it, it'll come up. You are what you eat, and I believe that if you feed those things into your spirit, that degrading music is going to become stronger, and it's going to dominate.

Music ministry, as I said, it opens up the heart. It leads a person to a place where, if you use a word, it may be harsh, and a person may not receive that word, but if the heart is prepared to receive, then no matter what you say to them, they'll accept it, or at least they'll listen. So when I say music is the veil of the church, in terms of ministry inside the confines of a church or an audience, it prepares the heart to receive what is to follow next. So, be it a sermon, be it a word of encouragement coming from somebody else, be it a word of exhortation, the heart is prepared. It kind of breaks up the fallow ground. It sets the tone. It lifts that hardness. It breaks away the shell and all the protective things that we have, the defenses, it breaks all that down, and it opens people up to receive.

I believe that when I'm busy about doing my Father's business, He takes care of mine. He makes sure that my children eat, my lights stay on. We have everything that we need, and it's amazing, and it didn't just start today and yesterday, three months ago; it's been going on since I gave my life to Christ.

So I'm really excited. I love God with all my heart. I wouldn't trade anything for my journey. I really wouldn't. It hasn't been easy, either. I mean, salvation and a walk with Christ is not a perfect walk. It's not something that you know how to do overnight. You have to learn Christ, and you have to put Him on every day, and so even as I'm growing, I'm learning how to put on Christ every day, and every day is a new day, and every day is a new experience with Christ.

Kelly Thomas is an advocate for children and youth. She recently moved from Marin County.

Gervaise Valpey, O.P., Story

CATHOLIC EDUCATOR

Following the Dominican Way

Over the years when I was in school, I thought at different times of becoming a religious, and yet didn't take it too seriously. But when I was in college, it was amazing that when I was enjoying the best of times I experienced the inner promptings of: "There's more to it, more to life than all of this." I felt very blessed and grateful for opportunities and experiences in life up to that time, and I really wanted to discover the best path in order to give back in some way.

I had been taught by the Dominican sisters, and as I was exploring religious life, it was the group that I resonated with the most. I saw the Dominican sisters as a group of individuals who were distinct from one another, and who used their particular gifts and talents in ways that seemed true to each of them. I felt much more comfortable with groups where individuals could be themselves, as opposed to a group that appeared to be very similar one to another. That didn't strike any chord of connection for me, so I moved ahead and met with the sister in charge in San Rafael. She took me on a visit to the novitiate, and I chose to try Dominican life, entering the convent soon thereafter.

I wanted to be a teacher, which was a predominant ministry for the San Rafael Dominicans at that time and I was able to earn my credential and started teaching elementary school. Later I was asked to consider an administrative position, which I agreed to, and was sent to study for an administrative credential. I moved into a principalship for our elementary school, and after a period of time I became principal of our high school, and then the head of school. In between administrative positions I was engaged in other ministries. I worked for a time at our hospital in Stockton, in the social service department. At Dominican Convent in San Rafael I initiated a development program for the sisters to raise funds for a new wing to our sisters' infirmary.

In response to your question about wearing the Dominican habit, I love to wear it–some days at school, and at formal and some public occasions where I represent the Dominican Sisters of San Rafael. I often wear the habit when I attend funerals of our graduates or of parents. However, originally, the white robes and black veil were the dress of the 13th century, when St. Dominic founded the order. Today we choose to wear the dress of our time and convey our desire to be one with our communities rather than individuals set apart from the community.

I have a group of eight advisees in the high school, and we meet every week. They're great because they ask all the questions: "How come you wear your habit sometimes, and don't wear your habit other times? How come some sisters wear short, simple veils, and some wear longer veils?" They invite the dialogue, which provides the opportunity for deeper conversation and explanation. I think it says something to them about being part of our Dominican community.

Being Part of San Domenico School

The school was founded in 1850, in Monterey, by Mother Mary Goemaere, a Dominican Sister from Paris. She was an outsider, if you will, coming into a community that was quite diverse in Monterey at that particular time. She established a classical education program for young girls. There were the daughters of the Spaniards in the Presidio; there were the daughters of ranchers from Santa Clara and Livermore Valleys; there were the Native American children attending. Students from all faiths were welcome, as they are today.

Young women weren't formally educated at that particular time. It was the young men who went off to school, and the young women learned to cook and to sew at home. Educating young women was one revolutionary aspect of the school and the other was that it was not restricted to Catholic children only. As the school moved over the years, from Monterey to Benicia, to San Rafael and now at San Anselmo, it remained all girls until 1973 when boys were included. We started with three and four-year-olds coming to the newly established Early Education Program. Now boys attend Pre-K though eighth grade. The high school continues its enriching programs for young women only.

I think what is most important for me about the school is that students at every level still learn how to tap into their own talents and resources, to recognize God's presence in themselves and in all of creation, to become their own best persons, meeting the challenges of the academic programs and addressing the critical issues of our times. As a Catholic school and as a Dominican school, the additional piece that we offer our students is the ability to explore the spiritual in their lives and in the world around them. We provide opportunities for dialogue, to question, to search, and to seek truth.

By the time students are ready to graduate from the high school, they have become very articulate young women. They have learned to study and to grapple with issues, to make choices and to be grounded in values so that they can move on to a college or university and be able to build communities wherever they live.

I have a great sense of hope in the recent graduates and in the generation coming up. They see the world and troubling situations across the globe, and they are willing to take risks, to go out and stand up for what they believe is right and to speak out against what they believe is wrong.

One of today's issues that I think is most critical is that of sustainability. Our mission as Dominicans and as an educational institution is to address the care of the earth and all who inhabit it. We ask, "How do we live in a world today where our planet is deteriorating rather than becoming healthier? How can we care for the earth so that it will be healthy for future generations? What can we do as an institution to respond to what we learn?"

Our Sustainability Program addresses the issues of food, transportation, recycling, use and reuse of materials, etc. and it works to integrate issues into the curriculum and into practices across the campus. Our children are bussed to school so that we reduce traffic and automobile emissions. We have an artesian well from which we pipe some of the water into holding tanks for watering landscaped areas. We have cut down on the use of electricity by installing compact fluorescent lighting across the campus. We've replaced some lawns with mulch and we involve the children in that process. Hands on activities are the primary ways for us to grasp the philosophy. Vegetables and fruit from the garden may be used in our dining room or shared in the community. Third graders grow daffodils to deliver to the Dominican Sisters in our infirmary and to other sites as well.

Finding Strength in Nature

The campus' natural surroundings, which reflect God's brilliant creativity fill my soul with gratitude and renew my spirit each day. The birds and animals on campus, at night time as well as during the day, reflect the awesomeness of God and make God's presence very real for me. There's a cycle of living and breathing, of death and new life, of drinking in and giving out, which shows us what our lives are about as well. I believe that we, as very conscious beings, can be inspired by what we experience around us, and can therefore very consciously respond by giving back to our world. If, for example, I stop and notice the redwood trees, I am reminded that their roots stretch down deep through the soil to find water. If I also go deep I can renew myself, readied to return to whatever I have to face. I believe the Creator has given these gifts to us to notice and to share, to learn from and most importantly to pass on.

We had Julia Butterfly Hill as our graduation speaker in June 2002. She described the two years and eight days she spent up in the redwood tree, as a deeply transforming time. Often she thought she just couldn't last one day longer, especially when the frostbite on her toes and fingers was terribly painful, or when the freezing winds chilled her to the core. She prayed very seriously and her strength returned when she went deep, deep down inside herself. She assured the graduates they, too, will gain strength and courage in life when they believe and keep drawing upon the God-given resources deep within themselves.

Creating Paths for Women in the Catholic Church

As far as dealing with the Catholic church and how it has not yet welcomed women for ordination and leadership positions in the church, the way I live with it is to read about it, dialogue with colleagues about it, and engage in the conversation with students. Obviously, within the Dominican sister community we dialogue about it often. Here at San Domenico, we prepare our students, Catholic and not, to be very articulate about issues and concerns so that they can speak out about them to the various groups or communities in which they live—readying them for possibilities of leadership in the future, too.

I believe there will be a time when women will be invited to ordination, and we need to be ready for it. We have sisters who are educated for it and are indeed ready. I'm not someone who is wishing to be ordained, but I support women's participation in whatever ways they can be involved now. And I think it's desperately needed within the Catholic church for women to be welcomed to leadership positions. Currently, the balance of men and women is not there. I believe the time will come, and I have to be respectful of the situation in the interim.

In the Mass, part of the ritual includes, after Scripture readings, a homily or reflection on the Old Testament or New Testament. Currently in the Catholic church, only priests or male deacons present a homily. However, it is allowable for women to give a reflection on the readings at some other time during the Mass. Some women accept that opportunity and our young women students at school, our liturgy classes and campus ministry program guided to be very articulate in sharing how Script readings connect with their lives. So, in the liturgy, in the Mass, there are opportunities for our students, for our faculty members, and for the Dominican sisters to participate minimally.

Additionally, at funerals or vigil services, sisters will share reflections about the individual whose life is being celebrated. We've had some lovely experiences, one here on this campus with one of our sisters who was dying. I have had the opportunity of joining our chaplain in offering a service with the family and friends of one of our parents who was dying. We read scripture and then invited the assembled group to share reflections about the readings and/or about the individual.

They were powerful religious experiences, where faith in their Creator, their God, and in the afterlife was spoken with a truly deep understanding and readiness for acceptance of death. We do participate in those ways, as well as in prayer services here on campus for various occasions.

We create the prayer services with the students for AIDS Awareness Day, or World Hunger Day, World Day of Peace, etc. We also offer what in the Catholic church was called the sacrament of Penance, now called the sacrament of Reconciliation. We have had a Jewish rabbi, a Lutheran pastor, and an Episcopal priest join our Catholic chaplain to offer the sacrament or experiences for reconciliation in different forms. Students speak with one of these church representatives, men or women, and ask for a blessing for some transformation in their lives.

History

Hospitals and schools were needed in the early years of the state of California, and the Dominican sisters staffed and administered those institutions. We continue in those ministries to a lesser degree today, moving into other relevant areas of serious need such as working with the elderly, young adults, with the imprisoned and the poor, and in social justice issues. Our Mission states that we address the needs and "critical issues of our times"—allowing us flexibility.

The Importance of Women's Leadership

I think it's extremely important for women to serve in leadership positions, and I'm pleased to see in the civil government that more and more women are seeking elected positions in the Senate and the House and locally. As I mentioned earlier, our Dominican sisters are more involved civically, too, particularly in the area of social justice—in prison ministry and reform, here in Marin and elsewhere, and working on affordable housing committees, etc.

In terms of women's leadership there needs to be a balance of women and men in all social structures, just as there needs to be the masculine and feminine operative in each of us. When women are kept down and their voices are not heard, that balance doesn't exist. Those men and women who understand its value invite the other to share in leadership. I think the communities that don't comprehend its value lose out because the shared perspectives are absent.

I think some of the specific qualities that women bring to leadership are the capacities to listen, to be inclusive, to be patient, and to work collaboratively. I think women also really possess a sense of justice. It's so important to them that there be justice in their families, in their communities, and in the world. Advancements for justice are happening around the world where women come together and work for change. I think change is difficult for all of us, but there is genuine power when women join together for change. I am very hopeful about the future, because I see how our young women are being educated and readied for leadership in all facets of life.

Gratitude for My Life

I love what I'm doing and I'm most grateful for my education, life experiences and opportunities to minister through leadership positions. I appreciate the people with whom I work. Everything isn't perfect, and when we have differences of opinion we grapple with issues, which is typical of Dominicans. We dialogue and resolve issues. We have reached deeper for understanding, to refine what we believe and to seek truth in and with one another. For Dominicans, study, prayer and action are critically important in this process. This cycle is life-giving.

I'm grateful to God for family, and for mentors and friends within and outside our congregation of Dominican sisters. For students and colleagues, from whom I learn volumes each day, I'm also most appreciative.

Sister Gervaise Valpey recently retired as principal of San Domenico School in Marin County. She now serves as their Director of Development.

Sara Vurek Story

MERGING TRADITIONS

The Evolution of a Call

I didn't go to seminary until I was thirty-nine, but I guess I would say that I've recognized myself on a spiritual path ever since I was in high school, but not ever, ever thought of being a minister. I was brought up in the Presbyterian church and decided pretty early on that they had it wrong; that their interpretation of Jesus was not correct, so I left the church and studied lots of different traditions, Hindu and Buddhism and native American and Judaism. Never really settled on anything, but it was in the seventies and I was looking, like everybody else.

Then I got married to my high school sweetheart, had two children, and my spiritual path became raising my children. As they got older, I knew that I wanted to do something more with my life. I had been involved in an intense meditation practice group for about six or seven years, and that had helped me clarify my own spiritual path. I had become involved in the Methodist church when I lived in Napa, because it was a very socially active church, and I was involved in all kinds of social action and justice things.

When I started thinking about what else I wanted to do, I thought of about ten different careers, considered them seriously, including social work and teaching. Then people started telling me, "Why don't you think about being a minister," or, "Have you ever thought about that?" And I just said, "No, no, no, no. My theology is too radical. Nobody would want me to be a minister in a church."

Anyway, I finally went to a workshop called Companions on the Inner Way, which was offered at San Francisco Theological Seminary. At that workshop, which was put on at a seminary, they had weird meditation, which I loved, and they had chanting, and they had movement, and they had all these things in the context of the church, and I thought, "Oh, maybe there is a place for me after all." And as soon as I came to that, it was "Okay, I can do this."

And I didn't think I'd be in a church. I thought I would be doing something outside of a church in a community organization. But I did my internship in this church. I was a member in this church during my seminary time, and I thought, "Okay, this church I could be in. There aren't many, but this one I could be in."

Then, right after I graduated from seminary, the minister who had been here retired, and so the church went through a long, a two-year-long search process. It was absolutely a full-on national search process, and I had the wonderful fortune of being called here.

Using Other Traditions

This church is hungry for a variety of wisdom from lots of different spiritual traditions. It's not a traditional church. They have been very open. I'm a very creative person, and one thing that that means is that I can't do one thing the same way twice, because I need to be creative when I do things, and they're fine with that. I have been able to use lots and lots of things, drumming, and chanting, and bringing in a lot of other traditions.

I have been interested in Buddhism for many years, and have done a lot of study of Thich Nhat Hanh and his work, have been to a number of retreats with him and have used a lot of his material here. I've got pictures of him on my wall, I've got a picture of him on my desk. He's very much a guide for me.

He's a Vietnamese Zen, but he's very not traditional Vietnamese Zen. He's very much into engaged Buddhism, action in the world, and he is very dedicated to peace, to creating peace and finding ways to do that. He's written books on Jesus and Buddha together as brothers. So I have learned more about my faith from a Buddhist, almost, than I have from almost anybody else. He's got some very wonderful insights into Jesus, not as a Buddhist, but Jesus wasn't a Christian either, so Jesus as a meditator and as someone who was very mindful and conscious. Thich Nhat Hanh's main theme is mindfulness and being very conscious of where we are.

About three years ago I got introduced to Tibetan Buddhism, and have found another home in Buddhism for me. As I look at what the teachings of the Buddha are, it gives me new insight into what Jesus said and what he taught. It gives me new ways to look at it, and I do not see any conflict; I see a blending, an amazing illumination of the Bible from the teachings of the Buddha in the ways that I have been studying him in the Tibetan tradition. It's been really wonderful for me to be able to, in this church, share what I've been studying and some of my insights in the Buddhist tradition and not have people think I was being non-Christian.

I've used Thich Nhat Hanh's prayers often. When I am writing my reflection, which is what we call the sermon, I will often turn to Buddhist writers to get more illumination on what I'm talking about. I recently did a sermon on anger, which I feel is something that we have to address in ourselves in order for us to be able to have a more peaceful world. Thich Nhat Hanh has recently written a book called Anger, and I did my sermon based on his book and Jesus' teachings. They go hand in hand, I think.

The last Sunday of each month is a contemplative service, and in that service we have readings and we have chanting and we have prayer time and we have healing. This is a hands-on healing component. That is one of the places where often we'll have readings from other traditions. We do chants with drum and often I accompany. They just are incorporated into the worship.

One of the other places where we express some of the differences that you would find here from other places, is on our altars. The practice of inspirational altars has been here for a while, but I have expanded the joy of creating beautiful altars. We don't just have a table with two candles and a Bible, or whatever other people have. We have a whole closetful of beautiful cloths and candles and candleholders and objects and baskets. We have people sign up to create altars, and we have the most incredible, beautiful altars. And I feel like bringing beauty into worship is really, really important. It helps us be in touch with the divine.

I had a sense when I came here that there was a little remnant the aesthetic of the Congregationalist, the Pilgrims, the Puritans. It really wasn't really a beautiful worship space. We've completely remodeled the worship space and it's now very beautiful, and bringing the beautiful altars in has been something that I have felt was important. You might find a Kwan Yin on the altar, or you might find a little Buddha, or you might find a picture of a woman in Guatemala. I try to have the altar tied in with whatever the theme for worship that day is. We bring in lots of different things on the altar. One of the ways that some of the richness and diversity comes in is visually in the altar.

I do feel that the attitude toward beauty is a feminine piece that I have brought here that wasn't here before. It's okay to have beauty in worship, and, in fact, it's great to have beauty. I don't think it's something that the men ever thought about.

I know a certain amount of the beauty and the Buddhism and the other traditions is going on in many people's lives and certainly in the private lives of most of the women pastors I've talked to. They study this, they think about this. But I can't think of anybody who is as up front or as integrated in their actual services with it. That's why this feels like such a fabulous match. I feel extremely fortunate that I can do this; I can share all kinds of things with them, and they are ready for more. It's great.

Being A Doula

Being at this church allows me to have a dual career. I am also a doula. Twenty-six years ago this August, I attended my first birth as a labor companion with someone, and I was hooked, totally hooked. And about a year later I had my first child and I went into training to be a childbirth educator, so I would teach Lamaze classes. In the course of doing that, I had the opportunity to attend births with women. I would always tell them, "If you need help, just call me. I'll be there." And they would.

Then gradually I got into doing private companion labor work, which meant that I would contract with someone to be with them at their birth. What that means is that you have to be available two weeks before and two after their due date.

I did that for a long time, and fortunately I have a very wonderful husband and he was very supportive. I went to a lot of births. I worked with a midwife for a while and attended home births with her, and it became a really important part of my life. I don't do home births anymore but work in hospitals.

The term doula is fairly new; we used to say labor companion or labor coach. Doula is a Greek word which means roughly servant or slave. But it was chosen because it can also have the meaning of handmaiden, and we are there to serve the laboring couple.

When I moved to this county and was in seminary, but before I had been called to this church, I discovered an association of women who were doing this work in a way that we could actually have a life. We have a call schedule. Each of is on call for twenty-four hours three or four times a month. So if somebody goes into labor on your day, then you go and be with them.

So I got hooked in with them, and when I came to this church I didn't want to quit that work. It's very spiritual work, and I really felt like it would enhance my work here. I'm always finding ways of being in touch with the sacred, and I have bazillions of ways of doing that, but going to births is a really great way for me to be in touch with the sacred. So I felt like that would be helpful for my work here.

But I also felt like it would be an outreach of the church, not overtly, although I don't hide the fact that I'm a minister, but I don't go in and say, well, "I'm a minister." I don't wear my minister hat when I'm there, but I hold a spiritual place, hold a spiritual atmosphere there. So I said to the church, "I want this written into my contract, that this is part of what I do here. It's part of my call and I want the church to support that."

And they said, "Okay." So it's written into my contract that I can do this work, and it's been fabulous. I bring stories of births into my reflection and I learn something. Every single birth I go to, I learn something new, not just about the process of labor and delivery, but about people and myself and life.

What I do is go and be a nonanxious presence. I don't know if you've heard that term before, but that's really what it's about. It's two things. I'm experienced, I have been to 150 births, so I've seen a lot. And there's a huge range of what's normal, so I'm there to say, "You know what? I know this is strange and intense and big, but it's normal what you're going through." The fact that I have lots of experience is helpful to people.

So I'm experienced and I'm nonanxious. That's our job. We are there to serve. Currently these births are all at Marin General Hospital, and the hospital loves having us there. They absolutely love it.

Sara Vurek is pastor of Fairfax Community Church in Marin County.

Jan West Story

EPISCOPAL PRIEST

Getting The Call

Why did I decide to become a priest? In one sense, I can say I didn't decide, that I felt it was God's decision. I felt it as a call, in a way to serve God, a different way to serve God than I had before. Prior to this vocation I was a homemaker, and I felt every bit as called to homemaking, being a wife and mother.

I had grown up in the church and done almost everything at that point that a woman could do, and was teaching some classes, particularly a class called Exploring Ministry. I was trying to help other people discover their ministries, and all of a sudden I began to feel very strange. I was crying all the time. I felt like I'd been thrown in a Cuisinart, couldn't figure out what was going on with me. It was my husband who said one morning, "I know what's wrong with you." And I said, "What?" And he said, "I think you want to be a priest." And I said, "Don't ever say that again."

I had been vehemently opposed to women in the priesthood. I was darn right nasty. I carried placards; I did a number of things. I had no rhyme nor reason, I mean, I couldn't find anything scripturally. I just had grown up in the church and there was always a man up there, dressed in black, and that's the way it was. Also, I'd met some women early on who'd come in the church, and I felt they were very, understandably, pushy, and just distasteful. So I thought, "I don't want those people pushing in here." And then when it happened to me, I thought, "There's something wrong with this picture." And I decided not to think about it again.

And then one by one, my friends began to say to me, "When are you going to become a priest?" And I said, "Don't say that again, ever." But the seed was planted. I tried not to think about it, and found that I couldn't think about anything else, and decided that I would spend a whole year trying to figure out why it was wrong, why it wouldn't work. So I did.

I took a legal pad, a yellow legal pad. I divided it, and on this side I put the reasons why I should, the reasons that I thought validated what I thought might be a call. And on the other side, I wrote everything in the world that was wrong with it: I was too old, I was forty-seven at the time, I was too old; I didn't want to go back to school. I went to college for two reasons: one was to get married and one was to have fun, and I did both, and thank God I got a degree on the side. But I didn't want to go back to school at that age. What would happen to my marriage? What would happen to our social life?

So I spent a whole year, and I came up with pages and pages of reasons why I should not do it. Would we have to move? My husband was in business in the city. I had only one thing on this side, and that was, "I feel called to the priesthood." So I also thought, "Well, what else could I do at forty-seven?" Obviously I was heading on to a new career. I could become a doctor. No, I don't do blood, messes, and so I couldn't do that. I could become a lawyer, but I wasn't interested in law.

The one thing I thought I could do, and I had other friends who were doing it, was I could go to Dominican College and get a degree in psychology and go on for my MFCC. That seemed like it would work, but it didn't interest me. So finally I thought, "Well, you know, it's not going to go away. It's not going to go away." And I thought, "God, if I've spent a whole year and God hasn't gone away, and neither has that feeling, that call, then I guess this is right." So I did it, and I was forty-eight when I went to seminary. My husband had two kids in college, our daughter and his wife, at the same time.

Women Ministers

Women who have been mothers bring a whole new attitude, and, I think, richness, to the ministry. Women have issues that men don't know about. They can't. And now there's somebody to go to, and talk to them. We've started here, as I know many Episcopal churches have, services for families, young families. And it's very inviting to have a woman on the staff for these young families. There's just a whole different sense of working, you know. It's not a power play. There's just, I think, more of a sense of "Let's work together and see how we can make this work," that the women bring.

What we're up against is patriarchy and hierarchy, and I don't think, generally speaking, that women are interested in hierarchy. We're interested much more in a team effort, a sense of mutuality, and I think it works better. I think it's a much more effective way of working with people.

The role of women in the churches is long in coming. I was born into the church, born into the faith, and I worshiped in this place when I couldn't sing in the choir because I wasn't a boy. I worshiped in this place when I couldn't carry the cross, or I couldn't be an acolyte, because I wasn't a boy. I attended Roman Catholic schools as a leader in those schools, when I couldn't receive communion because I wasn't a Catholic. And I think that's an injustice to God. I think the God we believe in is an inclusive God. For me, it's Jesus who shows that, who lives that, and I think that it's an uphill battle for women, still, in the church.

Retreats

I grew up an Episcopalian, but went many years to Catholic schools, and I went to Dominican convent in San Rafael. Every year we had a silent retreat for three days, and the Protestants could be excused if they wanted to be. And I didn't. I just loved it. I fell in love with making retreats when I was at the convent. I started telling people that I was interested in working retreats, and began to develop retreats for women, although for years I did the Advent retreat here, and the parish retreat, which is, of course, men and women.

But I really got into doing retreats for women. I took biblical characters, women, of course, and developed them, and put my imagination into it. I reversed the parable of the prodigal son to the parable of the prodigal daughter. I did another one called "Mary, Martha, and Me." I dramatized it. I'm a ham, you know. My grandparents were actors, and I loved to do that. I wrote the meditations so that I became Martha, spoke first-person, and I dressed like I thought Martha dressed. The same thing with Mary, and then applied it to myself as a twenty-first century woman. Then I was asked to do that by several different churches, for women's groups in churches.

The goal of the retreats was to help women see all sides of themselves. What I have heard most oftentimes is, "Well, I'm a Mary," or, "I'm a Martha." And particularly with women, "I'm a Martha," because Martha was the one in the kitchen, mad at Mary because Mary was sitting at the feet of Jesus. And so, "I'm just the Martha," women seeing themselves as the laborers, as the chief cook and bottle washer, rather than seeing that side of Mary, of the one who was in touch more overtly with her spiritual side, sitting at the feet of Jesus. And we are not, really, all Mary or all Martha; we're a combination of both. Maybe some of us have more Martha in us, or some more Mary, but the ideal feminine would be a balance between the Martha and the Mary.

Faith As A Need To Do

When I was going through the process for ordination, they're continually saying to you, "So, what are you going to do when you get out?" And I said, "Well, I'll go to work in a parish." And one of the questions to me early on was, "Coming from Marin County, how do you think you could ever go down south of Market Street and work in a church down there?" And I said, "Well, if that's where I end up, I would hope and expect that the people there would help me learn how to minister there." Never having a clue that I would end up in social justice ministry.

I had volunteered at the Canal ministry. The executive director said, "Why don't you come on over and hang your hat here." And so I did part-time there and part-time here, and realized that I was really being called over there, which was never, ever in my agenda. And it's funny, you know, when you let God mess with your life, where you find yourself sometimes. And I loved it. I absolutely loved it, and I felt that I could bring that here, and to try and afflict the comfortable, because, you know, we're called to comfort the afflicted, and afflict the comfortable. And I take that challenge.

We live in a very comfortable place, most of us. It's one of the wealthiest counties in the country. Oftentimes, when you have so much materially, you don't realize what you don't have. It's much easier to turn to God, I think, in times of pain and suffering. Everything is going along okay and you think you've got everything you need. Why would I need God? Why would I need to go to church?

So for me, it's a real challenge to try to help people find out what they're missing. This is where my experience with the Canal ministry is so helpful to me. Because I know that despite the wealth, despite the materialism in here, we have people who aren't making it. We have immigrants and refugees who want to go home. We have a lot of very poor. We have a lot of homeless.

And to me, the richness of our faith is, what are we going to do about it? Are we just going to sit and go to church every Sunday? Or are we going to realize what the gospel means? Because to me the gospel is a gospel of comfort, which indeed it is. You know, where is God? God's right here. But it's a gospel of challenge, too. Get out there and do something about it. Life is not okay in this county. Life is not okay in the world, and what are we going to do about it? How are we going to live it out? So I feel, because of my experience with social justice ministry, I am a thorn in the side of the church. And that's okay.

Liturgy

One great challenge is changing the exclusive language used in the church. It will take clergy who are totally committed to it. If you don't have your leadership passionate about it, it won't happen. You have to have clergy who are committed to it and who are willing to take the risk, to make a change and perhaps be unpopular.

Some people will squeal. Bob and I have made changes here, in the nine months that we've been working together, and we had a lot of squealing. And you deal with the squeals. You address them, and you invite people to come into your office and talk about it. You explain to them why you're making the change. We were using the 1928 prayer book here for years, and that's the really old one, and it's totally exclusive language. It's talks about a very judgmental God, and there are lots of reasons why the church changed from the 1928 prayer book to the 1979 prayer book.

There was a service using the 1928 prayer book. When Bob and I came in, we stopped the service, and we explained why. This isn't the kind of God that we worship. It's not an exclusive God. When we use exclusive language, we're picturing an exclusive God, and that's not the kind of God we believe in. Some people grumbled and growled for a while, and then we said, "Come on in and let's talk about it." And we did, and they haven't left. I think you have to have your leadership committed to it, passionate about it, and it's all in how you go about it, and time. Time.

So what I have been able to do, but not on Sundays, is I do liturgy with the women of the parish. I do liturgies that are printed in inclusive language, but also I do spontaneous liturgy, taking the essence of what's in the prayer book, but just speaking it in terms that are much more intimate, heart terms, not head terms. Heart terms, not head terms. That makes it so much more appealing and important, and they like it. It's so much more meaningful to them. But I can't do it at the regular services.

There is a blessing that the priest does at the very end of the service which is very formal. It's very Anglican, it's historical, and it's in the name of the Trinity, that goes like, "The peace of God, which surpasses all understanding, keep your hearts and minds in the knowledge and love of God, and of God's son, Jesus Christ. And may the blessing of God almighty, Father, Son, and Holy Spirit be with you, now and always." I don't use that one.

I use one that was found it on the wall of a little village church in England. It goes, "Life is short. We don't have very much time to gladden the hearts of those who walk the journey with us. So be swift to love. Make haste to be kind, and as we walk along the way together, may the blessing, the peace, the love, and the joy of the Holy One in our midst continue to be in our hearts, this day and always." The congregation loves it, and they have said, "It's so meaningful to us."

Place Of Religion

I feel sorry for people who aren't grounded in something, in some kind of faith, knowing that there is something more than just what's going on in this world, and I ache for the children who don't learn that. I think it's a travesty of justice for parents not to give that to their children. Now you know my bias.

Religion, to me—and in that I include spirituality—are vital to life. Not only do they give us the reason for life, but they give us a value system. They give us expectations, as far as compassion, forgiveness, mercy, justice. And to me, if the world had more of that, the world wouldn't be in the mess that it's in now. If we adults don't take that seriously, and if we're not passionate about our belief in those things that I just said, and if we don't instill those in our children, then where's the hope in the world?

I mean, I can't go out and save Afghanistan, but what I can do is hopefully raise my children and help other people to raise their children with a sense of values that lead to people loving each other, and not hating each other, to helping people open to having their lives transformed and not be stuck in the same situation of materialism all the rest of their lives. It gives us hope.

Faith involves contemplation, which is that personal relationship with God. I have to have that. But that's not all there is. It's not enough to love God. It's not enough to love Jesus the Christ. It's how that love translates into trying to make a difference in the world. In trying to help the world. It's helping the world to transform into what in Christianity is called the kingdom of God. That's what I like to say is the way God wants the world to be, and that is that God, love, compassion, justice, mercy, be at the center of our lives, and not ourselves.

I deal with people coming into this office day after day after day with the same question, and that is, "Where is the hope?" Well, if the hope isn't in our faith in a higher being, whom I call God, or the holy one in our midst, if the hope isn't there and then consequently because of that, with us and the little bit we can do, where is it?

So I just think that's where our responsibility is, particularly to the children, to our children, is to give them faith. And we must be examples if they are going to see it. I think that's the hope in an absolutely devastating world.

Jan West is currently serving at St. John's Episcopal Church in Marin County.

Denise Wylie Story

AMERICAN BAPTIST

Seeing Women In The Image Of God

I think it's critically important that we know God. The only way we can really know God is through those of us who were made in the image of God, and the way that most people connect is through experiences they've had with people. And if women are not seen as role models in the image of God, then we really have a limited understanding of who God is and who God can be, and how God can relate to each one of us and how God chooses to relate to us. There are a number of scriptures that talk about God as Mother, the mother eagle protecting her young, and the mother bear. There are several of those, but they're not the ones that are usually used in sermons.

There are amazing opportunities to talk about women with people. There was a man who didn't think women should be ordained. He came to my house and sat in a chair, knee-to-knee with me, and told me all the reasons why he didn't think that I should be ordained. And, I just got to love him and say, "Well, I'm sorry that your image of God is so limited, but let me share some things with you." I was able to process that with him and do it in a loving way so I'm not hitting heads with him and not fighting with him and not trying to argue my point. But I just say, "Well, let me just share some things with you for you to consider." God can use that to open up people's minds and hearts.

I don't think that in most circumstances, being strident and argumentative is helpful. I was around women that were in that place, and they turned me off, even though I agreed with what they were fighting for. It was not attractive in any way. If we're going to change people's hearts and minds about the place of women as spiritual leaders we have to model what we're talking about, that our spirituality is making a difference in our life and that we can come in an attitude of peace and love, because our actions speak louder than our words.

As a young girl it would have been helpful to see other females in leadership roles that were being affirmed and honored and respected. The women in the church that I grew up in were incredibly deep women that had a lot of spiritual connectedness, had a deep knowledge of the Bible, were very faithful, and worked extremely hard at all the things that they did. They were seen as second-class saints. But I have to say that there were a number of those women who made a huge impact on me from a spiritual perspective and who helped me on my own spiritual journey.

I later learned, when I came to seminary, that many of them were graduates of that seminary, but because of the time when they graduated, they didn't go on for ordination. They had the education and they were using it, and they were nurturing other people and helping them to grow in their faith, and I was a product of that.

Now I get to be a role model, a few weeks ago I preached, and we had a number of visitors who were in from out of town for a wedding, and three of them came up to me later and said, "I've never heard a woman preach before." They had always gone to churches that didn't affirm women preaching, and for them hearing me was a big step in their whole image of "Oh, what can this look like? How can God relate to me?"

Finding A Vocation

I had two careers before I went to seminary, so it wasn't my first career, but it certainly was my vocation. I did the other jobs and loved what I was doing, but really always kept a balance with what I was doing in and through the church.

I taught junior high home economics. I had always wanted to be Betty Crocker. Then I got a job working for a department store chain, planning all their menus and all their special events and catering events. After that I was in charge of all the restaurants gourmet food areas for a department store chain. I loved it. We had to eat chocolate and drink wine for part of the job. But it was also stressful, and the role of that position changed over the years. The bottom line became more and more important, and customer service became less and less important in the eyes of the corporate structure. The stress level skyrocketed.

Being involved in the things I was doing at the church were what kept me sane. It maintained a good balance in my life and it gave me a community to help me keep my values in a place that I felt comfortable with them being. It would have been hard to be in that corporate structure, especially in a retail environment where there were people with slimy morals. There were many opportunities to sell out, one way or another, and having a community that would hold me accountable for not doing that, and with whom I could process the struggle and the grief and the frustrations was very, very helpful.

I was ready to leave the corporate structure that I was in and knew that I didn't want to just go back into something that was the same. I went to a career counselor and processed what my gifts were, what my abilities were, what my personality was and how that all might fit with different kinds of jobs. I interviewed a lot of different people, looking at things that were not church-related, saying, "How can I use all the things that I love doing in the church in a secular setting, and helping people?"

I came to see that I always have been in ministry since I was really a young child. My mother was a Christian educator. She had some special training and had planned to be a missionary. So when she went around and taught other people how to teach Sunday school during the Sunday school boom of the fifties with the baby boom, she would always take me as part of a group of guinea pig kids that were in the class to demonstrate on.

Also before I went to seminary I was involved with helping other people who were lay people who were not ordained, to see that they had gifts for ministry and to help them to use those gifts. I felt strongly about that, that you didn't need to be ordained, you didn't need to be a pastor to be able to be in that kind of an encouraging role for other people, a teaching role, a training role. I did that throughout my life, and was involved in a number of aspects of doing that. It was my passion.

But it just kept coming back to me that this was where I fit. I was encouraged to go to seminary by people that were leaders in my church, my pastor and the person that was leading the small Sunday school group that I was in. I got a lot of affirmation from them, and decided that it was the next right step. I believe that God had been leading me in the kinds of things that I'd been doing. I had lead a number of women's retreats and was their main speaker, and planned the curricula and the content of the retreat.

I was very, very fortunate and blessed to be in situations where people recognized there was something in me and that they wanted to nurture that. I had a lot of people who would mentor me, or would open doors for me to have opportunities for training or opportunities to use the training afterwards. So it was a series of things. I saw how God's hand was at work in preparing me to be in this place at this time.

Helping People Help Themselves

I was at two other churches before I came to the Hillside Church of Marin. This actually feels like home to me. It has been a very comfortable place for me to do ministry. There are people struggling with the kinds of things I struggled with in the corporate world and trying to keep values in place for their families, and raise their children with a love for God and a knowledge of the Bible.

In our church people that are used to a traditional church wouldn't be any more at home or not at home than somebody who'd never walked into a church in their life. We don't do anything that's in a normal liturgical setting. We have developed our own liturgy. The music is upbeat. It's got a little jazzy edge to it and would be a comfortable music setting for most folks that listen to popular music today. The messages are very informal and they're always is an aspect of life application to it, so it's more "How does this affect me?" I preached last week, and the message was about friendship, and there certainly was scriptural basis for that.

One of the things that we do is a program called Alpha which is a short course in basic Christian theology. It's a ten-week course with a weekend retreat about two-thirds of the way through that goes through the basics of the Christian faith. It's designed for people who don't know anything about it, want to know about it, are questioning a faith that maybe they grew up with and want to own it for themselves, or people that are doubters and say, "You know, I'm not buying it. You better prove it to me."

We do three courses a year, and we've been doing it for about four years. And we have found that that has been a really important entrée point for a lot of folks in Marin. They are surrounded by all this talk of spiritual things, but there's not a lot of meat to it. So they get to a point in their life they say, "I really want to look into this." Or a friend says, "You know, this is really interesting. You might come check it out." They may not buy everything that they hear. They may still have some questions. But it helps them to process their questions in a safe place where they're not put down for any questions they want to ask.

Often folks will start to come on Sunday mornings as well, and they'll make friends and they'll become enfolded, and really feel a part of this community. Even if they haven't figured out all of the details of where they are theologically, they know this is a place that feels like a good place to be, and there're people that care about them here.

The other place we have noticed a lot of people coming to our church is through our children's program. Even if people aren't real clear on what they want in their life or they won't make time for it, they care that their children have some opportunity to explore. I have a number of people who drive up, and don't come themselves, but will drop their children off every week. Then over time they will get to know other parents from school who will invite them to something. They will come and start being part of the community, and then discover their own faith journey.

People in Marin are high achievers, they're overachievers, they tend to be, and they're very hard on themselves and they expect huge things from themselves. The women especially are in that place. They may have had a very high-level corporate job where they were really, really pushing, and they've taken some time off to raise their kids through a certain stage, and they are just as hard on themselves at home as they ever were when they were in the corporate world. They have the same high standards and they work hard at everything, and they want their children to have the best and to be the best.

That high expectation causes a huge amount of stress in all these people's lives. We see our role in this community as being a place of grace, and that theological issue of grace is a huge, huge component of what we are and what we do here. We see grace as being hugely important. We aren't afraid to call sin, sin, and we aren't afraid to confront somebody if that needs to happen, but it always happens in a context of grace where you're being surrounded by a loving group of people.

Maintaining Spiritual Health

As a pastor I need to work to maintain my spiritual health so that I can give people in the congregation what they need. Staying spiritually healthy is multi-faceted. Music is really important to me. I listen to music a lot, and I used to be a singer. I grew up singing and was always in choirs so a lot of my faith has had a musical component to it, and so that's still an important part for me. At times I'll just sit and sing through a songbook or a hymnal. The music comes first, and then the silence, the listening.

I've found that I'm one of those people that likes a variety of style. I know there are some people who are more introverted in the way that they connect with God, and others that really like to be out in a group and worshiping in a big group and a lot of noise. I tend to like all of them, and they all are important to me, and I like to have some of each in my life. Scott and I try and get over quarterly to walk the labyrinth on the nights that they have Taice at Grace Cathedral. That's something that we have benefited from, and love doing.

I need to have time alone, time for God to speak to me, for me to be in a listening place. How that looks varies. Sometimes it's taking a walk, and sometimes it's sitting quietly. It doesn't always look the same, but I need some downtime where I can be listening, where the TV and the radio and the CD player are not on, and I'm not processing content, but just have some time. One of the best places for me to do that is by the ocean. Water is one of those places that is very renewing for me.

Finally, I need to be in a community of faith, a small group of friends, that I can be honest with and that will hold me accountable and that will challenge me and that will keep me honest in my faith journey, that don't let me slide. It's important to be in a group of peers who can challenge me and say, "You know, are you really doing what you need to be doing?" and, "I'm noticing this in your life."

My husband does a little bit of that for me. He's very perceptive and he's trained as a spiritual director. Sometimes he'll ask a real pertinent question and it's exactly what God would have me process, and I'll have to take some time and go off and chew on that a little bit, and say, "Well, I don't know. I mean, let me see how that works."

Denise Wylie serves as a minister at Hillside Church of Marin in Marin County.

Allen Yan-Chamberlin Story

METHODIST MINISTER

First Part

My dad always said, "I would like to send my kids off to the States and pursue advanced education." I'm the third in the family. My sister came to the United States and then my brother. He sponsored my two aunts first, and they were the ones who paved the way. After my dad passed away, I decided I'm going to come and visit my family in the United States. So I came to visit and see how the U.S. looks. And then there are opportunities for me, so I decided to stay. I stayed, thinking that I'm going to just pursue my Christian education for two years.

I'm Chinese by ancestry, and grew up in the Philippines. The church was a major formative influence in my childhood and youth, along with my family. Grace Gospel Church, an independent mission-oriented church, provided me with a strong background in the Bible, personal faith, a life centered in prayer and commitment, and the meaning and power of being part of a faith community.

My call to the church was not like Paul in the Bible where he was blinded and heard the master's call. Mine is kind of gradual. I was brought up in a Christian school, but not a Christian family. I was influenced by missionaries from this country. On thing that was important to me was reading about the life of all these great missionaries, and all the missionaries that I have seen, who came from foreign lands to minister to us. That started my interest in being one of the ambassadors of the word of God.

I was first enrolled in a Christian theological seminary. In the first seminary I focused on Christian education. Then later on, became an intern in the United Methodist Church and I decided to pursue my master of divinity. That's how I became a parish minister.

When I was involved with the Methodist Church for my internship I found that I really liked the plurality of the Methodist Church, the balance of the personal piety as well as the involvement in social justice on a global scale. I decided to pursue further study, so that's how I continued my Master of Divinity program at the Pacific School of Religion in Berkeley. After I graduated from the Pacific School of Religion for my Master of Divinity program, I was in the process of ordination with the Methodist Church. I was ordained as a deacon, and then ordained as an elder, and this is my thirteenth year in ministry.

When I was going through my ordination process, we were being questioned by a group of folks. Somebody said, "What are you doing here? You know, you're a reverse missionary." So I was kind of taken aback by that question. But I just responded naturally by saying, "The founder of the United Methodist Church, John Wesley, says, 'The world is my parish,' and this is my parish."

My Church

My church here in Novato is challenging. It's especially challenging because it's in a very affluent community. As a pastor, I have to comfort the afflicted, right? The afflicted might be people who come to church because they need comfort. Or they might be the sick, the blind, or the crippled. But in this church in Marin County I have to afflict the comfortable, because they are too comfortable. At times I have to speak up and use my prophetic voice, and say, "This is not right. We have to move forward," and that's why I'm saying I'm afflicting the comfortable.

My church has mostly elderly folk, and I love them dearly, but sometimes it's just hard to make changes. But because they realize that I'm doing it out of love, I'm speaking the truth out of love, they don't feel offended. They kind of go along, and say, "Let's move forward."

I think as Methodists, we have our own heritage. We have our own roots, so I want to maintain that. And yet I'm open to new suggestions. So I'm making little changes, step by step, I cannot totally change the worship style, because it's the tradition. And yet I had to change a little bit because it's a new generation.

I have quite a few constituents who occasionally attend worship service but often they would rather go out in the country and worship God through the forest, through the ocean. That's their spirituality. It's okay, and yet I thought, "It's good to be gathered as a group because a group that gets together will be warmer, instead of being left all by yourself." But my conclusion is, I cannot serve everybody. I just have to use our assets and our strong points, and dwell on that, and let others do whatever they can.

Being A Pastor

People think that pastors just work one day a week, because they see us on Sundays, proclaiming the word, teaching Sunday school, leading. How about the rest of the week? What do you do? I'm not a smoker, so you don't see me with a pipe. But I spend a lot of time in my study.

Sometimes I receive calls that somebody's in the hospital, even when they're not members of the church. It might be somebody in the community who happened to register himself or herself as a Methodist, and then the chaplain, whoever is in charge of the ward, said, "Oh, better call." So since we are the closest Methodist church, they call me, and I hop into my car and go.

So sometimes you have to spend a whole afternoon on unexpected calls. But those surprises are very rewarding. Although I'd like to keep an appointment list, I just have to forget it and run, and come back and say, "Oh, what did I do for the whole day? I didn't do anything." I planned to do this and that for that day, but because there's an urgent need, I have to just put it aside and run. But as I said, it's very rewarding, because I see people being comforted.

Women

Women are not supposed to be in the pulpit in my tradition back home. You can be a Bible teacher. You can be a Christian educator, but not a full-time minister. So when I went to visit to my home church after I was ordained I was very disappointed. I came from a more conservative evangelical church. They don't acknowledge that I had been ordained a minister.

If I were to have gone home after my Christian education training I would not have been able to become a minister. As a "bible woman" we don't have the authority to proclaim the word in public. We can lead a small Bible study group. That's it. Or teach a Sunday school class, at most maybe lead a forum. But we could not do ministry the way I'm doing now. In the Methodist Church we proclaim the word. We conduct the order of the lives of the church. We do the word, the order, the sacrament. We administer the sacrament and we do the service, service in the community as well as the global scale.

It's important that women become ministers as role models for the younger generation. Sometimes it's hard for me to be a minister, because I don't have a lot of role models. There are other women in ministry who are Anglos, but not from the ethnic population, because it's not our upbringing to have women in ministry.

In this country women and men are more equal. But in the Asian culture, women are always to be supportive of the men. They are not really submissive, but are in a supporting role instead of a leadership role. So for an Asian woman like me to be in the leadership role, not striving to be equal with the men, but yet still to be on equal footing, that's very challenging.

I'm part of the California-Nevada Annual Conference of more than 350 churches, so I try to network with other clergywomen through the conference. There are seven districts in our annual conference. I try to keep in touch with them and have the support from my clergywomen friends. I also make friends with folks who are outside of the church, because day in and day out I deal with church folks. Sometimes I need to make friends with folks outside of the church, and get a different perspective.

Sometimes I want to be Superwoman. But I have to tell myself it's not the gender that counts. They have to see me as a person. So I tried not say because I'm a woman, that's why I'm doing it this way. I try to think a man would do it this way, too because it's the pastoral heart. Maybe men and women have different personalities. Maybe women are more towards the heart, and the men are more towards the head. But I try to make it balanced, you know, the meeting place for the heart as well as the head.

But I've come to realize that I have to be very sure that I am called and I am responding to this call, because at times in ministry, it seems that it's only God who cares.

Allen Yan-Chamberlin currently is the pastor at the Novato United Methodist Church.

0-595-31109-1

500300C

SIA information can be obtained at www.ICGtesting.com
ted in the USA
WW062138090513

142LV00003B/116/A

9 780595 311095